Audrey

May the Lord
continue to bless you
in every way.
Keep praising Jesus

Grace, Peace,

"Professor Antipas Harris has pointed us in a direction theology must move to penetrate the tissue of the church for days to come. Holiness ever has been an essential mark of the church. It is no less than exciting to ponder what its shape will take in our day. The crucial matters of personal piety in tension with life and death issues of justice promise to complicate the theological project in an exceedingly wonderful way. In this book Dr. Harris performs a splendid service by insisting that our work probes this complexity."

—WILLIAM TURNER JR.
Professor, the Practice of Homiletics
Duke Divinity School

"Dr. Harris' work speaks to the heart of the next generation of leaders about an absolutely essential element to the life-changing power of the biblical story—a life of holiness that is itself a reflection of God's love lived out in surrender and sacrifice to the transformative power of the Spirit in every aspect of our lives. This book is certainly an enjoyable read and a theologically provocative experience for all contemporary Christians."

—TOMMY A. CASAREZ
Systematic Theologian
President, Latin American Bible Institute

"*Holy Spirit, Holy Living* is informative, inspirational, and refreshing. The author's holiness and Pentecostal background undergirded by his deep faith in God of the Bible enables him to write with authority on biblical holiness. The book contains many insights and anecdotes from his spiritual journey. At the same time there is evidence of outstanding scholarly research. The author fulfilled his purpose to write on holiness in a way that would be useful both to the academy and the church. I strongly recommend this book to clergy and laymen and pray for a return to biblical holiness."

—GEORGE D. MCKINNEY
General Board Member
Bishop, Church of God in Christ, Inc

# Holy Spirit, Holy Living

# Holy Spirit, Holy Living

Toward a Practical Theology of Holiness
for Twenty-First Century Churches

ANTIPAS L. HARRIS

WIPF & STOCK · Eugene, Oregon

HOLY SPIRIT, HOLY LIVING
Toward a Practical Theology of Holiness for Twenty-First Century Churches

Wipf & Stock
An Imprint of Wipf and Stock Publishers
199 W. 8th Ave., Suite 3
Eugene, OR 97401
www.wipfandstock.com

ISBN: 13: 978-1-61097-930-6
Manufactured in the U.S.A.

This book is dedicated to the love of my life, Micah,
and to my parents, Bro. James L. Harris and Sis. Carolyn J. Harris
who have valued the message of holiness for many years!

May the words of my pen
and the meditation of my thoughts
be acceptable in Your sight,
Oh Lord, my Strength and my Redeemer, Amen!

# Contents

# Acknowledgments

FIRST, I WANT TO thank God for the opportunity to write this book. Although cliché sounding, I shudder at the thought: Where would I be without the Lord? To God be the glory!

Special thanks to my lovely wife, Micah, for keeping me grounded. You have been a source of inspiration and helpful in providing your proofreading skills. I owe a huge debt of gratitude to my mom, Mrs. Carolyn J. Harris; my dad, Bishop James L. Harris; my brothers, N. Andronicus Harris and Alonzo Harris; my sisters, Naomi Hines and Miriam Harris; Carla Glanton; my sister-in-law, Deborah Harris; Sebrina Brown; Sara Frazier; Jessica Huff; Briana Green; Jerry Adatsi; and my graduate assistant, Grace Arun Daniel for spending so many hours proofreading the manuscript and providing helpful feedback to bring this work to its current form. I thank God for each of you!

I am grateful to all of my colleges at Regent University School of Divinity for your support and collegiality. Either directly or indirectly, you have helped me develop as a scholar and in ministry. I must express my appreciation to Estrelda Y. Alexander, Dale M. Coulter, Kim Alexander, and Yabbeju (Jabez) Rapaka for reviewing parts of the manuscript and challenging me to think deeply and critically about holiness. Also, I want to extend additional thanks to Estrelda Y. Alexander for your passion and scholarship in pentecostal studies. I am blessed by your willingness to write the foreword for this work. What an honor! Also, on a personal note, I want to thank Vinson Synan, Michael Palmer, and Amos Yong, along with my other colleagues, for your friendship and inspiration. Your important work in renewal studies and leadership in theological education have inspired me in so many ways.

Last, I want to extend another thank-you to my parents, Bishop James L. Harris and Sis. Carolyn J. Harris, for raising my siblings and me in such a way that made it easy for me to say, "Yes, Lord!" at an early age. Your pursuit of holiness has been contagious. Your commitment to faith in practice has been my inspiration all of these years.

# Foreword

WHAT DOES IT MEAN to live holy? What does it mean to live out the biblical mandate to honor God with all of one's life? In a postmodern culture where this difficult subject gets little attention in the church or academy, Antipas Harris has chosen to tackle it head on and to try to work out what it means to live an inner-directed life of personal and communal virtue.

It is rare to find a young scholar passionate enough about the issue to invest time and intellectual effort to consider seriously its practical and social implications. Most scholars of his generation would consider it a mundane topic more appropriately left for the old folks to handle while they come to grips with the hot buttons of the day. They are seemingly unaware that many of the situations in which the church and the surrounding society find themselves are, in some ways, a consequence of abandoning this discussion. Yet, Harris attempts to return us, to guide us into conversation directly with this contemporary generation about this very matter.

Harris draws from the experience in a "sanctified church" in which life was circumscribed by a rigid holiness code—a list that directed one's actions in almost every area of life. There were strictures on dress, on food, and on social activities, and little room was left for personal conscience. In this work, Harris attempts to offer an objective critique of such outer-directed standards of holiness, asserting that they are not workable in the contemporary context.

He is committed to courageously revisiting a subject that once stood at the core of what it meant to be "sanctified" but lately has been pushed to the periphery, if not completely neglected within even the sanctified church. He clearly acknowledges that the church did not always get it right and often has only confused authentic holiness with rigid rules of personal piety that kept people in check but over time bore less and less genuine "fruit of the Spirit." He is also clear that the challenging times in which we live do not allow us the luxury of abandoning the notion of holiness or the challenge of living it out. Harris wrestles with new ways to understand the principles of an intrinsic holiness that is walked out in day-to-day life. Moreover, he wants to point us toward discovering biblical holiness of the heart that emanates from the transforming work of the Holy Spirit, and attempts to line out the contours of what such a holy life would look like.

At the same time, Harris takes on a second difficult task—encouraging a meaningful dialogue between the academy and the church, or more precisely between scholars and ordinary Christians, about a subject that effects all of us: How we, as Christians, are called to live our lives in relation to God and each other. He is attempting to frame the conversation in terms that are meaningful—indeed helpful—to the woman or man in the pew who is called, after all, to live out everyday practical holiness in the real world.

Harris offers us what he calls "a constructive theology to guide Christians of every age toward a greater emphasis on biblical holiness" in a world where neither Scripture nor the subject of holiness is taken seriously. He speaks with the heart of a pastor who desires to see the church he loves move in the power of the Holy Spirit to be what God intended. For Harris, such holiness brings with it a freedom that can never be experienced through any set of rules.

I may not always agree with Harris' conclusions or the path he takes to get there. Yet, in the end, what comes through in this work is Harris' love for the church, his pastoral concern for God's people, and a desire to see them walk in the fullness of life that can only be achieved through authentic personal and communal holiness.

Estrelda Alexander, PhD
President, William Seymour College

# Preface

## What Brings Me to This Subject

"A true love of God must begin with a delight in [God's] holiness, and not with a delight in any other attribute; for no other attribute is truly lovely without this."

Jonathan Edwards

OVER THE PAST CENTURY, particularly in the United States and the rest of the Western world, the theological academy and the church[1] have endured separation. In some circles, this separation seems more like a divorce. As a result, contemporary Christian seminary and university professors often find themselves writing to each other, discussing and arguing theory and theology among themselves with little concern whether their material is accessible to ordinary Christians. However, from Tertullian and Thomas Aquinas, to Martin Luther, John Calvin, and John Wesley, centuries of highly respected theologians directed their treatises beyond the academy toward enhancing practical ministry and the lives of everyday Christians. It is in this (seemingly) lost tradition that I write an academically informed work that is accessible and beneficial to the everyday Christian, seeking a deeper walk with the Lord and a stronger witness to their faith.

Late one evening, I was thinking about the opportunity for more books that draw upon scholarship for the purpose of edifying the church. I prayed for guidance about how I could do something to bridge this gap.

---

1. The usage of the term "church" here is not referring to a theological definition of the church. I am referring to the various institutions called "churches."

After deep contemplation, I felt an urge to write on "holiness" in a way that would be useful for both the academy and the church. Immediately, I told my wife, Micah, that I would write a book that calls Christians back to holiness.

The subject is not new to me. First of all, I am the second child, and first son, of eight siblings whose parents taught the importance of biblical holiness. In 1972, my dad was licensed as an evangelist in the Church of God in Christ (COGIC). Later, he separated from the denomination and founded a church named A House of the Living God, Church of Jesus Christ. Our church was an independent "sanctified church."[2] Over a span of approximately twelve years from the day my dad founded the church, it became an interesting mixture of several doctrinal influences. For example, our strict standards of holiness were an extension of COGIC teachings, as well as influences from the apostolic teachings at the Way of the Cross;[3] we used the Jesus' name baptism formula similar to the Apostolic "Oneness" churches; and we kept the Sabbath on Saturday like the Seventh-day Adventists. Additionally, our church acknowledged the major Jewish festivals, such as Passover, Pentecost, Feast of Trumpets, Day of Atonement, and Feast of Tabernacles, like the Worldwide Church of God.

The area where the church stood for more than twenty years was on the countryside of the city referred to as "across the mountain," between Manchester and Pine Mountain, Georgia. Our church was known in Manchester as the holiness or sanctified church "across the mountain." The other African American sanctified church in Manchester was the Bridge

2. The term "sanctified church" emerged within the African American community to distinguish congregations of "the saints" from those of other black Christians, especially the black Baptists and Methodists who assimilated and imitated the cultural and organizational models of European-American patriarchy. See Sanders, Saints in Exile. Throughout the United States, and particularly in the Deep South, the terms "saints" and "sanctified church" became analogous to black pentecostals. There is in fact no single notion of a "sanctified church"; there are in fact various "sanctified churches." Yet, the language in the singular is common nomenclature when referring to churches with the aforementioned description.

3. The term "apostolic" is codified language for sanctified churches that believed in the baptism in Jesus' name. They were often called "Jesus Only" or "Oneness" churches. Examples of Jesus Only churches include, but are not limited to, Pentecostal Assemblies of the World, Church of Our Lord Jesus Christ, Way of the Cross Churches, and United Pentecostal Churches. They refuted teachings on the Trinity, separating them from the Trinitarian sanctified churches, such as the Churches of God in Christ, Church of God, the United Holy Churches, and the Mount Calvary Holy Churches. Yet, they shared an emphasis on holiness, with strict dress codes and rules of conduct.

Street Church of God in Christ, affectionately referred to simply as, "Bridge Street." People who were members of the sanctified church were members either at the sanctified church "across the mountain" or the sanctified church on "Bridge Street." Many times, people went back and forth in between the two. Although there were some doctrinal differences, the two churches shared holiness as their common denominator.

Second, my doctoral dissertation at Boston University School of Theology addressed systems of belief, or the lack thereof, among independent pentecostal churches. My thesis was that twenty-first century independent urban churches would benefit from a stronger and more consistent belief framework by how they determined doctrinal practices. I proposed that the Bible, the Holy Spirit, and certain elements of culture are important for determining belief systems for church practice. During my doctoral defense, my advisor, Dale Andrews, asked me about the role of holiness in my theological treatment. I expressed that the issue of "holiness" is an important one, but I argued that such critical conversation should be treated in a separate discussion.

Third, when I decided to write this book, I spent some time trying to formulate my thoughts. The process has been long and complicated, as a discussion on "holiness" is rather complex. Then, Micah and I attended the annual "Man of the Year" Banquet in which New Jerusalem Church of God in Christ (COGIC) of Virginia Beach, Virginia, honored their senior pastor—the late Bishop Barnett Thoroughgood. COGIC Bishop Frank White of Long Island, New York, was the guest preacher. In the middle of his sermon, he asserted, "Holiness is right!"[4] The claim on holiness was not an idiosyncratic comment. Growing up in a sanctified church, I have heard similar sermonic assertions pertaining to holiness many times. Yet, this time, it did not sound like jargon in my ears. My spirit quickened; I experienced inner confirmation to write this book on holiness.

As I began to write, for several weeks, I considered who would be in my audience. What demographic? Then, I was invited to be a part of two youth / young adult panels—one was at a Baptist Church in Virginia Beach and the other one was at an independent pentecostal church in Newport

---

4. This comment was not merely sermonic rhetoric. COGIC historian David D. Daniels points out that "at the heart of COGIC's message is a love of holiness." See Daniels, "Forging." Also, for a wider discussion on COGIC doctrine on holiness and other doctrines, see Daniels, "By Sound Doctrine." Also, for a more robust discussion on ecumenical perspectives on holiness or sanctification, see Dieter et al., *Five Views on Sanctification*.

News, Virginia. The panels were on the same weekend. The targeted demographic present at each was similar—urban residents between the ages of eighteen and thirty-five—a rather broad age range. Also, there was a wide range of questions on the agendas to address. Soon after the panels began, there was a consistent challenge between both: we could not address all of the issues.

Commonly, when asked to participate on panels, the panelists discuss matters of success, education, professional development, money management, and such. However, the young people are often fired up with questions pertaining to how Christians should live and behave (i.e., sexuality, relationships, personal piety, how to get along with others, what type of music should Christians listen to, how to choose mates, what constitutes "worldliness," etc.). In retrospect, many of the youth and young adult conferences, retreats, and panels in which I have participated over recent years in Connecticut, Virginia, Georgia, and Florida have had similar demographics. Also, similar questions pertaining to pleasing the Lord dominated the discussions. It seems clear that young Christians in (but not limited to) urban environments have sincere concerns specifically about what it means to live godly and to make godly relationship choices.

In the spring of 2012, Converge 21 USA was held at Regent University. In one session, Dr. George Wood, General Superintendent of the Assemblies of God, commented that next generation Spirit-filled Christians place a premium on the importance of compassion for the poor, needy, victims of injustice, and so on. While he applauded the revival of compassion, he expressed serious concern on the "easing of personal piety and holiness."

In the mid-twentieth century, C. S. Lewis addressed the fact that sexual purity is becoming extinct among our churches. In *Mere Christianity*, Lewis said that, "Chastity is the most unpopular of the Christian virtues. There is no getting away from it: the old Christian rule is, 'Either marriage, with complete faithfulness to your partner, or else total abstinence.'"[5] Jumping more than sixty years forward, sadly the twenty-first-century Christian profile has not gained traction in regards to chastity. Relevant magazine reports that 80 percent of single Christians (20–30 years old) have had premarital sex.[6] David Kinnaman points out two skepticisms that are critical to the future of the church for the twenty-first century. The first is the young Christian's cynicism regarding the reliability of Scripture in light of

---

5. Lewis, *Mere Christianity*, 75.

6. See Charles, "Secret Sexual Revolution."

contemporary challenges. The second area of skepticism has to do with the role Christianity should play in public life and the broader culture.[7]

Kinnaman expresses concern that young Christians struggle to understand their call to peculiarity amidst a society that makes little room for religious commitment.[8] In short, there is an urgent need for twenty-first-century Christians to conceive of a faith that is distinct and unapologetically different from the world. An emphasis on biblical holiness will help the young Christian understand his or her place in a world that sometimes presents a benign apathy toward Christianity and other times exhibits a hostile rebellion towards God. In response to the growing challenges concerning public expressions of faith, I offer a constructive theology to guide Christians of every age toward a greater emphasis on biblical holiness.

This book is divided into two parts. Part 1 addresses the Christian need to pursue biblical holiness, a need to explore deeper the meaning of that holiness to gain knowledge of what it is and what it is not. Part 2 is a proposal on how to walk in that holiness in everyday life.

This work, explores teachings on holiness from the Old and New Testaments, church fathers such as Augustine, and early and later reformers such as Zinzendorf, Wesley, Fetcher, and Seymour. It brings their thoughts to bear on the significant question, what does it mean to be holy in the twenty-first century? Hopefully, this work will draw renewed attention to the biblical mandate for God's people to be holy and stir the conversation regarding a practical theology for holiness in the twenty-first century.

My thesis suggests some key elements that pertain to holiness. In a nutshell, holiness is neither legalism nor antinomianism; but rather, holiness is being and acting in a way that reflects both a regenerated life in Christ and the ongoing renewal in Christ by the power of the Holy Spirit. It is the conditioning of the heart; it means to be in love with God and to live out that love through obedience to God and by expressing God's love to a world that does not know God on its own terms. There are accompanying spiritual practices that help to foster holiness in the life of believers. First, the role of community in relation to holiness is observable in both the Old Testament through the nation of Israel and the New Testament through the church of Jesus Christ. The image of a person living alone either in a house or on an island far away—just she and Jesus—does not fulfill the biblical ideal of holiness. The biblical concept of the "people of God" is critical to

7. Kinnaman, *You Lost Me*, 53.

8. Ibid.

conditioning holiness. In community, holiness demarcates Christians from those who have not chosen Christ as Lord and Savior.

Second, holiness is a lifestyle that includes the three principles of rest, being, and doing. Rest is primary to biblical teachings on holiness; habitual rest and reflection are critical elements within the definition of what it means to be holy. Being implies that there is a divine outflow from what it means to be Christian. It includes behavioral choices and habits that flow from a transformed heart. Love for God, others, and self are principle elements of Christ-likeness. That love exists within God's idea of the church[9] but is importantly expressed beyond the community of believers to unbelievers whom God also loves. The pages that follow explore the splendor or beauty of God's holiness as expressed in the Bible.

9. Here I have shifted from using the term "church" to mean the institutions called "churches" to the biblical ideal type of church. I will explain the theological implications of this usage in chapter 1. Throughout the book, I switch back and forth with these two usages. It will be evident based on context when I am speaking of the institutions called "churches" and when I am speaking of the biblical ideal type called "church."

# PART ONE

Understanding Holiness

# 1

# Don't Throw the Baby Out with the Bath Water

A God-sent revival must ever be related to holiness.

—DUNCAN CAMPBELL

## THE SUBJECT OF HOLINESS: NOTHING NEW

WHEN I WAS GROWING up, the "sanctified churches," also called "holy rollers," placed epochal emphasis on holiness.[1] They proposed simple and often simplistic interpretations about what it means to live holy. The rules often varied from one pentecostal denomination to the next or even from church to church. One thing was for sure—the sanctified churches took seriously the biblical call to live holy.

Although their interests were biblical, some of the requirements for holiness seemed far-reaching, even superfluous at times. For example, some sanctified churches taught against drinking coffee and alcohol, smoking, going to amusement parks and Broadway (or Off-Broadway) shows, and playing sports. Even more of them emphasized what C. S. Lewis calls "social rules of modesty." Women were not allowed to wear makeup, trousers, jewelry, nor open-toed shoes. The men were only allowed to wear

1. In this book, I use the terms "holiness," "holy," "sanctify" and "sanctification" interchangeably.

long sleeves (even in the summer and on the beach), long pants, and shirts buttoned to the neck. I know the rules of modesty were not the "be-all" of doctrinal teachings on holiness, but it seemed so, at times—especially when new clothing styles came out. Women, in particular, were not able to wear them because they were considered "immodest" or because the outfits often included jewelry or trousers. Some sanctified preachers would spend significant time Bible bashing contemporary styles of dress. They also condemned other Christians who enjoyed these fashions, creating a wall between their own congregations and others that did not focus on dress.

Additionally, sanctified churches prohibited the usage of alcohol and tobacco. Many of them also discouraged social activities such as watching television, going to movies and theme parks, playing sports (except at home), attending high school games, and dancing in any other manner than the holy dance. They taught that "saints" should not listen to the blues, jazz, rock, country music, R & B, and hip-hop—only to Christian music.[2] We spent considerable amounts of time with people from the church, going to worship several times a week, praying, studying, and playing music. We did not feel like we were missing much; we were convinced that our peculiar practices reflected what it meant to live holy.

With the Church of God in Christ as our heritage, our church emphasized holiness and the baptism of the Holy Spirit with the initial evidence of speaking in tongues. While I was born into a Christian home, our church taught that the first birth was insufficient for salvation. It was necessary to be born again. To be born again meant to be saved, sanctified, and filled with the Holy Ghost. Receiving Christ into our hearts with the public confession of baptism was important but it was not considered the fullness of the rebirth. As in the Wesleyan tradition, salvation was the first step or initial blessing, holiness or sanctification was the second step or blessing, and the baptism of the Spirit was the third blessing.

We did not have a membership process. Cultured in the COGIC tradition, we practiced the belief that "You can't join in; you must be born in." Being members of our church meant that you must accept Jesus as Savior, receive the teachings on holiness, and receive the gift of the Holy Ghost (Spirit).

---

2. Sanctified churches referred to their church members as "saints." Unlike Catholic and other orthodox traditions that Christians are only eligible to become saints when they pass on, sanctified churches generally refer to all born-again, Spirit-filled Christians as "saints."

More than anything, our church emphasized living holy as part of what it meant to be a member of the church. The baptism of the Spirit was a matter of personal relationship with God. For years, I knew that I belonged to the sanctified church before I understood what it meant to be pentecostal. When I was fifteen years old, I received the baptism of the Spirit, expecting that experience would help me grow in Christ with greater passion for holiness, as I understood it.

These understandings separated young holiness-pentecostal Christians from members of the Baptist or Methodist Churches in our small town.[3] Most strands within the holiness-pentecostal tradition, in some way, associated holiness with "church sanctioned ethical, behavioral, and dress standards, which they saw as separating Holy Spirit-centered believers from other Christians."[4]

Historically, holiness-pentecostal churches have stood out because of their emphasis on the gifts of the Spirit and their unapologetic willingness to live out their faith with recognizable distinction. The sanctified preachers were often criticized for their Bible-thumping, strict preaching, and long church services. Families, coworkers, and former friends often ridiculed and criticized the saints for essentially abandoning them for the sanctified churches.

But, the more people talked about the saints, the more we praised the Lord. Oftentimes, the congregations grew stronger as a result of criticism because our communities found our identity in Christ rather than in the world. The more criticism from the world, the closer to God we felt.

For example, although I went to a parochial school, the homecoming queen at Manchester High School asked me to escort her to the prom. Since I had a crush on her, I was flattered. She was gorgeous. To have received that invitation was any high school boy's dream. However, as a son of the

---

3. The language of "holiness-pentecostal churches" is used interchangeably with "sanctified church" in this book. Yet, the language speaks to a broader category of pentecostal churches with the holiness tradition as their heritage. These include predominately white pentecostal churches, as well as the "sanctified" black pentecostal churches. To be clear, the term "holiness-pentecostal" should not be confused with the denomination called International Pentecostal Holiness Church or IPHC. Yet, they are included. Holiness-pentecostal churches are charismatic religious traditions within Protestant Christianity that arose in the nineteenth and twentieth centuries in the United States. Pentecostal and holiness churches are often characterized by their emphasis on a post-conversion encounter with God through an experience called the "baptism of the Holy Spirit." See Religion Library, "Holiness," n.p.

4. Jones, *Black Holiness*, 1.

sanctified church, I mustered up the strength to decline the offer. That decision became my testimony for that weekend's testimony service at church. I turned down the most gorgeous girl of all time for Jesus. As a zealous, sanctified teenage preacher, that was something to shout about!

During the worship services, our songs reflected the church's vision of Christian peculiarity. The choir sang out of the African American church tradition,[5] "This old world is not my home. I'm just a passing through. With each step, we're moving on. And from here we are going home." Or, we would sing the Albertina Walker and the Caravan's song, "I'm just a stranger here, traveling through this barren land. Lord, I know there's a building somewhere, a building not made by hand."

These songs expressed our theology about the end times. But more importantly, they highlighted our theology of holiness. The world in which we live is not our home. That was our eschatological hope. We wanted to be "in that number when the saints go marching in."[6] The commitment to living out holiness on earth directly connected with our awareness that the saints' ultimate citizenship is in heaven. So what on earth would we not be willing to give up to be in right standing with the Lord on Judgment Day?

Yet, living holy had immediate implications as well. The saints believed that it is important to live holy so that our prayers would not be hindered. Even people in the community believed that the saints could get a prayer through. Frequently, when families, friends, and coworkers had a need or were suffering with sickness or some other calamity, they would call on the sanctified church to pray.

Communal holiness was as critical as personal piety. Members of the community held each other accountable. In churches where there were peers of the same age group, it was easier for young people to obey the rules of holiness. It was harder for people who did not have a peer group with whom to share accountability and support. In my experience, various teachings on holiness established the foundation for what it meant to be a Christian. It is from this trajectory that I approach the subject of biblical holiness. The twenty-first century offers many opportunities and challenges for Christians and the church as a community of believers. The Church of Jesus Christ at large must ground its faith in sound teachings on biblical holiness.

5. The language of an "African American church tradition" is an ideal type. In fact, there is no "African American church tradition" per se. There are several traditions with particular elements of commonality in terms of ethnicity, history, and liturgy that make up the so-called tradition.

6. Lyrics taken from the traditional hym, "When the Saints Go Marching In."

## HOLINESS THROUGH THE WESLEYAN TRADITION

Strict religious guidelines seem a bit strange, looking through contemporary lenses. However, the connection between holiness and holy practices is not new. While the foundation for a message of holiness is biblical, twentieth-century pentecostal churches emerged from John Wesley's teachings on practicing holiness and the Wesleyan tradition. In the eighteenth century, Wesley had a list of General Rules for his Methodist Societies that were ultimately connected to monastic rules. The tenets for the monastic way of living were grounded in early Christian teachings. They sought to apply a practical appropriation of Scripture that they lifted from literal readings of certain passages.

As I reflect on the rule lists that were common among the sanctified churches, I have the same mixed emotions that I have when I reflect on monastic interpretations of Scripture. On the one hand, a focus on visible evidence of holiness with a list of "dos and don'ts" or "cans and cants" may seem frivolous. Given the times in which we live, they seem extreme. As Lewis contends, "I do not think that a very strict or fussy standard of propriety is any proof of chastity [or *holiness*, for our purposes] or any help to it."[7] On the other hand, as the serious Christian observes the church today, a spirit of lawlessness or antinomianism often replaces legalism. Immodest clothing becomes a distraction to others in worship. Provocative outfits are designed to entice, outshine, or draw flattery from others and distract from Christ as the center of worship.

Moreover, just as churches with fussy, visible standards do not prove holiness, churches with no standard of holiness or that bend to society's lustful sensuality do not prove spiritual liberty. Neither strict rules nor avoidance of practical standards of holiness reflect biblical principles of holiness. Rather, holiness begins as a condition of the heart. We need to balance a commitment to standards with the freedom to live out our faith from the heart. When it is not rooted in the heart, artificial human rules replace true holiness. As a result, we satisfy the flesh in odd ways rather than live out divine holiness from the heart.

7. Lewis, *Mere Christianity*, 74.

## HOLINESS: MORE THAN A NOTION

Recently, a friend who pastors a Hispanic pentecostal congregation shared the situation of an unmarried couple that had recently joined his church. They were from a strict Oneness pentecostal background. The classical pentecostal denomination emphasizes baptism in Jesus' name and focuses especially on physical manifestations of holiness, largely through dress and appearance. Women within the denomination are not allowed to wear trousers or excessive amounts of jewelry or cut their hair. Also, traditionally the men are discouraged to grow facial hair. This particular pastor, however, does not emphasize these rules as strictly as many other churches within his denomination. Rather, he emphasizes sexual purity and Christian behavior.

When the aforementioned unmarried couple came to the church, they were cohabiting and the young lady was pregnant. The pastor taught them that fornication and cohabiting are sinful behaviors. The couple was convicted of their sin and chose to repent of their ways. Soon, they got married. The pastor saw this as a wonderful testimony; two young people came back to the Lord and wanted to live holy.

The couple then met with the pastor to let him know that they were leaving the church. They felt that this church was not strict enough on dress. This news baffled the pastor. How could they find nothing wrong with fornication but be upset that the pastor did not emphasize a strict dress code? They explained that they felt closer to God with preaching that emphasized strict rules of dress. Although they had been living a sinful lifestyle prior to joining his church, they had viewed holiness as rules of dress more than as a lifestyle of chastity. So they were not satisfied with correcting the sexual indiscretion.

While classical pentecostal churches do not sanction sexual indiscretion, it can be easy for Christians to veer off into hypocrisy when the church places too much emphasis on fussy standards of propriety. Churches must stress the power of inner transformation and holistic chastity of lifestyle, which is central to a life in the Spirit. In Matthew 23:27, Jesus is recorded as saying, "Woe to you, scribes and Pharisees, hypocrites! For you are like whitewashed tombs, which outwardly appear beautiful, but within are full of dead people's bones and all uncleanness." Moreover, holiness should not be reduced to "social rules of modesty" or a list of dos and don'ts. Christians need practical biblical principles that both ground the identity of the church in holiness and help Christians know how to live holy in everyday life.

With all of its rigidity, there are redeemable qualities in both the sanctified church's dedication to being the church and the saints' commitment to godly living within an irreverent world. A testimony service was commonplace among the sanctified churches. During that part of the service, people would spontaneously stand up to share a brief testimony, as they felt led or as the pastor would select certain ones to testify. The classic ending of a testimony was, "Those who know the word of prayer, please pray that I be the saint that God is calling for in these last and evil days." The language of "the saint that God is calling for" emerged from the understanding that God requires personal piety as part of what it means to be part of the church. At the same time, the sanctified churches saw the church as bearing responsibility both to teach and to foster that peculiarity in the community. Grounded in a similar ideology as that of the saints, a twenty-first-century theology of holiness must be grounded in the old Christian adage, "We are in the world but not of it."[8]

## THE CHURCH, SOCIETY, AND HOLINESS

Certainly, the Bible warrants that the church of Jesus Christ has a critical role in society beyond herself. Reflecting on the history of the early church, Martin Luther King Jr. once wrote: "There was a time when the church was very powerful—in the time when the early Christians rejoiced at being deemed worthy to suffer for what they believed. In those days the church was not merely a thermometer that recorded the ideas and principles of popular opinion; it was a thermostat that transformed the mores of society."[9] Granted, King's lifestyle was, sometimes, a contradiction to this quote; yet, his words speak to the profound transformative nature of the church that God intends. It follows that if God calls a church to transform society's mores, the church must consist of people whose lifestyles are also transformed. The courageous, uncompromising, corporate image of Christ-like distinctiveness consists of people who are committed to living

---

8. See Sanders, *Saints in Exile*. The concept of *exile* included both a meeting space, a place of spiritual retreat, and spiritual warfare in their bout with what they experienced as frustration and injustice in American society. So to be "sanctified" or "holy" meant to find a sense of belonging in a world where they really didn't fit in. As times have changed, even the marginalized have found the courage to want to fit in. So, in the success of the civil rights movement, even Christians fight to be included and affirmed in mainstream society. For many, the idea of exile is no longer embraced.

9. King, *Why*, 80.

out faith in their everyday lives. The Holy Spirit enlivens our lives as the Spirit also enlivens the church to serve as a prophetic agent in society. In subsequent chapters, I will share more on the "prophetic church."

Peter and Paul address the need for believers to embrace the peculiarity of the church in their own personal lives. Peter speaks of the church as a chosen people (1 Pet 2:9) called out of the world and set apart as people of God. Paul charges the chosen of God to come out from the world and live a life of distinction (2 Cor 6:17). Therefore, whatever negative images of holiness have thwarted contemporary Christians' minds, whatever critique is appropriate to apply to certain rigidly legalistic traditions, biblical holiness remains a distinction that Christians must possess because we belong to the church of Jesus Christ.

## HOLINESS AS GOD'S IDENTITY

Holiness is central to biblical traditions (in both Judaism and Christianity). Though I will define the term more completely in later chapters, there are two keys to understanding holiness. We encounter the first one in the definition of the Hebrew term *kedushah*. As used in the Old Testament, *kedushah* suggests purity, or cleanliness. The Hebrew language of purity suggests communal and personal piety defined by God. In the Old Testament, the Hebrew people were chosen to be sanctified or holy unto God. We discover the second key in the meaning of the Greek term *hágios*. As used in the New Testament, *hágios* implies a divine setting apart, or to be made different as a result of divine identity. As with the Hebrew term, the Greek language for holiness is evocative of the Greek term *ekklesia*, which is translated as church. *Ekklesia* means "the called out ones."

In Hellenistic times, *ekklesia* was also the Greek term for a political assembly. The *ekklesia* consisted of designated men who assembled to make decisions about the city. The New Testament often borrows terms from the Greco-Roman world. The language was communicable within a first-century audience. Yet, at times, Jesus and his apostles embellished the meaning or even imposed new meaning upon expressions. As with the language of *ekklesia*, Jesus does not only borrow the political term, but more importantly proclaims a new "body politic" that involves his own agenda that includes his emissaries then and now. When Jesus says, "On this rock I will build my *ekklēsian*" (Matt 16:18), he is not speaking of a political body as the ones that were concerned with decisions and leadership in ancient

Greco-Roman society. Rather, Jesus' reference to his own *ekklesia* has to do with a "body politic" that is concerned with God's invitation for believers to separate themselves from the world in pursuit of God's agenda in the face of other religious or ideological opposition to it. There is a connection between the church of Jesus Christ, believers, and holiness. The church is called to govern herself according to standards which God establishes and Christians are expected to live by in our everyday lives.

In the New Testament, there is also an etymological as well as philosophical relationship between the church, believers, and holiness. God sets believers apart from the world to be formed into the likeness of Christ. In 1 Corinthians 12, Paul introduces the "body of Christ" metaphor interchangeably with "church."[10] The church is made up of a close-knit group of believers, which forms the body of Christ. God summons the "called-out ones" to be formed into the likeness of Christ. We are formed into Christ's likeness through the profession of faith, the transformation of the heart, behavior that is consistent with the teachings of Christ, and through participation with a believing community.

Philosophically speaking, the sum total of believers form the body of Christ, but also the impartation of holiness forms the community into Christ's body. In this way, holiness is the foundation of what I call a "body politic" that sustains the life and image of the church. Holiness is the distinctive that separates the life of the believer and the church from the rest of the world.

The church, as a whole, has a unique way of existing in the world. Ethnicity, gender, class, nor status defines the church. The church is defined by the profession of faith in Jesus as lived out in a world that is contrary to it. Holiness, as a lifestyle, necessarily involves the desire to think as God thinks, love what God loves, hate what God hates, and act as God intends.[11] At the core, holiness is love for God and everything that God has created—especially fellow human beings. Jesus is our chief exemplar of a holy life. He lived according to his Father's standards and loves unconditionally. The life of Christ that forms the body of Christ bears with it the attributes of God's holiness. All of those who profess to be a member of Christ's church are called to live and love like Christ in practical ways.

10. See 1 Cor 12:27 for Paul's reference to the church as the body of Christ.

11. Bernard, *Practical Holiness*, 32.

## HOLINESS, A CHRISTIAN'S NECESSITY IN POSTMODERNITY

Postmodernity has impacted the Christian lack of emphasis on holiness. Reformed theologian and pastor Bryn MacPhail correctly points out that any notion of postmodernity is complex and hard to pin down exactly.[12] Alan Padget, MacPhail, and others agree, however, that, although hard to fully explain, postmodernism has some identifiable characteristics. They include the celebration of "the demise of King Reason," affinity toward the "Independent Ego," and rejection to any "totalizing metanarratives."[13] Relativistic thinking makes it difficult for "postmodernists" to agree on criteria pertaining to objective reality. As a result, success exists on a materialistic continuum. Postmodern thinking, moreover, presents challenges for the twenty-first-century church on several levels: What is holiness? What is the church? What is authentic Christian identity? What is the relationship between the church and society? How should a Christian live in an increasingly pluralistic religious society? What is the distinct definition of a Christian life that is independent of Western ideologies and political parties?

These and other challenges translate into ambiguity among Christians about what it means to please the Lord. Contention emerges among churches, small groups, and even individuals on this subject. Relativistic thinking poses a challenge for any objective notion of holiness. In many church circles, preachers increasingly avoid an emphasis on holiness. For some Christians, these terms have become touchy subjects in these postmodern times.[14] Also, many young Christians are accustomed to neither the terms nor any practical meaning of holiness, consecration, sanctification, and godliness. It is hard to imagine a twenty-first-century church that pursues holiness when that language and concept of holiness is disappearing from the lips and lifestyle of believers.

12. MacPhail, "In Search," n.p.

13. Padgett, "Christianity," n.p.

14. See MacPhail, "In Search." The terms postmodern or postmodernity represent a broad spectrum of definitions. Bryn MacPhail is helpful to provide some characteristics of postmodernity. By postmodern, I mean that since the Enlightenment, cynical attitudes toward objective truth have tainted a single biblical metanarrative among Christians and has thereby veered western Christians toward resisting any consensus pertaining to important Christian ethics pertinent to pleasing God. Many systems and ideas about truth, what is right and what is wrong, have contributed to obscuring key terms that seem to speak to normative behavior among Christians—terms such as "holiness," "consecration," "sanctification" and "godliness."

Hearts that earnestly seek after God cannot refrain from asking, "How can I live to please God?" Living within postmodern frameworks, several other questions emerge: How do we know if we are living according to God's will? Even if we could know what it means to please God, could anyone claim to have achieved that goal?

As a result of these unresolved concerns and in an attempt to be relevant or politically correct, the term "holy" is often replaced with more contemporary, user-friendly language: "royalty with a swag," "on fire for God," "hyped for Christ," "sold out for Christ," "dare to be different," and "spiritual love affair." These catchy phrases capture a generation of what I call "enthusiasts." We look for something that excites us and keeps our attention rather than that which is good, healthy, and with soul substance. So, with effort to win over this generation to Christ, we adopt these catchphrases. Although commercially appropriate phrases for effective marketing purposes, they come coded with society's definition of what it means to be "cool" and "hip." Certainly, Christianity has always been adaptable to the vernacular. Yet, the meaning of the vernacular must also adjust to the depth and meaning of the words imposed upon it.

There often exists tension between the need to be culturally adept and to remain true to sound biblical teachings. Despite the negative baggage that the language has endured in contemporary times, holiness remains a divine requirement for every Christian in every generation, culture, and situation. So the language may be of contemporary vernacular; yet, what it means to be "on fire for God" or "saved with swag" must be clearly defined not by trending hype but by biblical principles for lasting holiness.

Regardless of what language we use, Old and New Testament teachings emphasize holiness as foundational to what it means to please the Lord. The two consistent categories for holiness in the Old and New Testaments are purification and separation. God has always intended for God's people to reflect divine purity and to live out that purity with boldness in predominantly "pagan" societies.

Divine purity is reflective of God's nature. Leviticus 20:26, records a divine command for the Hebrew people to "be *holy* to me, for I the LORD am *holy*" (italics added). In the New Testament, Peter teaches that holiness is associated with the new birth in Christ. He explains that God's mandate of holiness to the Hebrew people is extended to Christians. Because of Christ, we are endowed with power to live out that purity. New Testament scholar Everett F. Harrison comments, "In view of the general parallelism between

Israel and the Church, it is not unexpected that the New Testament children of God should be considered holy by virtue of their position."[15] Holiness is, moreover, fundamental to any consideration of the divine claim that by virtue of our faith in Christ we are God's chosen people.

## THE TENSION: RITUAL PURITY AND INTERNAL PURITY

Old Testament practices of holiness seem best revealed through ritualism. Such rites as sacrifices, temple laws, dietary laws, and more were examples of ritualistic holiness. The New Testament call to holiness draws out God's intentions from the foundation of the world that God's people commune with God in holiness. The coming of Christ and the outpouring of the Holy Spirit are part of God's plan to draw us back to relationship with God. In New Testament theology, God's activity in Christ cancels out the need for sacrifices, temple laws, and burnt offerings.

Yet, ritual purity remains part of the call to holiness. For example, baptism and Communion are new rituals that define the New Testament community of faith. Like in the Old Testament, however, these rituals do not create internal purity, but reflect and compliment it. More importantly, the Spirit endows us with power to live holiness as a daily lifestyle. Peter says, "as [God] who called you is holy, you also be holy in all your conduct, since it is written, 'You shall be holy, for I (God) am holy'" (1 Pet 1:15–16). Peter is teaching that personal piety must connect with how we live and the choices we make on an everyday basis. Purity is not just an attribute of *who we are* as believers but *how we act* as believers.

Furthermore, just as the Hebrew people were called out of Egypt to serve God, Pauline theology teaches a holiness that separates the church from the society in which she finds herself. In 2 Corinthians 6:16b–18, the apostle says, "For we are the temple of the living God; as God said, 'I will make my dwelling among them and walk among them, and I will be their God, and they shall be my people. Therefore go out from their midst, and be separate from them, says the Lord, and touch no unclean thing; then I will welcome you, and I will be a father to you, and you shall be sons and daughters to me, says the Lord Almighty.'"

This passage begs for exegetical and practical clarity. Does Paul mean that Christians should withdraw entirely from society to be part of the church? Does separation mean alienation? How could the church influence

15. Harrison, "Holiness," 2:727.

a society in which its members are entirely alienated? Bobby Jamieson points out that Paul is encouraging us that in Christ we are God's treasured possession, set apart, for the Master's purpose in the world.[16] Paul relies on God's message to Israel to express his concern that believers would be distracted in a world in which there are incompatible, competing loyalties. The commotion would, inevitably, foster conflicting interests to God's agenda. Paul, moreover, challenges us with God's call to submit, obey, and reflect God's character within a world that is full of distractions.[17]

## HOLINESS IS RIGHT! GO GET THE BABY!

The sanctified church tradition, moreover, offers a way of thinking about what it means to maintain a different way of living in the world. I am now convinced that many of the rules that defined the sanctified church were not particularly biblical. Yet, their willingness to forsake the world for the sake of Christ is plausible. As contemporary Christians, we often profess to be saved but fail to live with that kind of willingness to be ridiculed, ostracized, and criticized by the world. We would like to maintain a sense of contemporary relevance to faith in Jesus Christ. But, in the words of an old saying, we must not "throw the baby out with the bath water." In other words, we should not throw out holiness (or the second blessing) while trying to get rid of artificial visible proof of holiness.

Pentecostal historian Vinson Synan explains that in the early days of the pentecostal movement in America there was a move to throw out the teachings on holiness to which the founding revivalist William Seymour held.[18] Seymour believed and taught that people must be "saved, sanctified, and filled with the Holy Spirit." William H. Durham of Chicago was an obdurate opponent of the "second blessing" (sanctification/holiness), the teaching that salvation and the baptism of the Spirit without sanctification were not sufficient.[19] Those who were receiving the baptism of the Spirit but had not been schooled in holiness theology or those with non-Wesleyan backgrounds (e.g., Baptists) quickly ascribed to Durham's teachings. He

16. Jamieson, *Built*, 18.

17. Ibid.

18. For more on the historical criticism and controversy about the teaching of holiness among classical pentecostal churches, see Synan, *Holiness-Pentecostal*, especially chapter 8, "Criticism and Controversy (1906–1920)," 143–66.

19. Ibid., 149–50.

called his teachings the "finished work" of Christ, suggesting that there is no need to emphasize a need for ongoing development of holiness, thereby claiming that sanctification is automatic at the moment one receives salvation.[20] Synan explains that Durham's theory eventually not only attracted non-Wesleyans but also independent pentecostal missions, including the Assemblies of God. But the Church of God, Pentecostal Holiness Church, and Church of God in Christ held firmly an emphasis on the necessity of the second work of sanctification.[21]

Today, many Spirit-filled churches, including those who once held firmly to a theology of holiness, have veered away from the second work of sanctification. Although not theologically adverse to holiness, in practice they do not emphasize it. They rather focus on "getting saved" and "being filled with the Spirit," the first and third blessings. Yet, there are independent Spirit-filled or charismatic churches that value the gifts of the Spirit with little or no emphasis on biblical teachings of holiness. Postmodern relativism flies in the face of biblical norms of holiness. Churches that lean toward accommodationist and materialistic notions for success become more "seeker friendly" than theologically sound. They produce Christians who are attracted to charisma more than conscientiousness about holiness; they seem more interested in playing the numbers game than producing disciples—how many people got saved this week? Or, how many people were baptized in the Spirit this week? More importantly, churches should ask, are we teaching people to live holy? The lure of temptation seems stronger than an emphasis on escaping from it. A statement of faith in Christ does not always reflect the commitment necessary to live the peculiar life to which Christ calls the believer.

Our contemporary culture is a culture of fitting in. A common phrase is, "Everybody is doing it." Conversely, Christ calls for us to forsake the world and be different from the world. Jesus says to us, "If anyone would come after me, let him deny himself and take up his cross daily and follow me" (Luke 9:23). At its simplest form, denying the self and taking up the cross speaks to a willingness to be a non-conforming spectacle for Christ. In a society that is increasingly pluralistic and relativistic, being a unified spectacle for Christ seems more challenging than in the last century. Flipping the adage, moreover, it is appropriate to say, "Go back and get the baby that is being thrown out." In other words, let's consider another look at what

20. Ibid.
21. Ibid., 152–53.

it means to live selflessly and to take up the cross of Christ in the twenty-first century. So before we completely dismiss the sanctified church tradition, let's consider their indefatigable attitude about their faith. Coupled with close reading of Scripture, careful reflection on the sanctified church, at best, shows this generation an example of what it means to live with unashamed abandonment for Christ.

## REFLECTION

Early Christians did not live in a so-called Christian society. This means that they did not have the option of hiding their faith. They knew that when they chose to follow Christ this could mean severe persecution. But they chose to abandon everything to follow hard after Christ. For them, that was what it meant to be a Christian. Because the church consisted of such loyal and committed people to Christ, the church was in a better position to impact society. Today, the problem is not so much the world as it is the church. Are you willing to stand for Christ even when the world criticizes you? Or, are you trying to live out your faith without distinction from the world? Are you willing to be part of a church that consists of people who are decidedly followers of Christ with complete abandonment?

## PRAYER

If you are willing to live for Christ despite the odds, pray this prayer with me:

> Dear Lord, my heart is fixed on you. May you speak to my heart as I read through the pages of this book. Quicken my heart; inspire my soul. Open my understanding to your holiness. Give me holy boldness to follow you even when it is not popular, in Jesus' name, Amen.

# 2

# In the World but Not of the World

This is the will of God, your sanctification.

—1 THESSALONIANS 4:3

MANY CONTEMPORARY SPIRIT-FILLED CHURCHES emphasize getting saved and being filled with the Spirit. There seems to be less and less emphasis on what it means to live a sanctified life as a Christian. Among Spirit-filled, pentecostal, and neo-pentecostal charismatic churches there has come to be an emphasis on "getting saved" and what Holiness ministers of the late 1880s[1] distinguished as the "baptism of the Spirit," also called "fire baptism."[2]

1. Harold Hunter explains, "It was with the birth of the idea of yet a 'third work' of spiritual experience, distinct from Wesley's salvation and sanctification (first and second blessings) which, in my view, ultimately gave rise to the phenomenon we now know as the 'Baptism in the Holy Spirit.' During the 1880's this novelty became quite defined: 'The Western Kansas Ministerial Association discussed sanctification, and some of its members thought that there were three works: regeneration, sanctification, and the baptism of the Spirit. W. H. Kennedy, later to serve as general mission secretary, distinguished at one time between entire sanctification on the one hand, and the baptism with the Holy Ghost on the other, saying they were distinct experiences which might or might not occur at the same time; he declared this baptism to be a special impartation of power, repeatable many times.'" Quoted from Haines, "Grander," 136; see also Hunter, "Beniah," footnote 56.

2. "Baptism of the Spirit," or "fire baptism," involves the gifts of the Spirit—namely, speaking in tongues as the Spirit gives utterance. Benjamin Hardin Irwin was a former Baptist minister who became a member of the Iowa Holiness Association. He became convinced that there was a distinction between the baptism of the Holy Spirit at entire sanctification, and the baptism of fire, which subsequently brought down power to the

However, in recent years, the Wesleyan concept of *entire* sanctification has not been the focus of conversation among Spirit-filled Christians, or even the emphasis of much of popular Christian teaching. Confession of faith in Christ serves as an important element of redemption; the empowerment of the Spirit in spiritual gifts is critical for personal and ecclesial spiritual development; yet, sanctification speaks to the way we live, act, and relate to the world around us.

Wesleyan scholars Stanley Hauerwas and William Willimon point out that the church need not be concerned about whether to be in the world. The church's most important concern is *how* to be in the world, in what form, for what purpose.[3] While they speak about the communal presence of the body of Christ in the world, the "how" question has profound implications for individual Christians' lives, as well as for the church collectively. Paul states plainly, "This is the will of God, your sanctification" (1 Thess 4:3). All contemporary Christians must wrestle with questions pertaining to how to live in the world but still be set apart (sanctified) from the world in the twenty-first century. How can we live a sanctified life when the society in which we live is dramatically shifting? What does it mean to be *in* the world but not *of* it? What is the church's role in helping to foster Christian distinction in a world that does not have much respect for Christians nor the church anymore?

The church, by virtue of her continued, visible presence of Christ (Acts 1:8), reserves a place in society where living Jesus' teachings, sustaining his work, and possessing his Spirit mark the separation between society and the church. Twentieth-century theologian Karl Barth elegantly explains that the church is the "Christian community" that exists within the world but must be distinct from society, or what he calls "the civil community." In Barth's own words,

---

believer. He used the term "fire baptism" for the "baptism of the Spirit." The notion of the "baptism of the Spirit," or "fire baptism," in American pentecostal history is the confluence of the Keswick doctrines of an "enduement of spiritual power" grafted onto the Wesleyan/Holiness concept of sanctification. This "third work," or "third blessing," of Spirit baptism became the language and theology that distinguished many Spirit-filled, classical pentecostal, neo-pentecostal, and charismatic churches of the twentieth century. See Hunter, "Beniah." Growing up in an independent holiness-pentecostal church, the saints were used to being "saved," "sanctified," and "filled with the Holy Spirit" (some would say, "filled with the Holy Spirit and fire").

3. Hauerwas and Willimon, *Resident Aliens*, 43.

The church must *remain the church*. . . . The Christian community [or the church] has a task of which the civil community can never relieve it and which it can never pursue in the forms peculiar to the civil community. It would not [contribute much] to the welfare of the civil community if the Christian community were to be absorbed by it and were therefore to neglect the *special* task which it has received a categorical order to undertake. It proclaims the rule of Jesus Christ and the hope of the Kingdom of God. This is not the task of the civil community [society]: it has no message to deliver; it is dependent on a message being delivered to it. It is not in a position to appeal to the authority and grace of God; it is dependent on this happening elsewhere.[4]

In other words, continuing Christ's presence in the world requires that the church (or "the Christian community") maintain the type of dissonance that Christ had with society, while presenting eternal hope that Christ extends to the world. As such, Hauerwas and Willimon point out that Christianity is an invitation to be part of an alien people who see something that cannot otherwise be seen nor experienced without Christ.[5] Plainly stated, the church's greatest witness is that Jesus makes the difference. This confession of faith is the formation of the visible community of faith and the Christian's lived reality. The difference that Christ makes serves as the fundamental separation between the Christian lifestyle and that of the rest of the world.

## CHRISTIANITY REQUIRES DIFFERENCE

The church as a whole, and at times individual Christians, have wrestled with the relationship between confessing Christ and the practical meaning of Christianity. As stated above, "What does it mean to be *in* the world but not *of* it?" Today, the question of peculiarity reigns as increasingly significant in our society, wherein there is an upsurge of political, social, and religious plurality. What does it really mean to live out the Christian faith amid so much ideological, philosophical, and theological diversity? Relativism has become the order of the day. The lyrics to the Isley Brothers' song are an appropriate description of the common lifestyle: "It's your thing; do what you wanna do." Contrary to ruling pluralistic ideals, Scripture offers

---

4. Barth, *Karl Barth*, 272 (italics added).

5. Hauerwas and Willimon, *Resident Aliens*, 24.

foundational standards by which all Christians live. The sinful nature of humankind cannot determine what it means to live the Christian life or to be sanctified. The Bible exposes God's vision of what it means to be sanctified. God requires the church both to teach and to encourage those principles.

The issue of sanctification or holiness is two sided: What is a holy church? And, what is a holy Christian? With so many versions of Christianity and denominational differences, there needs to be a critical look at what it means for the church to exist in the unity of holiness; but also, an emphasis on holiness remains a pertinent concern for the Christian's everyday life.

## HISTORY: AN INTERPRETATION, A COMMENTARY, A WAY FORWARD

From the New Testament forward, church history presents many examples of how Christians have wrestled with what it means to be the church and the issue of living the faith in everyday life. Until the early fourth century, Christianity was known as the religion of the persecuted followers of Christ. This means that converts not only made a public confession of faith in Jesus, but Acts 6:7 says that they became "obedient to the faith." The language of "obedience" suggests that there was a specific discipline, a unique lifestyle, that followed their belief that Jesus is the Messiah. Because of their Christ-oriented way of living, they became originally known as "the Jesus people," "Jesus' disciples," or "the Jesus followers." The term "Christian" was a slanderous term that eventually "the Jesus people" proudly embraced. Because it was illegal to be a Christian, the church was a scattered population of believers. Our idea of a local church was the gathering of believers in houses and other incognito places.

Notably, there was no such organization as an institutionalized church in the earliest days of Christianity. There were many churches. New Testament scholar Raymond Brown observes that the earliest apostles left behind at least seven local church paradigms.[6] Yet, they were unified by the common faith in Jesus Christ. Together they spread the gospel, taught believers what it meant to live a sanctified life, and nurtured them in fellowship and faith against the backdrop of varying levels of persecution. Believers took full responsibility for their countercultural and illegal commitment to Jesus. Their only political, social, ideological, theological, and philosophical commitment was to their faith in him.

6. See Brown, *Churches the Apostles Left Behind*. See also Dunn, *Unity and Diversity*.

While there might not have been as many competing ideals, religions, and philosophies in their world as there are today, the few that did exist were very strong and often severely hostile toward Christians. Yet, the believers' commitments to Christ were not only revealed through their confessions of faith but also through their character and lifestyle choices. The gospel spread from the East to the West, throughout the Roman Empire. A decision to follow Christ was not culturally accepted; yet, persecution did not stifle the expansion of the faith. These decisions emerged as deeply personal.

When Constantine became a believer, the world started to perceive the religion differently. More importantly, Christians began to understand their own social and religious place in society differently. This shift in perception made a profound impression upon the world and Christianity as a whole—especially in the Western world. I will explore three important times in Christian history: the Eastern monastic tradition, the Constantinian Christian tradition, and the slave Christian experience, out of which the "black church" tradition emerged.[7] In a broad sense, these three traditions have in varying ways influenced religious views among American Christians. They shed light on the state of Christianity and provide constructive insight into what it means to be Christian in a world that does not subscribe to Christian beliefs.

## The Holy Recluse: The Church as Alienated from Society

Early Eastern monasticism is the first paradigm that I wish to explore. The monks present us with a Christian way of being in the world that is alienated from society. Although my thesis defines Christianity as peculiar to the world rather than alienated from the world, monastic life inspires serious reflection on God's call for his people to live holy when the world is full of alluring unholiness. Times have changed but the issue of holiness, as antithesis to worldliness, remains a similar problem for Christians as it did in the times of the early Eastern monks.

---

7. The earliest form of the black church emerged from the situation of African American Christians who were not allowed to worship freely with white Americans; nor were they allowed to participate in the established churches as full participants of the communion of faith. They started their own churches that evolved into what became known as the "Black Church" because the theology, ways of worship, customary practices, and ecclesiology was organic to the African American experience and influenced by both what they learned at the White churches and their indigenous African religious heritage. See Lincoln and Mamiya, *The Black Church*, 20–46.

The desert fathers and mothers developed a reputation for their pursuit of holiness and wisdom through asceticism. They subscribed to an astute, trenchant interpretation of Scripture. Through solitude, cultivated within an atmosphere of critical engagement with the spirit world—made real through their experiences—and oriented toward matter-of-fact application of Scripture, holiness and wisdom became their legacy.[8]

It all began on a Sunday morning in 270 or 271 CE in a small Northeastern African village in Egypt. The congregation listened to the reading in Matthew 19:21 that records Jesus saying, "If you would be perfect, go, sell what you possess and give to the poor, and you will have treasure in heaven; and come, follow me" (see also Luke 12:33). These words deeply moved a young man named Anthony of Egypt. The words resonated as a divine order for him to pursue a life of relative poverty and radical solitude.[9] From a young man until his death at 106 years old, Anthony lived a common lifestyle and with radical self-denial. He fought with demons in deserted places. His lifestyle marked the beginning of several monastic traditions in which men and women dedicated their lives to prayer, meditation, and the strict reclusive way of living.

The early monks believed that true intimacy with God involves living with simplicity as hermits in a desert, seeking God. Importantly, they discovered value in living according to a divinely inspired system of beliefs, uninterrupted concentration on seeking God, complete abandonment, and dependence on the Holy Spirit. As Jesus defeated the demons in the desert (Mark 1:12–13; Matt 4:1–11; and Luke 4:1–13), early monasticism held that defeating demons by the power of the Spirit marks the ultimate goal of holiness. They believed that holiness becomes perfected when Christians confront their demons.[10]

While the manner in which the monks expressed their principles of faith was eccentric to our modern minds, there is an important biblical lesson to learn from them. An important part of Christian particularity includes the mastery of temptation. In an extreme way, the monks' way of life teaches us that other human beings are not our ultimate enemy—evil spirits are. Therefore, being "in the world but not of it" entails the power of the Holy Spirit to overcome temptations, like Jesus did in the Wilderness of Temptation. The model of sanctification among the monks was quite

---

8   See Burton-Christie, *Word*, especially 33–75.

9.  Chryssavgis, *In the Heart*, 15.

10. Cassian, *Conference*, 19.12; see also *Institute* 5.36.

bizarre, particularly to our contemporary minds. Yet, their understanding of the relationship between sanctification and overcoming demonic spirits becomes helpful in a world that is full of temptation. They did not merely rebuke spirits; rather, they believed that asceticism helped them to live in a way that prepared them to defeat their spiritual enemies.

## Constantinian Christianity: A Distortion of the Faith or the Biblical Way?

Another form of Christianity came into play in 313 CE, when Constantine became the first Roman emperor to convert to the Christian faith. Since then, Constantinian Christianity has had a profound impact on all Western forms of Christianity. Traditionally, Roman emperors were not only seen as kings but as gods with final authority. In the worldview of the Roman world, it was a severe crime to go against the dictates of the emperor. Moreover, when Constantine ruled and declared Jesus as king, this marked a significant shift in Roman society. The king was Christian, so everyone must follow suit. This change was good news to the Christians because Constantine would sign the Edict of Milan and declare Christianity a legal religion.[11] Christians were no longer victims of national war, but rather protected by Roman law. They could express their faith publically without the threat of imprisonment, torture, or the death penalty.

Furthermore, zealous of his newfound faith, Constantine went a huge step further and decreed that all of Rome become a Christian society.[12] In a short time, Christianity went from being the religion of persecuted believers in Christ to being the official religion of the empire. As the official religion of Rome, the first so-called Christian society was born. Constantinian Christianity would impact the world, indeed. But also, Constantinian Christianity impacted the church and marked a transition from the church as the body of believers in Christ to an institutional church. Additionally, the shift in society from faith by personal conviction in a world of indifference to Constantine's Christian empire marked a shift in Christians' self-understanding, such that over time, the institutional model of faith undermined the original emphasis on deep-rooted personal faith in

11. Miller, *Peculiar Life*, 24.

12. In the first century, Paul and Peter paid the ultimate price in Rome for the sake of the gospel. Paul was beheaded and Peter was crucified upside down. Amazingly, four centuries later, Christianity was the religion of the empire.

Christ. Although good news to the suffering Christians, the challenge was that Christianity would lose its peculiarity to the world.

The reign of Constantine marked a transition from the church being a body of believers who lived out her own body politic defined by Christ and empowered by the Spirit, to the leadership of Rome calling all of Rome to profess Christianity. This was a massive shift that altered both the church and what it meant to live as a Christian.

For three hundred years, Christian identity had meant forsaking the world for Christ. Under the rule of Emperor Diocletian (245–313 CE), the state had declared war on the church to eradicate Christians. In this and other ways, Constantine's conversion to Christianity had a positive impact on the history of Christianity. To summarize a few of them: From a historical perspective, it marked the first time in history that a leader of an empire was converted to the Christian faith. As a result, from a social perspective, it was an important time in history, in which the Western world fostered public respect for the Christian faith. From a missional perspective, the Christian faith was placed on the world stage. Finally, from an ecclesial perspective, and as a direct result of Constantinian leadership, the first official councils were held. These positive effects of Constantinian Christianity should not be undervalued.

While there are more positive reflections upon Constantine's efforts to treat Christians with dignity in society, a so-called Christian society was not the worldview into which the church was born. An authentic Christian society seems impossible. The church is a collection of believers who find identity in the peculiarity of Christ while surrounded by a society that does not share his way of being in the world. While every society needs rules and regulations to enforce civility and respect for self and for others, a civilization cannot produce a nation of "believers" by force of rules and regulations.

## The "People of God" in the New Testament: A Holy Society or a Holy Church?

The New Testament, moreover, calls for a holy church and not a holy society or nation like that of Israel. The church that God intends must by necessity exist with indifference to the world, both to guard herself from the pollution of the world and to advance God's mission to impact the world. Hauerwas and Willimon coin the metaphor for the church as "a Christian colony" in the world.[13] For them, the message that sustains the colony is Christ for the world. Hauerwas and Willimon explain that as a colony, the church is "God's means of a major offensive against the world, for the world."[14] But also, as a "Christian colony," the church consists of Christians who must conform to Christianity through personal piety and self-denial. Jesus says, "If anyone would come after me, let him deny himself and take up his cross and follow me" (Mark 8:34). Although radical in practice, the Eastern monks also provide a way to think about self-denial in pursuit of Christ. In principle, we learn from the monks that in order for the church to advance the work of Christ in the world, we must choose God's way of living despite the thinking and dictates of the world around us. James 1:27 states, "Religion that is pure and undefiled before God, the Father, is this . . . to keep oneself unstained from the world." Biblical Christianity is most authentic when we choose the marks of Christ's teachings, behavior, and yes, even Christ's sufferings.

Christ's goal for Christians is holistically transformational. When Christianity's goal becomes legislation of the masses by institutionalized regulation, the divine focus on heart transformation is compromised. The example of Constantinian Christianity shows that legislation of the masses toward Christian devoutness does not work. Authentic Christianity is a divine invitation of the heart. The Christian faith starts and ends in love.

## America: A Post-Christian Society?

Today, we live in an increasingly religious and socially pluralistic society. Some have dubbed the world of the twenty-first century "post Christian." Many American Christians believe that it is their divine mission to get America back on track with a Christian identity. *Charisma* magazine dedicated an entire edition (October 2012) to the need to pray America back to God. These prayers are not only for the church to return to Christ, but carry the assumption that America once was such a Christian society. Those who hold such assumptions tend to interpret Old Testament prophecies pertaining to the nation of Israel as proclamations of judgment and blessing on any nation—but particularly America—that was once "Christian" but has "turned its back on God."

Despite original sins of racism, greed, and elitism, many American Christians believe that as a nation, America has been an authentic Christian

13. Hauerwas and Willimon, *Resident Aliens*, 51.
14. Ibid.

nation, trusting God, for 240 years.[15] The executive director of the Congressional Prayer Caucus, Lea Carawan, says, "The spirit of America is derived from deeply held Judeo-Christian values."[16] The very idea that a nation could be Christian traces its roots back to the fourth century's emperor of Rome, who used his authority to declare Rome as a Christian society. Constantine's authority to make such a declaration was from the state, not God.

The biblical concept of Christianity is rooted in a personal encounter with a risen Lord. As a result of that encounter, God invites the believer's life and lifestyle to the privilege of conforming to the likeness of Christ. In his reflections, called "Paul's Conversion," interestingly, Pope Benedict XVI emphasizes, "We are Christians only if we encounter Christ."[17] He elaborates, "Christianity is not a new philosophy or new morality. . . . Only in this personal relationship with Christ, only in this encounter with the Risen One do we really become Christians. . . . Therefore, let us pray to the Lord to enlighten us, so that, in our world, He will grant us the encounter with his presence, and thus give us a lively faith, an open heart, and great charity for all, capable of renewing the world."[18] The Christian experience is compromised when we expect a nation to have the capacity to embrace Christ without having such an encounter with the risen Lord. The Christian encounter with God is a call from God to extend help to a world that desperately needs the same experience.

## Slaves Discover Christ in a World of Hate

The third model is the emergence of the "black church" paradigm. Ironically, the slaves learned about Christianity from the white people that enslaved them; but they were able to discover a different interpretation of the faith than that of the oppressors. Theologian Nancy Lynne Westfield explains that slave Christians were able to subordinate white people's sacred rhetoric to their own way of interpreting personal salvation, conviction of sin, charismatic praise and worship, the equality of all peoples, and the divine promise of heaven.[19] From the repulsive experience of jam-packed slave ships to the most dehumanizing and devastating enslavement known

15. See Carawan, "In God We Trust."

16. Ibid.

17. Pope Benedict XVI, "Paul's Conversion."

18. Ibid.

19. Floyd-Thomas et al, *Black Church*, 4.

to humankind, millions of Africa's children turned their souls to an un-known, unnamed God that might hold the answer to their present fate.[20] They heard about Jesus and sought him fervently. From the foils of human debauchery, somehow, they were able to discover a Christ who cared for them, loved them, and would someday, somehow emancipate them.

Forbidden to learn to read and write, these "field theologians" ex-pressed deep insights into spirituality through the mediums that "the world didn't give them and the world couldn't take away"—music and poetry.[21] They found ways to build community among themselves through worship, music, and poetry. Even when Willie Lynch's philosophy of control through division sought to cripple the slaves, they persisted in the power of unity. Their common experiences and love for music and poetry was not merely for the sake of entertainment but were central to fostering their community of faith. Such faith in God drew them together in a unified hope.

The slave church was a tightly woven faith community that understood the relationship between their faith in God and their everyday life, work, and play.[22] Their faith was deeply rooted in hope that one day God would make things better for them. It was the "already and not yet" theology of the New Testament. God would make life better on earth; at the same time they were aware that the real joy would come beyond the rivers of this life. With shameless conviction in the God of their hope, they boldly sang songs that helped them to maintain faith and a sense of community for more than four hundred years. Their theology was revealed in song lyrics like, "I got shoes, you got shoes / All of God's children got shoes"; "We're marching to Zion / Beautiful, beautiful Zion / We're marching upward to Zion, the beautiful city of God"; and "We shall overcome / We shall overcome / We shall overcome some day / Oh, deep in my heart, I do believe / We shall overcome some day."

20. Ibid.

21. For more on African American theology and sociology as imbedded in the spiri-tuals and the blues, see Cone, *Spirituals*. Cone was one of the earliest systematic theolo-gians who wrote on the theological implications of the spirituals. Most slaves could not read or write. Much of their history, including the music and poetry, was passed down through oral tradition.

22. See Cone, *Spirituals*, 30. See also Hollenweger, *Pentecostalism*, 2. Foremost histori-an Walter Hollenweger describes the oral and African roots of American pentecostalism. He says that the movement was mediated through African American slave Christianity. So the holiness-påentecostal movement is not only Wesleyan but also African American in that it weaves spirituality with concern for how Christians live their daily lives.

Their faith was communal. The communal element of faith was revealed in lyrics that emphasized the "we" and not the "me." This emphasis is supported by Hauerwas's point that an authentic "embodiment" of holiness exists, not through personal claims on holiness by individually rationalized truth, but rather through the life of habitual faith practices through community.[23] Slave Christians formed a community of faith in which each one saw oneself (at least in large part) as connected with another slave through common experiences and their common faith in God. As integral to the "African American experience," this shared faith propelled them forward as a community, against all odds.

## Slave Christianity: The Search for Pure Religion, Separate from Slave Master Religion

The history of American Christian slavery reveals another vision of Christianity. Unlike the desert fathers and mothers and the Constantinian Christians, slave Christians experienced faith against a backdrop of racial bigotry and hostility. While there were certainly slaves who propagated retaliatory violence in the name of Christ, the majority of slave Christians interpreted the faith as a nonviolent religion. Faith in God through worship, prayer, and treating people "right" was their primary escape from the hard life that slavery inflicted upon them.

It should be noted that the majority of white Americans during the slave era also proclaimed Christianity as their religion. The predominant form of white Christianity, however, validated bigotry and oppression of the African American people. For the most part, white slave masters did not allow slaves to participate in the full communion of their churches. Many of the white churches excluded slaves from attending services altogether, while others of them did allow slaves to come to their churches but reserved their seating in the balcony of the church rather than in the main sanctuary.[24]

---

23. See Hauerwas, "Sanctified Body," 22–23. In his essay, Hauerwas uses the Catholic peasants as an example to build his argument. However, I think that the slave Christians are equally as appropriate as an example to show the power of habitualized faith in community.

24. The only exception was probably the Society of Friends, later known as the Quakers. For more on the Society of Friends, see Fox, *Journal*.

*Slaves Discovered the Relationship between Faith and Everyday Life*

Furthermore, slave Christians understood the relationship between their claim of faith and their everyday life. In contemporary, individualized society, where the probability of achieving communal holiness is questionable, slave Christians help us think critically about individual responsibility to achieving a holy life acceptable to God. The slaves sought to translate their faith into everyday practice.

Slave "practical theology" is observable through their music as well. Two songs illustrate this point very clearly. "I'm gonna live so God can use me; anywhere, Lord, anytime! I'm gonna live so God can use me; anywhere, Lord, anytime" has become a favorite contemporary gospel song, but it has deep roots in the spirituals tradition. In its lyrics, one can find four theological points that are pertinent to this discussion. First, there is the acknowledgement that God's reign is supreme. The slaves believed that divine favor rests on those who honor God as "the big man upstairs," a colloquial way of acknowledging that God is above "the big man in the big house" or the slave master. So pleasing God in all things is the highest priority. Second, God desires to use human beings to advance God's agenda on earth. The slaves believed that ministry leaders are God's chief agents on earth. So it is to every person's advantage that God would choose him or her for God's service. The third theological notion is twofold. On the one hand, a woman or a man must conduct his or her everyday life with commitment to divine values. On the other hand, essentially religious affairs (singing and praying) require earnest engagement from a heart of deep earnestness. Sincerity is essential to honoring God. Authenticity is a divinely profound and conditional criterion for divine choosing. The fourth theological concept is that God is willing to use even the slave for divine purposes. Even the lowest-class person (so to speak), the slave, is a candidate for God's choice. The only requirement is that one conducts her or his everyday life in sincere devotion to God.

We learn from slave Christians that as we are desirous of divine favor with blissful eschatological expectation, there is a divine requirement to live and worship in reverence to a holy God. Another spiritual, "Everybody talkin' 'bout heaven ain't goin' there," is relevant to this discussion. There are two tenets of faith exposed here. First, although mostly illiterate, they had a type of spiritual intelligence that taught them that lip service is not enough to please God. They feared God more than their masters. No doubt their oppressive and often cruel masters were part of the reference to those with vain lip service. There is an essential connection between our everyday behavior and our profession of faith. As they say, "We must do more than talk about it. We have to be about it." Second, the slave Christian believed in another world that is better than the one they experienced. That world belongs to a people who are in this world but not of it. The song "Everybody talkin' 'bout heaven ain't goin' there" reveals the belief that life as they knew it was only temporary. For those who pleased God, who is the ultimate Master, there remains the promise of a better life than the one on earth.

There is an observable commonality between the themes conveyed in these two songs. In both, the theology suggests a divine expectation for Christians to behave in a manner that consecrates us for service to God and prepares us for life with God after death. Also, these spirituals teach that God expects more from Christians than mere confessions of faith. The second spiritual, "Everybody talkin' 'bout Heaven ain't goin' there," conveys the message that the Christian's lifestyle must back up confessional statements—else, "talk is cheap."

## Slave Lessons on Being Prophetic

Much of slave Christianity teaches us that to be different from the world does not imply the ceasing of social action and engagement. Slave Christian leaders like Isabella Baumfree (Sojourner Truth), Harriet Tubman, and Frederick Douglass were prominent leaders in the abolitionist movement. There was, of course, a minority group of angry militant slaves like Nat Turner and others who professed to be Christians but sought their freedom through a response of violence. Their approach mirrored the hostility of many white oppressors. However, Baumfree, Tubman, Douglass, and many slave ministers maintained a distinctly Christian nonviolent approach in the uphill struggle toward freedom. Now we look back on the work of abolitionists, such as Harriet Tubman's Underground Railroad and the writings of Sojourner Truth and Frederick Douglass, with gratitude as well as awe of their very fine Christian work. Their struggle of faith was arduous; yet, their distinctively Christian approach to the fight made the difference.

The work of nonviolent Christian slave ministers teaches us that the Christian call to distinction from the world becomes the first step toward our own meaningful engagement and influence in contemporary society. Where there is no distinctive action, influence loses strength. Acts 1:8 defines the role of Christians as bearing an unapologetic witness to the world.

Being a witness means to continue the presence of Christ in the world. By doing so, we collectively affect the world as Christ did. What was unique about Jesus was his willingness to love his "haters." In the face of utter brutality during the days before his crucifixion, Jesus maintained a nonviolent approach in the face of hate. He could have retaliated with hate but chose the power of love instead. A serious look into the history of slave Christianity reveals an expression of the faith that mirrored the loving Christ, who, without violence, has positively impacted the history of America.

## HOLINESS AS FORSAKING THE WORLD: IDENTIFYING WITH CHRIST

In *Holiness by Grace*, Chapell rightly comments that the love of the Savior draws us from the lure of temptation.[25] God's love is the power that transforms people from the inside out. The Savior's transformative love empowers us to walk away from sin's clout. In Paul's own words, legalistic, rigid religion develops followers with no internal change, who have no transformative power to sustain them during difficult times, and have "the appearance of godliness, but deny its power" (2 Tim 3:5).

As characterized by the writer of Ephesians, true holiness is Spirit-enlightened holiness, for he prays that members of the Ephesian church would have "the eyes of your hearts enlightened, that you may know what is the hope to which [Jesus] has called you, the riches of [God's] glorious inheritance among the saints" (Eph 1:18). This enlightenment is the ideal, which God intends for all believers to experience. This ideal involves a lifestyle that can only be discovered in Christ. The biblically operative word that defines that ideal is "holiness." Yet, again, the ideal of "holiness" has become a taboo even in some contemporary church circles. Especially where the language has historically been excessively infused with "can't do this or that," within these contexts, a new Christian feels more oppressed than liberated in Christ and may refuse to submit to such rigidity. The problem, however, is that when one truly identifies with Christ, one becomes willing to forsake the world. The biblical idea of forsaking the world has to do with the orienting of the self toward God rather than a rigid list of dos and don'ts. When one truly becomes the inheritance of Christ, a holy lifestyle becomes a desire of the heart and not a burden that others should place upon the believer.

25. Chapell, *Holiness*, 108.

## NOT OF THE WORLD BUT CALLED INTO THE WORLD

Furthermore, the church has both a missional and a prophetic role in society. Missions is Christ's invitation to the world, not only to accept his gracious offer of salvation but also to become part of the "called-out" ones—the church. As missional, she bears the responsibility to call people out of the world for transformation in Christ. Then, she sends them back to extend God's love and grace to the world. Holiness properly understood through the lenses of love and grace requires the love of the neighbor. This means that holiness must focus on the fullness of the Great Commandment—the love of God and neighbor.

## The Church as Missional

The first part of the Great Commandment is "Love the Lord your God." The second part is "Love your neighbor as yourself" (Matt 22:39). More than the "love of God" focus of the reclusive Eastern monastic tradition's approach to holiness, sincere social engagement is also required for the purpose of penetrating the darkness with the light of Christ's love. John Wesley teaches that as we pursue holiness for ourselves, the neighbor is an essential part of both our own holiness and that of the neighbor. In Wesley's own words, "So widely distant is the manner of building up souls in Christ . . . from that taught by the Mystics. . . . For contemplation is, with them, the fulfilling of the law, even a contemplation that 'consists in a cessation from all works.' Directly opposite of this is the Gospel of Christ. Solitary religion is not to be found there. 'Holy solitaries' is a phrase no more consistent with the Gospel than holy adulterers. The Gospel of Christ knows no religion but social; no holiness, but social holiness."[26]

The church's mission in the world involves the integrity of a body of believers who care for personal piety and the religion of a people who are concerned for others—believers and unbelievers—particularly those who experience distress and disenfranchisement and for an entire creation that is in need of God's love expressed in tangible ways. New Testament scholar and Anglican Bishop N. T. Wright critically asserts, "The church has been divided between those who cultivate their own personal holiness but do nothing about working for justice in the world and those who are passionate for justice but regard personal holiness as an unnecessary distraction

26. Wesley, *Works*, ed. John Emory, 592–93.

from that task. This division has been solidified by the church's unfortunate habit of adopting from our surrounding culture the unhelpful packages of 'left-wing' and 'right-wing' prejudices, the former speaking of 'justice' and meaning 'libertarianism' and the latter speaking of 'holiness' and meaning 'dualism.' All this must be firmly pushed to one side. What we need is integration."[27] Vital to this mission is that Christians live lives of high moral character. Wright further comments, "The high calling of Christian morality is therefore the necessary handmaid of the still higher callings of Christian worship and mission. The virtues which constitute the former are the vital components of the latter."[28] In other words, on the subject of holiness, the love of God and love of neighbor are not mutually exclusive.

The penetrating love of Christ as manifested through the church gently calls and influences the world, calling people out of darkness into the light of Christ. In a lecture to pastors, former attorney general of the United States of America John Ashcroft captured the mission of the church in the following profound quote: "The church is called to inspire and not to impose."[29] The church, therefore, must position herself to draw positive attention to a humble and loving Christ rather than a suspected hostile and coercive Christ.

## The Church as Prophetic

Furthermore, the prophetic nature of the church involves being called to open the eyes of a society to the love, hope, and grace in Christ. Walter Brueggemann's thesis in *Prophetic Imagination* is helpful here: "The task of a prophetic ministry is to nurture, nourish, and evoke a consciousness and perception alternative to the consciousness and perception of the dominant culture around us."[30] The experience of Christ flies in the face of competing philosophies inculcated in societies that are tarnished by sin. Christians, moreover, live in a world into which we were born the first time. However, when we accepted Christ as Savior, we were born again. John 3:1–7 teaches that this rebirth does not constitute a reentering of the womb to be born again; rather this rebirth constitutes a birth from above. By virtue of the new kind of existence in the world, we are part of the church. We share the

27. Wright, *After*, 247.
28. Ibid.
29. Ashcroft, "Hymns and Scripture."
30. Brueggemann, *Prophetic Imagination*, 3.

consciousness and perception related to our new existence. We are in the world but no longer of it.

Emphasizing the difference between being "in the world" and "of the world," pastor and religious columnist Timothy Jones correctly comments, "Christianity is at its best when it is focused on building the church and allowing the church to speak against the evils of its context."[31] Jones posits that the best prophetic work that has been done in North America has come from a church that has stood apart from society. He points out, for example, "Senator King" has a nice sound to it, but Martin Luther King Jr. would not have been able to spearhead the Civil Rights Movement as an instrument of society. King functioned as a prophetic voice of a prophetic church.[32] There are two critical points of note in Jones' characterization. First, in a time in which people, particularly Westerners, are infatuated with individuality, albeit challenging, it is important that Christians rediscover the meaning of being part of a universal church. Second, it is necessary for the church to exist in contrast to society in order to fulfill her role as the continued presence and power of Christ.

Christianity is a faith that aggressively extends itself to the world. Thus, it is important for Christians to embrace our peculiarity without excluding ourselves from the rest of the world. Practically speaking, Christians must always hold *strategy* in tension with the divine calling to *peculiarity* in line with 1 Peter 2:9, which reminds us that we are "a chosen race, a royal priesthood, a holy nation, a people for his own possession" so that we "may proclaim the excellencies of him who called [us] out of darkness into his marvelous light." The church is not called to the likeness of the world. Rather, the church should call people who are called out of the world to know and live like Christ did.

The Christian life demands that faith crystallizes our everyday lifestyle and attitude in a way that reflects Christ. From an evangelism perspective, my dad often told my brother and me that to win the sinner to Christ, we must not be like them. He often admonished us, "You can't be a fish and catch a fish. You must be the fishermen." This is the only way the Christian is able to impact the world for Christ. We cannot be like them to win them. Biblical Christianity is revolutionary—either people will love us or hate us for what we stand for. The sooner we grasp the countercultural realities of Christianity, the more effective we become in impacting society.

31. Jones, "Christmas Tree."
32. Ibid.

Chick-fil-A is an example of a Christian business that seeks to live out biblical Christian peculiarity. Samuel Truett Cathy and his family are devout Christians who have sought to live out their faith despite society's increased moral plurality. Cathy established that all of the family's Chick-fil-A franchises be closed on Sunday in observance of the Lord's Day. Although I have argued that Sunday's observance of the Lord's Day is a historical misconstrual of the biblical Sabbath in Constantine's Christianity, Cathy's stand for contemporary Christian practices is a plausible one. Most businesses have no respect for any "holy day." Rest is not considered sacred in our society. Greed is a tremendous vice in our society; making money is more important than the sanctity of rest. The Chick-fil-A model stands as a beacon in the night because it defies common economic sense during the current recession. Money and business are not more important than a religious stance on what's holy and what's not as pertaining to Sunday business. Americans have a history of misappropriating the pursuit of meaning and value. True fulfillment does not emerge from making a busy life of making money. True fulfillment occurs when we develop a rhythm of life upon the foundations of God's holiness.

## A PERSONAL YEARNING FOR HOLINESS

Words from Bishop Augustine of Hippo's *Confessions* inspire me in my own desire to live a life of Christian fulfillment. He says, "Man desires to praise thee, for he is a part of thy creation; he bears his mortality about with him and carries the evidence of his sin and proof that thou dost resist the proud. Still he desires to praise thee, this man who is only a small part of thy creation. Thou hast prompted him, that he should delight to praise thee."[33] Like the bishop, there are times when I work continuously; but I remain discontent. What I have is not enough. What I have accomplished is not enough. Where I am going is not enough. Accepting my calling to ministry is not enough. Helping others is not enough. I find myself yearning for more—not for more church services, not more ministry assignments, not more stuff or more accomplishments but more of something else. In the words of philosopher Blaise Pascal, "What else does this craving, and this helplessness, proclaim but that there was once in man a true happiness, of

33. Augustine, *Confessions*, 5.

which all that now remains is the empty print and trace? This man tries in vain to fill with everything around . . . though none can help."[34]

There are two notions that emerge from Augustine's prayer coupled with Pascal's observation. First, all human beings—both Christians and non-Christians—must wrestle with human vulnerability to sinfulness. Second, there is a part of each person—Christian or non-Christian—that yearns for enduring substance, which human standards cannot satisfy. Two questions emerge. The first is whom will we worship? The second is how will we worship? Pascal asserts that this infinite abyss can be filled only with an infinite and immutable object—in other words, by God alone.[35] When we answer Christ's invitation to be part of the church, we enter a new way of living in the world. God's way is one in which God's people enjoy the fullness of life in a world that is in search of the same fulfillment. Christians experience fulfillment when we discover that life is fullest when we worship God and live according to the teachings of Christ. This is what it means to be *in* the world but not *of* it.

## SUMMARY

The life of holiness requires a posture of distinction in a world that cannot be holy without Christ. First, from the Eastern monastic tradition we learn the role that individuals play in the pursuit of holiness. They placed an emphasis on personal piety in which the everyday life of Christians participated in the stride toward holiness. Second, Constantinian Christianity teaches us that the institutionalization of Christianity does not achieve a desired Christian nation. In fact, it undermines the unique purpose of the church that God intends to be countercultural. Third, the slave Christian tradition was born among an ostracized people who found meaning in Jesus. We learn from them that identity in Christ brings meaning and hope for this life and the life to come. To borrow again from Barth's sentiment, the church shares in the task of society precisely to the extent that she fulfils her *own* task.[36] It is within the framework of Christ's agenda for the church where we find Christian *particularity* as well as *peculiarity*, defining what it means to be *in* the world but not *of* the world. The language of Christian *particularity* points to the distinctive way of living in the world—a way that

34. Pascal, *Pensées*, 45.
35. Ibid.
36. Barth, *Karl Barth*, 273.

reflects Christ, as expressed in Scripture. Christian *peculiarity* expresses the difference that the Holy Spirit makes in the life and lifestyle of the believer.

## REFLECTION

### Questions to Ponder

Have you ever wondered what it means to be in the world but not of it? Have you ever found yourself resistant to the subject of "holiness" because of past affiliations with churches with many rules but no real insight on biblical holiness? Does your soul ever seem empty and in search of something more, even when you seem to accomplish something for which you are grateful? Since you accepted Christ, have you felt a longing for greater understanding about what it means to be a Christian?

## PRAYER

If through the pages of this chapter you have become inspired to pursue God's holiness, pause and pray the following prayer.

> Lord, I want to be holy! None of my worldly pursuits could grant me full reflection of you. I want to be holy. Please help me be holy as you are holy. Amen.

# 3

## Biblical Holiness: A Theological Reflection on Selected Passages

Holiness is not merely a doctrine or dogma.
It is part of divine revelation.

—Noel Brooks

### BE HOLY: A DIVINE MANDATE

From Genesis to Revelation, holiness surfaces as a biblical theme. The subject of holiness is sometimes explicit, and at other times, implicit: God is holy; God makes certain days holy; God requires holiness from his people— the nation of Israel; through Jesus, God extends the invitation to Gentiles to be holy; the Holy Spirit empowers people to live holy; the bridegroom, Jesus Christ, will return for his holy bride, the church. A close reading of the biblical narrative reveals critical insight for holy living. Scripture claims that the ontological nature of God is holy. Importantly, God summons his people to share in the holiness that defines God's own essence. Admittedly, the divine requirement that we live holy seems overwhelming. How can frail and sinful human beings become like God? It is simply impossible. Theologically, God's summons to holiness is an invitation to rest in God's grace and love.

Moreover, holiness is best understood not merely as a descriptive teaching or dogmatic doctrine, but more prominently as divinely transcendent revelation.[1] God's creativity in creation, grace in redemption, love as expressed toward us again and again, and his truth that guides us are all attributes of divine holiness. The old wise saying seems appropriate: "Some things cannot be taught; they have to be caught." I often reference this quote in my homiletics classes at Regent University when explaining the process of translating the academic study of preaching into the preaching moment. There is a process of "catching" the knowledge in one's soul more than simply learning with the mind. In a similar fashion, I wish to express that the transcendent nature of holiness is "caught" in the soul; it is both initiated and translated through divine revelation.

Already, in the first five books of the Old Testament, we discover God's requirement for God's people to be holy. *Torah* and *Pentateuch* are the Hebrew terms, both referring to the first five books of the Old Testament. *Pentateuch* means "first five books." In them, Jews count approximately 613 laws and call them *Torah*. The term *Torah* refers to God's instructions, or God's laws. In the Old Testament, God requires the Hebrew people to obey all of what God instructs. These rules define holiness for every area of life—public and private—in ancient Hebrew history. They mark a way for God's people to be different than the other nations. God has always expected God's people to be different than those who are not part of the community called "God's people." The most divine way to be different is through living a life of holiness.

On the central issue that God's people—the church—be holy, Old Testament Christian scholar John N. Oswalt posits that the fate of the Christian church in America and around the world depends upon what the church does with the biblical teaching on holiness.[2] If Oswalt's inference is correct, Christians must search the Scripture to discover the vitality and longevity of the church.

## Two Aspects of Biblical Holiness: To Be Set Apart and to Be Pure

Scholars have observed that throughout the Old and New Testaments there are at least two broad categories as pertaining to the issue of holiness: the first one has to do with being set apart for divine purpose; the second one

1. Brooks, *Scriptural*, 9.
2. Oswalt, *Called*, 1.

is holiness as divine purity. Throughout Scripture, one or both of these perspectives of holiness come to light. In both aspects holiness requires communal and individualized attention. The Old Testament bears record that God sees all of Israel as the "Chosen People." Yet, God is concerned that individuals live God's Word. One person could desecrate the community through violation of God's commands. Therefore, everyone is expected to subscribe to holiness for the communal notion of holiness to be in full effect. Similarly, in the New Testament, God extends the invitation beyond the Jews to all people. The call is as communal as it is personal. Everyone is invited to partake in the community of faith where there is one Lord, one faith, and one baptism.[3]

As new believers transition into this "household of God," they must understand what it means to be part of this newfound household or common community of faith. Admittedly, in a highly individualized society, it is hard to overcome the idea of the church as a collection of individuals who have individually decided to follow Jesus. But, such a concept of the church is contrary to a biblical vision of the church. Emphasis on personal salvation eschews the ancient Middle Eastern worldview of community that exists in the backdrop of the biblical narrative. The ancient common understanding of community and faith seems rather foreign to contemporary Western thinking. At the same time, young people yearn for community today more than ever in Western history. Contributing factors include the broken family, young peoples' desire to be accepted, and a raging stride toward popular appeal. From a positive perspective, this generation teaches us about the essentiality of community to all of life, including what it means to feel fulfilled. The tragedy is that Western churches are lacking in our theology of community. We can learn from this generation that there is fulfillment in community.

The sacred call to be in the world requires that this glaring gap in Western religious life be closed. For example, evangelism and worship remain stuck in the individualization of the past. The emphasis on church growth has prioritized numbers over community. The individual as a number added has become more important than the quality of the community as a whole. Such church-growth efforts are a testament to life as we have known it—to an obsession with individualism. Religious life, moreover, has been relegated to individuals' own private devotions. While personal piety

---

3. See Eph 4:5. It follows that while there are many angles to discern truth in community, there are not many different truths in Christ's church.

serves as an essential element of faith and holiness, we discover the fullness of life in Christ when we understand that we belong to a body. In doing so, we learn the power of self-abandonment to embrace our communal identity in Christ.

Identity in Christ requires self-abandonment. If we are to live holy, we must come to terms with the self-abandonment principle. Self-abandonment does not involve violence, as was thought by the early gnostic Christians, who held to the necessity to separate the body from the spirit. Conversely, for the contemporary believer, "dying to self" means as body and spirit we live in such a way that separates us from the world. Submission to God includes fellowship with a community of selfless people of faith. As such, we form a community joined together by faith in search of a lifestyle that pleases God. That is the church of Jesus Christ, called to a life in constant quest of God. The global community of faith is joined together through the Eucharist, Bible study, prayer, and a commitment to the leadership of the Holy Spirit.

## Old Testament and the Notion of Holiness

Over the past forty years or so, an increasing number of Evangelical and Spirit-filled churches are finding contemporary relevance of Old Testament teachings on practices ranging from the financial benefit of tithing to the health-related importance of dietary restraints. Both are laws in Torah that were previously rejected as unnecessary, particularly in Western Christianity. I often hear testimonies from people who tithe that there is benefit in it; many people report that they don't miss the ten percent, suggesting that there is a divine increase related to the practice. This message has taken off particularly within the Word of Faith movement, but also in classical pentecostal churches such as COGIC, Assemblies of God, UPC, and PAW, to name a few.

Additionally, as society has become more health conscious, more and more people do not eat pork and shellfish. Research shows that there are health benefits in refraining from them. More and more restaurants are cooking with less pork products. Traditional theological claims suggest that biblical teachings on dietary consumption were done away with in the New Testament. However, many Christians have begun staying away from pork and shellfish.

It strikes me as strange that society often sets the framework for Christian theology and practice. Sometimes the practices are biblical, and other times they are not. In a society that is driven by benefits, it concerns me that the attraction to a message on tithing and dietary restraints may be more accurately driven by the perceived material benefits than by a hunger for God's holiness. If so, as society changes, the church follows society's lead rather than maintaining her theological and philosophical particularity.

Moreover, following God's instructions has benefits that are material but also beyond the material. There are, more importantly, spiritual assets in obeying what the Lord says. There is such a nature of holiness inculcated in divine instructions that, when we obey, we experience a quality of life that the world can't give and the world can't take away. So, while Christ fulfills the ceremonialism in the Old Testament, a closer read of the Old Testament reveals a wealth of information as pertaining to holiness that might translate into spiritual vitality and practical application of holiness for Christians today.

A key difference between the Old and New Testaments is revealed in the shift from defining God's people exclusively as Israel to defining God's people as the church, which bridges God's promises to anyone who believes in Jesus Christ. Through Christ, believers (whether Jew or Gentile) become the people of God by faith. While the New Testament altered the definition of what it means to be the "people of God," there is no evidence that the requirement for holiness ever changed. The New Testament, in fact, draws upon the Old Testament to define what it means for the church to be holy. A close reading of both the Old and New Testaments is crucial for our understanding of holiness.

## Torah

The command to live holy and teachings on holiness are prevalent throughout Torah. Biblical scholarship notes that the third book of Torah, Leviticus, emerges as the seedbed for Hebrew lessons on holiness. Torah, as holiness, helps us understand God's intended relationship with humankind, on the one hand; on the other, we, God's people, gain greater appreciation for divine grace through Christ (see Rom 12:1).

Late second- and early third-century theologian Tertullian[4] argues that the Spirit as sanctifier makes the waters holy in Genesis 1:2b by virtue

---

4. See Johnson, *Religious*. Tertullian was from the north African city of Carthage. He was converted when he was thiry years old in the church of Carthage, then later left the church to join the Montanists. Montanists were a stricter group of Christians who

of touching them. His point is that the lower substance must take to itself the quality of higher substance. This suggests that upon encounter, the Spirit (higher substance) possesses material reality (lower substance).[5] Tertullian's thought reminds me of the old song we used to sing, written by Bill Gaither, "He Touched Me," which says, "He Touched me, Oh He touched me / And oh the joy that floods my soul! / Something happened and now I know / He touched me and made me whole."[6]

Genesis 1:2b implies that the Spirit purifies the whole earth in preparation for the six days of reordering and creating in Genesis 1 and 2. In doing so, the Father reveals the Spirit's power to sanctify all of creation.

For Tertullian, the initial moving of the Spirit in Genesis 1:2b does not include the fullness of cosmic sanctification. It, rather, implies the divine desire for all of creation to be holy. As a result of the foretaste of God's glory, all of creation yearns for the infilling of the Spirit. In a similar way, baptism in water prepares us to receive the Spirit.[7] First Peter 3:21 states, "Baptism, which corresponds to this, now saves you, not as a removal of dirt from the body but as an appeal to God for a good conscience." Thus water baptism does not sanctify the believer. It signifies one's desire for the fullness of the Spirit. As the Spirit descends upon the water for baptism, she prepares us to receive the baptism of the Spirit—the sanctifying power of God. I mention this here because the early mention of the moving of the Spirit in Genesis becomes the antecedent to the sanctifying work of the Spirit. I will return to this theme of the sanctifying work of the infilling of the Spirit in the chapters to follow.

Besides Tertullian's and others' theological insights on holiness in Genesis 1:2b, the *term* "holy" first appears in Genesis 2. Genesis 2:3 states, "So God blessed the seventh day and made it holy, because on it God rested from all his work that he had done in creation." The narrator uses the word "holy" to describe the unique nature of the seventh day of the week. God

---

intensely sought the power of the Spirit and taught about the life and work of the Spirit. For them, the Spirit provides freedom and openness to new revelations and ecstasies. Some scholars like Luke Timothy Johnson point out that in Tertullian we discover that early Christians, post-New Testament times, exercised glossalalia (speaking in tongues) as part of their worship in the Spirit.

5. Tertullian, *On Baptism*, chapters 4–8.

6. Although the song is Christocentric, speaking of Jesus, the sanctified churches (especially the Oneness churches but also Trinitarian churches) understood the lyrics as referring to the moving of the Spirit.

7. Tertullian, *On Baptism*, chapters 4–8.

ordered the world in six days and rested on the seventh day. The Sabbath's chief theological implication in Genesis is that God gives rest as a holy gift.

## SABBATH, THE FIRST THING GOD DECLARED HOLY

I want to note several insights as pertaining to the holiness of the Sabbath day. First of all, the initial thing that God declares holy in Scripture is the Sabbath day. God set apart the seventh day from the other days of the week, distinguishing it as God's blessed day because it is God's own day of rest. Genesis 2:3a expresses the relationship between God's blessings and God's holiness. In other words, the blessing is holiness, and holiness is the blessing. If a believer wants to obtain the ultimate blessing from God, that blessing is holiness, the very essence of God that permeates the fullness of life. As Christians, many times we ask for and expect material blessings from God, but less often, we seek for divine holiness. The second chapter of the Bible reveals that divine blessings and holiness are inextricably intertwined in God's vision of maximized human experience and satisfaction.

Second, God rests on the seventh day. God's calling of the seventh day as blessed and holy is associated with God's own state of peace, suggesting that true peace comes into play when we abide in a place of blessings and holiness. Note that in Genesis 1, at dusk of the six preceding days, God declared that what He had created was good, but *not* holy. It should be noted that God did not choose to rest in the beautiful goodness of the preceding days of creation. Rather, God purposely set apart an extra day to rest in the beauty of its holiness. When we discover the beauty of holiness, we experience peaceful rest. Augustine sheds insight on this point in saying, "Thou hast made us for thyself and restless is our heart until it comes to rest in thee."[8]

Third, spiritual rest must be coupled with practical rest. God created the Sabbath day as a gift for spiritual and physical rejuvenation. The old saying goes, "We can work ourselves to death." It is true. While work is sacred, rest is equally as sacred. God created six days for us to work and one day for us to rest. On the issue of work and rest, Claire E. Wolfteich notes the necessity of rest, particularly as it is critical to women's spiritual lives. Yet, her commentary on rest is insightful for everyone. In *Navigating New Terrain,* she emphasizes married women's rigid work ethic, and is critical of religious institutions, namely churches, for not addressing the moral and

---

8. Augustine, *Confessions*, 5.

spiritual implications of working too much, a problem that plagues many people.[9] People work too hard and have too little time to enjoy the fruit of their labor or the splendor of creation. We become slaves to our work. Although good, sacred, and holy, work has the tendency to compromise the sanctity of rest.

Fourth, the Decalogue, also called the Ten Commandments, reminds God's people of the sanctity of rest from creation. The fourth commandment states,

> "Remember the Sabbath day, to keep it holy. Six days you shall labor, and do all your work, but the seventh day is a Sabbath to the Lord your God. On it you shall not do any work, you, or your son, or your daughter, your male servant, or your female servant, or your livestock, or the sojourner who is within your gates. For in six days the Lord made heaven and earth, the sea, and all that is in them, and rested on the seventh day. Therefore the Lord blessed the Sabbath day and made it holy" (Exod 20:8–11).

Most of the other commandments, with the exception of the fourth and fifth commandments, begin with "You shall not." The fourth commandment is the only one that begins with the word "remember." This commandment calls God's people to the remembrance that from the beginning the Sabbath day has been holy. We should, moreover, rest on that day as God also rested on it. It is unlikely that the one who made the universe, who crafted the stars and the sun and moon, who made the oceans and the sky, needed to rest. God's rest demonstrates the need for us, who are created in God's image, to rest. God was creative and then rested. This order shows us how to live out our calling to creative work and to be at peace with our work!

Importantly, after a week of work, the gift of Sabbath rest revivifies us for a more productive workweek, as well as repositions our minds toward God, who is aware of the needs of the human family. Jesus points out that the Sabbath day is a gift to us (Mark 2:27–28; Matt 12:8; Luke 6:5). Wayne Muller insists, "Because we do not rest, we lose our way. We miss the compass points that would show us where to go; we bypass the nourishment that would give us succor. We miss the quiet that would give us wisdom. We miss the joy born of effortless delight."[10] Muller's point is well taken that Sabbath is essential to spiritual vitality, but also to reorienting the self toward a renewed journey. Additionally, Sabbath, as spiritual renewal,

---

9. See Wolfteich, *Navigating*, 111. See also Schor, *Overworked*, 8.

10. Muller, *Sabbath*, 1.

extends beyond simply preparedness for a continued journey or the work ahead. Sabbath rest is an end in itself.

Fifth, Sabbath rest symbolizes true peace when we rest in God's blessings and live out God's holiness as a rhythm of life. This point was brought home in a talk delivered by the former dean of my institution at a faculty retreat. In his keynote address, on the subject of "Sabbath Living," pentecostal philosopher Michael Palmer put forward that Sabbath living orients us to respond to God in gratitude and faith, and to our fellow human beings with compassion and understanding.[11] Palmer arrives at this conclusion as he critiques Steven Covey's seventh habit, "Sharpening the Saw," in his famous book 7 *Habits of Highly Effective People*. It relegates physical, mental, spiritual, and social/emotional renewal merely as a means toward effectiveness in other areas of our lives. Palmer argues that Covey's underlying principle for "Sharpening the Saw" is results-oriented and suggests that "sharpening the saw" helps keep one fresh to continue producing. This results-oriented language, explains Palmer, reinforces the preeminence of work, with rest as simply a means to an end.[12] So, if we pause at Muller's emphasis on Sabbath rest as a kind of restorative repose, we obstruct Palmer's emphasis on the fullness of biblical Sabbath as the celebration of the holiness of the moment of rest.[13] Just as tithing is more than an instrument to greater material gain, and as dietary restraints are more than a means to healthier bodies, the Sabbath day should be understood as more than a means, or an instrument, for continued work or enhanced work potential.

Jürgen Moltmann explains that the whole work of creation was performed for the sake of Sabbath, rather than the other way around. The Sabbath day, therefore, is the feast of creation.[14] Here the emphasis is on the celebration of what God has done—the holiness of Sabbath involves joy in rest. Within a similar framework that "the Sabbath is the pinnacle of creation,"[15] Palmer coins his term "Sabbath Living." This language suggests that Sabbath observance becomes part of what it means to live out the rhythm of divine order—work and joyful rest.

Sixth, the biblical Sabbath is not only a concept for living, as Moltmann suggests, but also a specific day of the week—the seventh day. Throughout

11. Palmer, "Sabbath," 9.

12. Ibid.

13 Ibid.

14. Moltmann, *God*, 277.

15. Ibid.

Scripture, God's timing is as important as God's will. The Sabbath day accentuates this point more profoundly than any other example in Scripture. The Sabbath day is a time that God has designated from the foundations of the world for God's people to reorient our lives back to God and to remember God in the midst of our busy lives. Sabbath is associated with divine holiness because holiness reorients us back to God. We maximize the divine blessing when we align our will and timing with God's will, God's way, and God's timing.

Seventh, the Sabbath day is a gift from God, a sign that God loves and favors humankind above all of the rest of God's creation. Dorothy Bass states, "The commandment to 'observe' the Sabbath day is tied to the experience of a people newly released from bondage. Slaves cannot take a day off; free people can."[16] So while God's command, "You must observe my Sabbath" (Exod 31:13) sounds like another rigid rule to be kept, the true essence of the Sabbath has to do with freedom. Just as God commands Israel to observe their freedom by keeping the Sabbath day holy, Christians have an opportunity to observe our freedom in Christ through observance of the Sabbath day.

Eighth, Jews and Christians have an eschatological understanding of the holiness of the Sabbath. The Talmud, two third-century CE to fifth-century CE books of Jewish origin that focus on the teachings of God's Word, refer to the Sabbath using the Hebrew words *me'en 'olam ha-ba*. The Hebrew translates loosely as *somewhat like eternity or the world to come*.[17] In the New Testament, the writer of Hebrews reasons, "For if Joshua had given them rest, God would not have spoken of another day later on. So then, there remains a Sabbath rest for the people of God, for whoever has entered God's rest has also rested from his works as God did from His" (Hebrews 4:8–10). Therefore, from a Christian perspective, the Sabbath serves as a reminder that "Some glad morning when this life is over, we will fly away" to a heavenly freedom!

## God Gave a Holiness Code

In Hebrew tradition, Leviticus is the second book of *Torah* and is known as the "Holiness Code." Holiness remains an overarching theme of all of Torah, particularly Leviticus. It explains holiness as a way of life for God's

16. Bass, "Keeping Sabbath," 79.

17. Heschel, *Sabbath*, 74.

people.[18] God communicated to Moses and Aaron instructions by which the people were to live. The Holiness Code provided divine governance for them during the nation's formative years. Within the book of Leviticus there is a shift from the blessed, divine, restful holiness in God as viewed in Genesis 2:3 to a divine mandate that God's people be holy because God is holy.[19] Repeatedly, God beckons for the people to "be like God." This divine invitation is a summoning for reentry into the "likeness of God" that Adam and Eve knew in the Garden of Eden before they disobeyed God.

Three key verses that clearly state God's expectations for the people to be holy are Leviticus 19:2, Leviticus 20:7, and Leviticus 20:26. Leviticus 19:2 states, "Speak to all the congregation of the people of Israel and say to them: You shall be holy, for I the Lord your God am holy." The first part of this verse, "You shall be holy," is the starting point for understanding human beings' whole purpose in life—to be holy. God is speaking to the Hebrew people that which is not restricted to them, but is God's ultimate desire for all of humankind—to be holy like God. The holiness of God is God's gift to the people of God so that our lives might reach a level of inner peace and joy infused with happiness, trust, and love.

Anthropologist Alan Morinis records that during the second half of the nineteenth century in Lithuania, Rabbi Yisrael Lipkin Salanter started a movement that he named after the Hebrew word *mussar,* which means to conduct oneself morally.[20] The *Mussar movement* was grounded in Leviticus 19:2.[21] In this current discussion, the reference to mussar suggests that the principle points to Leviticus 19:2 as a divine indicator that the Bible teaches wisdom for everyday life. The Mussar movements shine Bible light on the causes of suffering and expose how to realize our highest spiritual potential, including a daily experience of life that is infused with joy, trust, and love.[22] In other words, human beings are here on earth for no other

---

18. Levine, *Leviticus*, xxxi.

19. See Willis, *Leviticus*, 176. Willis points out that Lev 20:25–27 is clear that "the Lord expects holiness of all the people of Israel, not just the priests."

20. See Morinis, *Everyday Holiness*, 20, 437. The word *mussar* first appears in Deut 11:2 and occurs several times throughout the Old Testament. The term is used on a continuum. Alan Morinis explains that sometimes the term is used to indicate "moral instructions" or "ethics," but other times it is used to convey a stronger connotation, such as "rebuke" or "reproof" or "reproach."

21. Ibid., 21. Also, the term *mussar* is used in Prov 1:2. It speaks of wisdom for moral conduct.

22. Ibid., 17.

purpose than to grow and blossom spiritually—to become holy. So the command in Leviticus 19: 2 to "be holy" is not simply a sanction. Rather, it suggests that only God's advice is capable of helping people to understand the people's divinely ordained potential.[23] This serves as a divine summoning to the inner person to draw closer to God, a precursor to the apostles' advice in James 4:8: "Draw near to God, and he will draw near to you." Rabbi Yisrael Lipkin Salanter, moreover, discerns correctly that it is God's will for everyone to live at our maximal potential.[24] That potential is realized in the lives of those who activate biblical teachings in everyday life.

Yet, there is a prerequisite to activating biblical teachings. Leviticus 20:7 states, "Consecrate yourselves, therefore, and be holy; for I am the Lord your God." Divine responsibility is laid on the shoulders of the people of God to cleanse themselves of manners of living that are contrary to a godly lifestyle. God not only invites the people to be like God, but also expects them to make godly choices. God's people must abandon worldly ideals and the people who live by them in order to embrace and activate God's ideals.

Expanding upon the premise of Leviticus 19:2 and 20:7, Leviticus 20:26 states, "You shall be holy to me; for I the Lord am holy, and I have separated you from the other peoples to be mine." These passages are essential to God's instructions on purity throughout Leviticus. They indicate that Torah is not only a book of laws to govern the Israelites, in the way that every nation needs laws in order to be a nation; Torah, rather, consists of instructions to maintain an intrinsic linkage to divine order. It articulates a way for God's people to be, live, and worship God in ways that distinguish them from other nations.

## Holiness is Not Impossible

God knows it is impossible for frail human beings to live holy on their own effort. Whereas on the one hand we see a divine command, or a demand of

23. Ibid., 22.

24. What is absent in Rabbi Yisrael Lipkin Salanter's mussar is an emphasis on following God. He focuses on gleaning principles from the Hebrew Bible. As he is Jewish, he does not see the New Testament as important because he does not accept Christ as Savior. Therefore, in the Mussar movement there is no acceptance of Christ's teachings as continuation of God's instructions. So, while mussar is limited, it does help us understand that God intends for all of humankind to maximize our potential. And, biblical holiness is God's way of guiding God's people toward that end.

sorts, on the other hand we hear the voice of a loving parent as she teaches a child to walk, a voice of authority saying, "Come on; you can do it." The message that emerges is that we were created to live holy—but only with divine help.

In Leviticus 20:26b, the writer briefly explains what it means to live holy: "I have separated you from other peoples." Old Testament scholar Timothy M. Willis points out that Leviticus 20:22–27 helps us to understand that the instructions in Leviticus define holiness in terms of what people do on a daily basis, away from the sanctuary. They present the belief that the Lord's home is not restricted to a sanctuary. There are at least two key lessons here.

First, the divine call to be "separate" suggests that holiness means a parting from people who are not in pursuit of what God wants. Subscribing to "practices of the nation[s] I am driving out" (v. 23) will yield the same result—divine alienation—within those God has called to be holy.[25] The practices of the ungodly are abhorrent to God, for Torah plainly sets forth a lifestyle converse to those of the other nations surrounding God's people.[26] The emphasis on being a "separated people" serves as an enduring principle for divine holiness. It underscores holiness in both the Old Testament and in the New Testament. God's power liberates and calls us to a set of values over and against those of the broader culture. Such a struggle is never easy, and it is continuous. Yet, it is crucial to being set apart, to being a holy people, as the Lord is holy.[27]

Second, there is no way to live holy without God's instructions. Just as in the case of the ancient Hebrews, we cannot fabricate holiness based on our own understanding apart from God. Only God determines what it means to be holy. Our journey does not end when God delivers us from the bondage of our past. As God's power delivered Israel from Egypt and then called them to holiness, God calls all of us who have been delivered by God's power to obey God's instructions for achieving holiness.

Undoubtedly, the New Testament standards of holiness supersede certain practices in Leviticus; yet, the New Testament maintains a divine call for Christians to live holy. As believers, we believe that Torah (the law) is fulfilled in Christ. What does that mean? We might ask, moreover, does the Bible give evidence that God's instructions in the Old Testament apply to

25. Willis, *Leviticus*, 176.
26. Ibid.
27. Ibid., 178.

the New Testament church? If so, in what way? Or, does the Holiness Code merely contain spiritual lessons and implications rather than prescribed practices for today? Do some literal rules of holiness, such as instructions against homosexual practices, apply today? Are there any other rules of holiness, such as dietary restrictions, that do not apply today? If so, how do we know which ones apply today and which ones do not? These questions are difficult to answer definitively. Yet, they are questions worth considering if we desire holy living.

Leviticus 20:26c explains that the divine goal in setting the Hebrew people apart is for God's own purposes: "to be mine." This brief rationale suggests that there is a privilege of divine Lordship extended to the lives of the persons who are willing to accept the peculiarity of holiness. The distinction is a divine claim of being called to the leadership and Lordship of divine order.

## THE BLESSEDNESS OF HOLINESS

The book of Deuteronomy explains that the divine requirement to live holy comes with benefits. God desires to bless God's people. As with other laws, holiness has causes and effects. For example, the law of gravity says that everything that goes up must come down; and the law of seedtime and harvest says that after seeds are planted, a harvest will follow. In like manner, following the law of holiness brings results. Deuteronomy 7:1a and 6a states, "The Lord your God brings you into the land that you are entering to take possession of it, and clears away many nations before you. . . . For you are a people holy to the Lord your God."

Torah establishes that when God's people subscribe to holiness, God regards their efforts as priceless. Imagine a loving parent who observes that a child is following his or her pattern of success. The parent looks at the child and says, "She is growing up to be just like me!" The parent smiles with priceless contentment. Nothing satisfies God more than a life that seeks to imitate God.

### The Book of Psalms

Scripture is clear that God is holy. Psalms goes to great lengths to glorify the holiness of God, "Ascribe to the Lord the glory due God's name. Worship the Lord in the splendor of holiness" (Ps 29:2). First Chronicles 16:29

echoes the need to give God the glory that is due God's name. The biblical instruction to give glory to God is humbling. How can human beings who are vulnerable to sinfulness give anything of value to the majestic Creator of the universe? Yet, God accepts our insufficient gifts, for in essence, God makes our unholy gifts holy.

God the Creator gives of God's self in the Spirit of holiness, a holiness that is unattainable by human efforts alone. Isaiah 64:5 states, "All our righteousness is as filthy rags." Human attempts at forging holiness by placing a premium on legalistic approaches (as mentioned earlier) create self-righteousness. Self-righteousness is a kind of pseudo-righteousness in which one glories in one's own efforts and achievements. Conversely, Clarence Earl Walker points out that the righteousness of Christ (not self-righteousness) envelops our hearts, protects our emotions, and secures our feelings amid Satan's assaults.[28] No one who subscribes to outward expressions of righteousness alone will succeed in their everyday bouts with evil. Walker further explains that living self-righteously is similar to wrapping one's hearts in "filthy rags" and going out to spiritual battle. These rags offer no adequate protection for spiritual battle.[29] When we seek to create a life of holiness for ourselves, we create a world of dark oppression. God's holiness is eternally beautiful. It liberates the soul. No wonder Augustine and Pascal insist that there is an innate desire in all human hearts, a longing that they identify as a yearning for God—a search for holiness that is defined and only obtained according to divine measures.

For centuries, both scholars and non-scholars have agreed that every human being has an inner yearning for wholeness. Some of us try to fulfill the hunger through a passion for work, promiscuity, substance abuse, exorbitant material gain, unhealthy relationships, notoriety, and money. Some believers even throw themselves into ministry as a search to fill the deep desire of the soul. After twenty years of ministry, thirteen years of college education, and five years as a seminary professor, I am learning that ministerial, academic, and professional accomplishments are rewarding. None of the preceding accomplishments, however, fills the central yearning of the human soul.

Repeatedly, the psalmist provides us with an understanding of our own frailties in the presence of God. The psalmist also helps us to see that only God's presence sanctifies God's people. Leviticus invites the believers

28. Walker, *Breaking*, 56.
29. Ibid.

into the magnitude of divine holiness. Moreover, those who hunger for holiness can appreciate how the Psalms teach that obeying the Lord's instructions becomes the only path to holiness.[30] Brueggemann notes that the book of Psalms' emphasis on obeying God starts in Psalm 1 and dominates much of the book, concluding in Psalm 73.[31] After that point, there is a shift in theme to an emphasis on praising God. However, a clear reverence for God's holiness remains a clear motif that suffuses all of Psalms.

Psalm 1 opens the book of Psalms with a recapitulation of Hebrew historical relationship with God—the Hebrew people had been God's chosen ones with divine commission to obey God for good success.

> Happy are those who do not follow the advice of the wicked, or take the path that sinners tread, or sit in the seat of scoffers; but their delight is in the law of the Lord, and on his law they meditate day and night. They are like trees planted by streams of water, which yield their fruit in its season, and their leaves do not wither. In all that they do, they prosper. The wicked are not so, but are like chaff that the wind drives away. Therefore the wicked will not stand in the judgment, nor sinners in the congregation of the righteous (Ps 1:1–5).

Notably, the psalmist expands the concept of a divine blessing in obeying God's instructions by delineating the adverse misfortune for those who disobey God's instructions beyond the Hebrew people. Psalm 1 presents this divine promise as a general principle for all of humankind. Prophetically, Psalms invites all of humankind into divine leadership and Lordship. Any blessing that God promises to the Jewish people in the Old Testament becomes a viable promise for everyone who chooses to follow God's

30. For the Hebrew people, the entire book of Psalms is a symphony of music compiled by David's administration to compliment God's instructions set forth in the first five books of the Old Testament. Torah (the first five books of the Old Testament) is a five-book cannon—the Word of God for the Hebrew people. Also, the Psalter is a cannon of five books that parallel Torah. As such, for the Hebrew people, following David's administration, the Psalter is the official worship that accompanied and sought to promote adherence to Torah. Hebrew scholar Gerald Wilson argues that Psalms is divided into two groupings: the first is Psalms 2–89 (books 1–3) and the second is Psalms 90–145 (books 4–5). In Wilson's view, Psalm 1 is part of the first book but serves as an introduction to the entire book of Psalms. So Psalm 1 is not designated as part of the first grouping. Also, Psalms 146–150 are part of the fifth book but serve as a conclusion to the entire book. So these Psalms are not designated as part of the second grouping. See Brueggemann, "Bounded," 88.

31. Brueggemann, "Bounded," 88.

instructions. Obedience to God is the central tenet of holiness. Brooks points out that a summation of the message of Psalms is that holiness is love for and devotion to pursuing God.[32]

Psalms also suggests that the divine invitation to holiness is an invitation to intimacy with God. All too often, people struggle with feelings of failure because of doubts and anger. Life squeezes so tight that we find it hard to breathe. Situations pressure us so heavily that some of us sometimes wonder if there is a God who truly cares. In his article "Holiness in the Psalms," Dwight Swanson points out that Psalms invites us to offer these emotions to God as prayer. God will then turn feelings of living hell into miraculous healing. The rhythm of life is a constant presentation of ourselves, just as we are, to the Lord. Then, we seek to learn, try to obey, and grow through this experience of divine intimacy.[33] Furthermore, Psalms draws out insights as pertaining to the truth of holiness. God's Word is truth and God's very words are holy, as God is holy. Listening to God's Word is the first step, then, to walking in holiness.

In Psalms, as in Leviticus, God is the possessor of all holiness. Psalm 22:3 states, for example, "You are holy, enthroned on the praises of Israel."[34] The psalmist invites all human beings to praise the holy God. Divine holiness is beautiful and deserving of all praise. The psalmist writes, "Let them praise your great and awesome name. Holy is God!" (Ps 99:3; see also Ps 99:5). Dwight Swanson correctly notes that in Psalms, the divine encounter invokes constant awareness that God is holy.[35] Repeatedly, the psalms reminds us that everything about God is holy. God's way is holy (Ps 77:13). God's very name is holy (Pss 30:4; 33:21; 145:21). God commands God's people not to desecrate God's name (see Exod 20:7). In the Old Testament, people meet God in the holy place—the temple where God dwells to encounter those who come.[36] That specific place is holy because it bears God's name (see Jer 7:11). Conversely, in the New Testament, the transcendence of the Holy Spirit creates a space in the believer's hearts and minds for God to dwell and for God to make a home.

32. Brooks, *Scriptural*, 21.

33. Ibid.

34. An additional reference is Ps 71:22: "I will also praise You with the harp for your faithfulness, O my God; I will sing praises to you with the lyre, O Holy One of Israel."

35. Swanson, "Holiness," n.p.

36. "Extol the LORD our God, and worship at his holy mountain; for the LORD our God is holy" (Ps 99:9). Ps 93:5b states, "Holiness befits your house, O LORD, forevermore." Ps 134:2 says, "Lift up your hands to the holy place, and bless the LORD."

## NEW TESTAMENT

Unlike the Old Testament, in which God's laws serve as rules to legislate holiness, the New Testament requires no need to legislate holiness. Instead, the commandments serve as a guide to show believers what is right and wrong. By the confession of faith in Jesus Christ and the infilling of the Holy Spirit, the believer professes and, indeed, possesses the power to do God's will. Ezekiel prophesied of the day when God would dwell in God's people's hearts and minds by the Spirit. By doing so, our minds would be regenerated and our lifestyles transformed to live out God's will. Ezekiel records God saying, "I will give you a new heart, and a new spirit I will put within you. . . . And I will put my Spirit within you, and cause you to walk in my statutes and be careful to obey my rules" (Ezek 36:25; 27). The Spirit that was poured out at Pentecost (Acts 2) fulfilled this prophecy and marked the birth of the church, but it was only the initial outpouring of the Holy Spirit, which is the Spirit of holiness, or the "sanctifying Spirit."[37] In this sense, in the New Testament, the life of the Spirit empowers the hearts of believers to carry out the age-old divine mandate of holiness.

Today, the Spirit of holiness remains the foundation of the church, and the central purpose of the outpouring of the Holy Spirit at Pentecost was to empower people to live sanctified lives. New Testament teaching, particularly in the letters of Paul and Peter, explain that, although the divine household has been extended to Gentiles, God continues to require holiness. New Testament preachers use the Old Testament as their textbook on holiness. In like manner, the contemporary church must take seriously both the Old Testament and the New Testament teachings on holiness.

In his writings, Paul considers the Holy Spirit to be the sanctifying spirit that cleanses everyone who becomes a part of Christ's church, as in 1 Corinthians 1:2, for example. Luke Timothy Johnson points out that Paul's basic message to the Corinthian church was that of holiness. [38] He explains that along with Paul's affirmation of the gifts of the Spirit, the apostle insists that these gifts mandate that the Holy Spirit must lead to personal transformation.[39] In essence, through regeneration, a mind enlightened through

---

37. The Spirit of holiness or the "sanctifying Spirit" discussed here is reminiscent of John Fletcher's interpretation of the second blessing. Fletcher believed in multiple baptisms of the Spirit, part of the experience of the Holy Spirit is the experience of the sanctifying Spirit. See Fletcher, *Works*, 230–32.

38. Johnson, *Writings*, 298–99.

39. Ibid.

biblical preaching, prayer, and fellowship, the Spirit's goal is to sanctify us in preparation for "the day of our Lord Jesus Christ."[40]

A wider vision of Paul's theology includes robust examination of holiness from the standpoint of personal piety. Individual Christians have a responsibility to live according to the Spirit as a direct result of Christ's triumph over sin through his death on the cross. Moreover, for Paul, holiness is the exclusive privilege of those regenerated through faith in Christ. He elaborates more on the relationship between Christ and holiness in his theology of the Spirit in Romans.

## Paul on Holiness

Romans 8:3–5 zones in on the crux of Paul's doctrine of New Testament holiness: "For God has done what the law, weakened by the flesh, could not do. By sending his own Son in the likeness of sinful flesh and for sin, he condemned sin in the flesh, in order that the righteous requirement of the law might be fulfilled in us, who walk not according to the flesh but according to the Spirit. For those who live according to the flesh set their minds on the things of the flesh, but those who live according to the Spirit set their minds on the things of the Spirit." Christ made it possible that the fullness of life in the Spirit, poured out at Pentecost, is the ultimate reality of divine holiness for all believers. Paul's teaching distances the Old Testament legalistic approach to achieving holiness from a new and more accessible process of holiness in Christ—though the standard remains the same. Romans 5:1–5 says, "Therefore, since we have been justified by faith, we have peace with God through our Lord Jesus Christ. Through him we have also obtained access by faith into this grace in which we stand, and we rejoice in hope of the glory of God. More than that, we rejoice . . . because God's love has been poured into our hearts through the Holy Spirit who has been given to us." Christ is both our holiness and our justification that fulfills God's law. Spiritually, the fullness of obedience to God's instructions is possible through the outpouring of Christ's love as the Spirit of Christ is imputed into the lives of believers. Christ's Spirit is the Holy Spirit. In Romans, the Spirit compels a lifestyle that flows from the heart, which is transformed by faith in Christ. By the Spirit, God's requirement to love is written upon the heart, and this internal inscription of love compels us to love God as well as others.

40. 1 Cor 1:4–8.

### Divine Promise of Inheritance for the Sanctified

Holiness becomes the rite of passage to divine inheritance. Acts 20:32 states, "And now I commend you to God and to the word of [God's] grace, which is able to build you up and to give you the inheritance among all those who are sanctified." God redeems us through Jesus Christ our Lord; God's Word cleanses us from sinful ways and teaches us holiness. The Holy Spirit empowers us to live according to the will of God. First Corinthians 6:9–11 states: "Or do you not know that the unrighteous will not inherit the kingdom of God? Do not be deceived: neither the sexually immoral, nor idolaters, nor adulterers, nor [people] who practice homosexuality, nor thieves, nor the greedy, nor drunkards, nor revilers, nor swindlers will inherit the kingdom of God. And such were some of you. *But you were washed, you were sanctified* [made holy], *you were justified in the name of the Lord Jesus Christ and by the Spirit of our God*" (italics added for emphasis). Paul assumes that God intends for us to have access to God's entire kingdom. While in places he seems ambiguous about what God's kingdom entails, he appears optimistic that what it does entail emerges from royal inheritance. Paul emphatically explains that our divine royalty is achieved by far deeper confession of faith than mere verbalization—though verbal confession has significance.

The church belongs to those who want to be cleansed and earnestly seek to walk in holiness—a lifestyle of integrity, empowered by God's Spirit. So then, while Christ justifies and sanctifies us (makes us holy), human cooperation with what God has done through Jesus Christ fulfills God's law. In other words, through what Christ has done for humanity on the cross, and by the power of the Holy Spirit, God has made it possible for human beings to live holy before God. God invites the believer to respond to God's gift through faith and obedience.

## Peter's Teaching on Holiness

Peter connects the divine call to the Hebrew people in the Old Testament with the believers in Christ of the New Testament. He explains that life in Christ calls for practical lifestyle changes. The apostle explains that holiness defines the believer's new way of life and behavior in the world. In his first letter, he says, "Therefore, preparing your minds for action, and being sober-minded, set your hope fully on the grace that will be brought to you at the revelation of Jesus Christ. As obedient children, do not be conformed to the passions of your former ignorance, but as he who called you is holy, you also be holy in all your conduct, since it is written, 'You shall be holy, for I am holy'" (1 Pet 1:13–16).

Oswalt observes that, in Peter, holiness is a principal connection between Christian faith and the faith of Israel pronounced in the Old Testament.[41] The Spirit poured out on all flesh at Pentecost in Acts 2 is the *Holy* Spirit. God is holy and those who believe in God are called to be likewise. Additionally, Oswalt notes that Peter's theology sees the principles that God lays out in the Old Testament for the Hebrew people as having immediate relevance for believers in Jesus Christ.[42] It is clear that God requires holiness both then and now.

Furthermore, Peter charges us: "As obedient children, do not be conformed to the passions of your former ignorance, but as he who called you is holy, you also be holy in all your conduct, since it is written, 'You shall be holy, for I am holy'" (1 Pet 1:14–16). Peter presupposes that divine holiness maintains internal norms, as well as a lifestyle consistent with the enduring nature of God's character, to which the apostle summons believers.

In 1 Peter 2:9–12, the apostle further expounds that, as believers in Christ, the church belongs to God. So the language of "people of God" is not a cliché. Believers are God's own possession. Marked as such, they have privileges as well as responsibilities. The greatest privilege is to be considered "chosen by God." The chosen people of God bear the honor of God's presence within, which therefore makes them an attractive people.

The apostle affirms the advantage of holiness among the most oppressed and often abused within ancient Greco-Roman society, namely the women: "Do not let your adorning be external—the braiding of hair and the putting on of gold jewelry, or the clothing you wear—but let your adorning be the hidden person of the heart with the imperishable beauty of a gentle and quiet spirit, which in God's sight is very precious. For this is how the holy women who hoped in God used to adorn themselves." (1 Pet 3:3–6).

The female believer discovers her beauty in holiness. Within the framework of a first-century misogynistic society, wherein women were pressured to look a certain way to feel attractive, to be called beautiful, and to be affirmed as persons, Peter's message came undoubtedly as

41. Oswalt, *Called*, 1–2.
42. Ibid., 2.

both liberating and affirming news to them. He explains that in Christ, a woman's beauty is not contingent upon her external assets, her hairstyle, her clothes, or the jewelry she wears. She is beautiful regardless of what she wears because her beauty exudes from her inner holiness.

Holiness bears inherent attractiveness. All of God's people possess the advantage of God-defined beauty. Imagine the relief that Peter's message of holiness brought to the women in his immediate audience! Today, God still offers women freedom from the need to work hard to look any particular way for men. They are beautiful no matter what hairstyle they choose, what clothes they wear, and what jewelry they adorn themselves with. Peter is not teaching a legalistic message. On the contrary, it is a liberating message for women who deeply desire to move beyond oppressive social expectations that disapprove of their natural humanity. God accepts women as equal parts of the church and affirms their humanity as equal to that of men.

Furthermore, holiness bears essential responsibility. Peter reminds us that God's standard for living requires believers to publically magnify God through how we live in community with each other before a watching world. In this sense, God has chosen believers to be his representatives by manifesting divine presence in the world.

## REFLECTION

## Questions to Ponder

Have you found yourself resistant to the subject of "holiness" because of past affiliations with churches that have many rules but offer no real insight into biblical holiness? Does your soul ever seem empty and in search of something more, even when you seem to accomplish something for which you are grateful? Since you accepted Christ, have you felt a longing for more? To borrow from the words of the song, "To be like Jesus, to be like Jesus, All [you want is] to be like Him."

## PRAYER

If this chapter has helped you gain insight into the biblical call for God's people to be holy, pause and pray the following prayer:

Lord, Scripture is clear that Christians are called to be holy. I recognize that human holiness is as filthy rags. I need your holiness—that which is initiated in you and fulfilled by your power and direction. Even now, my heart is restless until it fully embraces the joy that comes in true holiness. Lord, I want to be like Jesus in all that I say and do. Please grant me the humility to live like Jesus. Amen.

# 4

## Holiness: Understanding Its Complexity

The starting-point for the development of a holy character
is the realization that the mercies received from God
call for an adequate human response.

—EVERETT F. HARRISON

### THE WORK OF CHRIST: SALVATION AND
### SANCTIFICATION

BECAUSE OF OUR HUMAN failures, the radiance of God's glory is not something that we deserve. It comes to us as a gift. God loves and eagerly endows us with grace. He expressed the ultimate display of love through the
gift of his only begotten Son—Jesus Christ. The story of Jesus' birth, life,
death, and resurrection spells love. Psalm 149:4 states, "For the Lord takes
pleasure in his people; He adorns the humble with salvation." Apart from
a vibrant relationship with God, we endure the hopeless journey of life.
In a life wherein sustainable, enduring relationships are seldom reliable,
salvation brings hope for a continued relationship with God. Referencing
several New Testament Scriptures—1 Peter 1:2; Romans 8:29; Ephesians
1:4; 2 Timothy 1:9; and Hebrews 12:10—nineteenth-century Bishop of
Liverpool J. C. Ryle comments, "We must be holy, because this is the one
grand end and purpose for which Christ came into the world. . . . Jesus is

a complete Savior."[1] Ryle's notion of holistic salvation invites the believer to live out the practical implications of salvation beyond the confession of faith. It includes engaging and responding to everyday life situations with the fervor of Christ-like character.

Since I was a young boy, Christians have repeatedly asked a catchy and seemingly simple question, which has become a sort of mantra: "What would Jesus do?" To some degree, this question seems to be a cliché; but to others, it expresses a desire to be like Christ. Relating this question to the current discussion, the Bible unequivocally states that Christ is holy. To do as Christ would do requires both accepting Jesus as Savior, being filled with the Holy Spirit, and committing to Christ as Sanctifier. The life and work of Christ extend God's order of holiness beyond the Hebrew people to everyone. This chapter: (a) explores the intricacy of holiness as exemplified and personified through Christ and extended to us through life of the Spirit; and (b) explains how the church facilitates holiness through community formation and an emphasis on preaching.

## Hope of Christ's Salvation

In the cross of Christ, we discover the "positive" in the "negative"—the "yes" in the "no."[2] Like a criminal, Jesus was lifted up on the cross to serve as a public example to all who disdained the first-century Roman Empire. This was the worst punishment of all. Yet, God took the Roman symbol of shame and depravation and transformed it into a symbol of hope. The cross was not the end, but the beginning of the best. Through the cross, God brought forth glory and resurrection from the negativity of shame and death. The cross, then, became an emblem of majesty and power. In it we discover the message of hope in Christ, which comes as good news amid a host of negative human experiences. This is the beautiful hope emerging from the middle of a world filled with the ugliness of evil, a reality with which all of us have to contend in one way or another.

---

1. Ryle, *Holiness*, 49. See also 1 John 3:8: "The reason the Son of God appeared was to destroy the works of the devil."

2. "For Barth, the cross of Christ represents the locus in which the righteous judge makes known [divine] judgment of sinful humanity and simultaneously takes the judgment upon [God's self]. . . . By undergoing the cross Jesus expiated our sins, propitiated our maker, turned God's 'no' to us to a 'yes' and so saved us." McGrath, *Christian Theology*, 331.

Salvation is the only prerequisite to God's gift of holiness. Many churches place an emphasis on getting saved without an equal emphasis on the importance of sanctification. However, Scripture warrants the importance of salvation and sanctification. In Wesleyan terms, sanctification is a necessary part of the Christian life, both instantaneous and an ongoing work of grace.[3]

## Hope of Christ's Sanctification

Wesley explains, "At the same time that we are justified, yea, in that very moment, sanctification begins."[4] His theology teaches that holiness, or "sanctification," is an entire work to which the believer must submit.[5] It is a work that God does; but to receive it, we must recognize that we are nothing without God, become convicted that only Christ can change our condition, and accept Christ as Savior. As sanctification begins, God's Word plays an important role in cleansing our hearts and purifying our lifestyle, daily. The story is familiar. An unbeliever was invited to church. He said, "I am not ready. I need to get myself right first. If I go over there, the wall would collapse when I walk in the door." This common illustration represents the misconception that people possess the power to ameliorate their own lives.

Those who seem possessed with addicting sins (drug addicts, promiscuous persons, kleptomaniacs, habitual liars, and cheaters) or those with secret sins (the prideful, envious, hateful, or unforgiving) will never be free to live holy by their own power. Not one of us can ever emancipate ourselves from whatever "weight, and sin, which clings so closely" (Heb 12:1). Importantly, the psalmist asks the rhetorical question for which he provides an answer: "How can a young [person] keep his [or her] way pure? By guarding it according to Your word" (Ps 119:9). The emphasis here is on the Word of God as the divine cleansing agent. When we receive God's saving grace, we must submit to biblical teachings that are able to develop within us a godly lifestyle.

---

3. Wesley, "Scriptural," 372.

4. Ibid.

5. See Wesley, "Circumcision," 23–32.

## The Relationship between Salvation and Sanctification

Understanding holiness is complex. It's like a prism. There are many angles to explore. Yet, there is one starting place. That is the moment we receive God's gift of salvation. Salvation as the beginning of holiness is not a new concept. Paul explains salvation as a gift of God's grace. The believer's involvement is not meritorious, as though it could become a contributing factor to our acceptance by a holy God. However, the believer must involve herself or himself in the process of continual sanctification—not as in a repeated process but as a progressive one.[6] While salvation is the initial gift, holiness is a progressive opportunity into which God invites the believer to participate. As children of a holy God, it is necessary for God to reproduce the family likeness.[7]

Harrison points out that the starting point for developing holy character is when we realize that God's mercies call for us to respond adequately.[8] Although salvation is complete in the cross, divine gentleness compels Christ to reserve the experience of salvation for those who choose it. Neither the work of the cross nor our response to it should be taken lightly. When we respond to Christ's love, we must also submit to the process of continued sanctification. It is a life-long progression. Along these lines, the thirteenth chapter of the 1646 Westminster Confession of Faith, entitled "Of Sanctification," states:

> They who are effectually called and regenerated, having a new heart and a new spirit created in them, are *further sanctified*, really and personally, through the virtue of Christ's death and resurrection, by his Word and Spirit dwelling in them; the dominion of the whole body of sin is destroyed, and the several lusts thereof are more and more weakened and mortified, and they more and more quickened and strengthened, in all saving graces, to the practice of true holiness, without which no [person] shall see the Lord (WCF 13.1).

Regeneration occurs through the confession of faith in the Lord Jesus. While the confession of faith begins the salvation experience, holiness is not an instantaneous work. "Further sanctification" is necessary for a life of faith. It requires spiritual discipline and Christian formation.

6. Harrison, "Holiness," 727.
7. Ibid.
8. Ibid.

Most Evangelical and pentecostal/charismatic traditions promote doctrines of salvation that are rooted in the angel Gabriel's prophecy to Mary in Matthew, who says that Jesus saves his people from their sin (1:21). In the ears of a young first-century Jewish peasant girl, salvation probably would have meant redemption from Roman-imposed political and social oppression. But more importantly, salvation would have also meant divine redemption from punishment as a result of disobedience to God. Certainly "sin," from which Christ would save his people, would speak of separation from God, caused by disobedience to God's instruction set forth in the Torah.

The Greek root for the terms "saved" and "salvation" is *soterion*. In the context of the Greco-Roman world, the word *soteria* would have brought to mind the goddess *Soteria*. In Greek mythology, *Soteria* was the goddess of safety, deliverance, and preservation from harm. So the notion that Christ would "save" communicates a type of rescue from oncoming danger. Scriptures such as John 3:16 ("For God so loved the world, that He gave His only Son, that whoever believes in [Jesus] should not perish but have eternal life") and 1 Timothy 1:15 ("The saying is trustworthy and deserving of full acceptance, that Christ Jesus came into the world to save sinners") reveal that Jesus was born to provide salvation for all of humanity, Jews and non-Jews alike. Christ comes, moreover, to provide a holistic salvation that surpasses first-century Jewish expectations. Christ comes to redeem all of humanity from the curse of disobedience to a renewed relationship with God. Redemption brings internal and existential liberation and preservation from eternal harm.

Holistically speaking, salvation becomes divine deliverance from unholy lifestyles and habits, as well as poverty, pain, agony, depression, and oppression that separate human beings from their maker. These conditions and vices are endangering our spiritual, as well as physical and psychic well-being; thus we need *soteria tou theos* (the salvation of God) to rescue us from this situation. Our separation from God inhibits the free flow of the highest quality of life that God provides for humanity. Christ came to redeem us from that separation.

When Christ is formed in us, his character preserves and draws us into the abundance of life that only he can give. Since the sin from which Jesus saves his people is ultimately separation from God, salvation reunites us with God. Anyone can be saved when he or she simply accepts that God accepts all people through the cross of Christ. Regardless of one's past or present state of affairs, salvation is God's invitation to everyone. This gift serves as the ultimate opportunity to begin a new life of holiness with God. Our only job is to accept God's acceptance.

## PARTICIPATING IN A GODLY COMMUNITY

Accepting God's gift is both a personal and public profession of faith in Christ as Savior. But, the journey does not end there; it only begins. The local church has an important role in helping us to form into Christ's image. My parents passed down to my siblings and me some wise sayings that have helped to shape my outlook on life. One of them was "association brings on assimilation." This one is quite fitting here. Whether good or bad, we affect our surroundings, and they affect us, as well. This is true from multiple perspectives, including sociologically, ecologically, psychologically, and spiritually.

Kinnaman's research concerning twenty-first-century Christianity reveals that young adults look to their peers to be their moral and spiritual compass. They tend to base their views of morality on what seems fair minded, loyal, and acceptable to their friends.[9] Kinnaman further notes the historical contradiction between the emphasis on the individual over the group in the Western church and the cultural emphasis of the group over the individual among young people today. Concerning the contemporary Western Evangelical churches, he says, "We focus on personal responsibility to a fixed standard, rather than on collective negotiation with a world absent of absolute truth. This is the exact opposite of how young people relate to the world. . . . Christians are Christians in community, and the next generation can teach us a thing or two about what that means."[10] If we are to impact this generation with holiness, we have to think communal holiness. Communal holiness does not de-emphasize personal sanctification, but rather accentuates the power of community in our walk toward the biblical call for the church to be holy.

When we spend time with people, our thoughts, behavior, mannerisms, accents, and way of walking are all vulnerable to assimilating to their ways. So adaptability can serve as a virtue and a vice. We must consider it wisely. Acts 4:13–16 presents a good example of how personal interactions could be healthy: "Now when they saw the boldness of Peter and John, and perceived that they were uneducated, common men, they were

9. Kinnaman, *You*, 172–73.

10. Ibid., 173.

astonished. And they recognized that they had been with Jesus. But seeing the man who was healed standing beside them, they had nothing to say in opposition. But when they had commanded them to leave the council, they conferred with one another, saying, 'What shall we do with these men? For that a notable sign has been performed through them is evident to all the inhabitants of Jerusalem, and we cannot deny it.'" This pericope follows the narrative of how Peter and John extended a hand up for the lame man at the gate called Beautiful in Jerusalem. The man received a miracle from God. He was so excited that he praised God publicly and attracted attention. Of course, Peter and John became a spectacle in the eyes of the onlookers. As a result of the man's miracle, the Jews concluded that Peter and John had spent time with Jesus. Their boldness of faith and commitment to helping even the least among them was evocative of Jesus' behavior. The narrative reminds us of the impact that good, wholesome behavior can have on the lives of associates. However, the same principle applies to associations with evil behavior.

Paul exhorts the Christians in Thessalonica that, if a brother or sister behaves in contradiction to godly teachings, they should separate from them.[11] The principle of association is the appropriate interpretation for the pastor's exhortation. Paul's concern is that certain Christians' disorderly conduct would negatively influence others. Paul also writes to the Christians at Corinth, admonishing them regarding unbelievers, to "go out from their midst, and be separate from them, says the Lord, and touch no unclean thing" (2 Cor 6:17). Here, Paul is not suggesting that we should assume that we are better than non-Christians. Neither is the biblical directive a transmittal of arrogant, judgmental attitudes upon us.

Paul relies on the Hebrew tradition and quotes from the Old Testament to communicate firmly that holiness is not only a personal virtue, but is also communal. The community to which we belong participates in the process of holiness. Therefore, associating with those who do not participate in the growth toward holiness has an adverse affect on the outworking of that development. In the Old Testament, God instructed the priests to refrain from touching unclean things in order to avoid desecrating themselves. The idea is that uncleanness and cleanliness cannot mix without compromising cleanliness.

---

11. 2 Thess 3:6: "Now we command you, brothers, in the name of our Lord Jesus Christ, that you keep away from any brother who is walking in idleness and not in accord with the tradition that you received from us."

## LIVING A SANCTIFIED LIFE

Beginning with the early days of the Reformation, the sanctified life has been the subject of many thinkers. To name a few, John Calvin saw this sanctifying "process" as one in which the believer conforms to the image of Christ. Later on, John Wesley and his friend John Fletcher argued over the subject of sanctification. Fletcher argued that at the moment of salvation, sanctification is completed. Wesley, however, argued that sanctification is a second blessing after salvation. Later in his life, Wesley concluded that sanctification is a lifelong progression toward perfection.

As a Wesleyan, I propose that the sanctified life consists of constantly learning, growing, and conforming to the image of God. John Wesley frequently referenced the image of God, seemingly connecting the *image of God* to his *doctrine of holiness*. Theologian Theodore Runyon points out that in Wesley's 1730 "University Sermon," he makes use of a metaphor stemming from the Eastern fathers: "Humanity as the image of God is a mirror that reflects what it received from God, reflects it both back to God and into the world."[12] Runyon reasons, "The image (for Wesley) is not, therefore something that humanity has or that is lodged within the human being but is an ongoing relation in which humanity receives and gives. And what is received is love."[13]

People grow and change in the progression of sanctification at varying rates. While we are in various places of our journey of faith, throughout this process of sanctification, there are inevitable challenges and even obstacles. Sanctification is, moreover, a goal that every Christian must "press" toward. Holiness exists on the continuum, faithfully pressing toward a sanctified life. Importantly, sanctification is not simply a script that the faith prescribes to us, but it is hearing, understanding, and internalizing God's will for everyday life. It is this outworking of biblical sanctification that endures struggle with the flesh. Indeed, as stated in Matthew 26:41, "The spirit is willing but the flesh is weak." Paul faces his own limited strength and learns that placing greater priority on spiritual matters helps him to overcome the limitation of the flesh. In at least two places—1 Corinthians 15:31 and Colossians 3:1–6—Paul says, "I die daily" to develop a life like that of Christ.

12. Runyon, "Holiness," 80.
13. Ibid.

## PREACHING

Ancient religions, including Chinese Confucianism, as well as Judaism, bear record that ethical living requires the role of a teacher. A quotation from ancient Confucian philosopher Xunzi rings appropriate to the relationship between preaching, holiness, and the people of God. Xunzi says,

> A warped piece of wood must wait until it has been laid against the straightening board, steamed, and forced into shape before it can become straight; a piece of blunt metal must wait until it has been whetted on a grindstone before it can become sharp. Similarly, since [people's] nature is evil, it must wait for the instructions of teachers before it can be made upright and for the guidance of ritual principles before it can become orderly. If [people] have no teachers to instruct them, they will incline toward evil and not upright; and if they have no ritual principles to guide them, they will be perverse and violent and lack order. . . . In this way, [teachers cause people] to become orderly and to conform to the Way.[14]

Although not a Christian quotation, the Chinese reference sheds light into the process of human develop. From it, we can learn something constructively applicable to Christian discipleship in holiness. Holiness is more than words on a page or theological ideals. It has to do with the process by which God's people learn to live ethically. As the teacher has a central role in Confucian ethical and philosophical thought, teachers—preachers—have a vital role to play in equipping Christians in holiness. Preachers cannot take the place of the Spirit but must work as agents of the Spirit to teach Christians God's lifestyle.

More closely related to Christianity, the Old Testament sheds light on the essentiality of teaching. The prophet Ezekiel explains the responsibility of the priest in the temple as "teach[ing] [God's] people the difference between the holy and the common, and show[ing] them how to distinguish between the unclean and the clean" (Ezekiel 44:23). Connecting Hebrew through with the New Testament, Paul commissions Timothy to "preach the Word; be ready in season and out of season; reprove, rebuke, and exhort, with complete patience and teaching" (2 Tim 4:1–2). The holiness of God exemplified in the life of Christ is discerned and communicated to the believer through preaching. Romans 10:14c states, "And how are they to hear without someone preaching?"

---

14. Xunzi, *Basic Writings*, 162.

The Holy Spirit empowers the preacher to teach holiness. Although Spirit-filled, without preaching, the believer experiences spiritual neglect. Nineteenth-century Baptist Preacher Adoniram Judson Gordon, who decried the absence of the Holy Spirit, insisted that "our generation is rapidly losing its grip upon the supernatural; and as a consequence, the pulpit is rapidly dropping to the level of the platform. And this decline is due, more than anything else, to ignoring the Holy Spirit as the supreme inspirer of preaching. We would rather see a great orator in the pulpit, forgetting that the least expounder of the Word, when filled with the Spirit, is greater than he."[15] Our generation still hungers for preaching that makes a difference in how we perceive the world, as well as in how we live our lives. Contemporary preaching must still rely on the Holy Spirit to communicate the message of holiness applicable to everyday life. Holiness means to *be* and to *act* in a way that reflects both a *regenerated* life in Christ and the *ongoing renewal* in Christ.

Historically, the "black church" placed a premium on preaching. The pastor was the community leader during slavery until the Civil Rights Movement. W. E. B. DuBois reports that the African American communities depended heavily on their preacher as "leader, politician, orator, 'boss,' intriguer, and idealist."[16] James H. Cone adds that the African American preacher's most important office was that of a prophet. In this role, they "speak God's truth to the people. The sermon therefore is a prophetic oration, which 'tells it like it is,' according to the divine Spirit who speaks through the preacher. . . . In order to separate the sermon from ordinary human discourse and thereby connect it with prophecy, the ["black church"] emphasizes the role of the Spirit."[17]

In depending on the preacher to "tell it like it is," "call and response" was integral to the preaching moment. Spontaneous outbursts throughout the sermon of "hallelujah," "glory," "praise the Lord," or "amen" have always characterized African American worship, as congregants bear witness to the Spirit's presence in their midst to bring a transforming Word from God.[18] Cone posits that when people say "amen," they feel involved in the proclamation. It commits them to the divine truth that they hear. It means that the people recognize that what the preacher is saying is not just

15. See Heisler, *Spirit-Led*, 7.

16. DuBois, *Souls*, 141. Also quoted in Cone, "Sanctification," 180.

17. Cone, "Sanctification," 180.

18. Ibid., 182.

Reverend So-and-So's ideas. It is the message from God for the people.[19] Then, they would encourage the preacher at the close of the service with comments like, "That's right Reverend! Don't sugar coat it; tell it like it is."

However, today preachers seem to avoid the subject of holiness. Perhaps they fear that as soon as they say the word "holiness," some people would turn a deaf ear, because holiness bears the stigma of the forbidden "L" word—legalism. Many preachers offer polemics against "being religious," contending that "God doesn't want us to be 'religious;' we need 'relationship.'" Televangelism has made the language of "kingdom living" popular. There is often a desire in contemporary preaching to mingle contemporary jargon and ideology with preaching, and many young preachers attempt to be relevant by using language that is considered "hip." Instead of insisting that Christians live godly, they might say "Let's get crunk for Christ," or "We need to be on fire for Christ." In doing so, they avoid the language of "holiness." In the postmodern, pluralistic climate that characterizes our contemporary culture, many people assume that the language of "religion" or "holiness" comes loaded with ulterior motive. Thus, using the language of holiness and godliness in sermons is often seen as off putting. It is not considered inviting to the ears of the congregation, particularly any people who are not Christians.

Making the gospel practical to people of all walks of life, while also using multiple vernaculars and being cognizant of the changing times, is essential for translating the gospel message with relevance. Perhaps the use of alternative popular language makes the gospel seem "cool." Further, cultural translation is crucial to effectively communicate the message of Jesus Christ, and language is important to translating the message of Christ. On the other hand, the message and life of Christ require that preaching maintain a commitment to emphasizing the difference between holiness and unholiness.

There is a thin line, however, between communicating a profound biblical message and worldview through the use of cultural signs, symbols, patterns, and languages and drawing from the secular worldview to reduce our witness to one that is syncretistic and not authentically biblical. So, while we use relevant vernacular, contemporary signs, symbols, patterns, and other tools to communicate God's Word, we must remain in tune with the enduring nature of God's character—the holiness to which all believers are called.

19. Ibid.

Donna Orsuto, a scholar of spirituality, observes the role that preaching played in the earliest Christian community's life and sees the image of the church in Acts as exemplary for the contemporary church: "And they devoted themselves to the apostles' teaching and the fellowship, to the breaking of bread and the prayers. . . . Wonders and signs were being done through the apostles. . . . [They] were praising God and having favor with all the people" (Acts 2:42–47).

Orsuto notes that this ideal picture still has drawing power and models God's ideal for the church today. "First," says Orsuto, the assertion that "the early Christian community devoted themselves to the apostles' preaching means that the Christian community [was] not a chance gathering: it [was] summoned and unified by teaching. The central teaching [was] about the death, resurrection and glorification of Jesus, that He [was] the Messiah and His life and teachings are the sure way that God has planned to lead us to holiness. . . . The Christian community," she adds, "still gathers to be taught."[20] It is important to note that preaching, like teaching, is essential to learning principles for living a holy life.

The Word of God is still powerful to transform the believer's life from unruliness to holiness. This power is noted in Paul's first letter to the Corinthian church—that though "the word of the cross is folly to those who are perishing . . . to us who are being saved, it is the power of God" (1 Cor 1:18). New Testament scholar Gordon Fee points out that Paul's language of "the word of the cross" draws attention to redemptive history as wisdom beyond human understanding, and that such wisdom is scandalous to the wisdom of the Greco-Roman world.[21] Paul draws attention to the fact that the wisdom of redemptive history is distinctively divine, exemplary, not only of an "otherworldly" or heavenly wisdom, but the fullness of God. Fee explains that no mere human would have dreamed up salvation as God's way of doing things.[22] Redemptive history is one example of how God's will is inherently inconsistent with society's logic.[23] Just as God's working out of redemptive history seems foolish to the Greco-Roman world, holiness is inconceivable in the minds of unbelievers. Preachers must focus their preaching on the essentiality of God's Word and not on the wisdom of the world. God's holiness is humanly outrageous, but it is power to those of us who believe.

20. Orsuto, *Holiness*, 153.
21. Fee, *First Epistle*, 68.
22. Ibid.
23. Ibid.

Isaiah's words offer us insight: "Cry aloud; do not hold back; lift up your voice like a trumpet; declare to my people their transgression, to the house of Jacob their sins" (Isa 58:1). The called-out, peculiar people of the New Testament are no longer referred to as "the house of Jacob" but the community of believers—the church. The early church gathered to study the Old Testament to learn the principles of holiness.[24] God requires that preachers grab hold of the life of holiness and sanctify the church through that message.

In John 17:17, Jesus prays that his followers would experience divine sanctification, which comes only by the truth of God's Word. Jesus' prayer is that God would set them apart for holy service. It is consistent with the divine requirement in the Old Testament. The words of Christ in John 17:17 become, moreover, a crucial moment in salvation history, in which the Christ of the New Testament is concerned that his followers align themselves with the holiness required by the God of the Old Testament. In the New Testament, God extends a divine hand to include Gentiles into the family of God. Yet, God still requires us to sanctify ourselves and become holy.[25]

Three points in this verse are worthy of note: first, only the truth can sanctify; second, God's Word is truth; and third, there is no sanctification beyond God's Word. A theme in John's Gospel is "truth." Christ is that living truth incarnate. Christ's prayer is that his emissaries inherit the life of divine truth. Yet, truth comes through the preaching of the Word of God. The Word of God in the Old Testament was the law. The Word of God in the New Testament includes the Old Testament but focuses on how Christ fulfills the law. Therefore, as Paul indicates, God inspires all Scripture, and it serves as schoolmaster in explaining the truth of God—that is, Jesus. At the hearing of the Word, we receive a spiritual transference of its truth into our hearts.

## LIVING THE FRUIT OF THE SPIRIT

Although not a proponent for the charismatic gifts in the church today, Dwight L. Moody was indeed a believer in holiness. He once said, "It is a great deal better to live a holy life than to talk about it. We are told to let our

24. Orsuto, *Holiness*, 154.

25. Leviticus 11:44 states, "For I am the LORD your God. [Sanctify] yourselves therefore, and be holy, for I am holy."

light shine, and if it does we won't need to tell anybody it does. The light will be its own witness. Lighthouses don't ring bells and fire cannons to call attention to their shining—they just shine."[26] In other words, it is far more popular to talk about Christ and to say, "I have the Holy Spirit," than to live out the fruit of the Spirit that bears witness to the faith confession. Paul expressed a similar concern toward the Christians at Galatia and Ephesus. Drawing a line in the sand between the acts of the sinful nature and the assets of living by the Holy Spirit, Paul describes the productive life of the Spirit as a fruitful one. In Galatians 5:22–23, he explains, "The fruit of the Spirit is love, joy, peace, patience, kindness, goodness, faithfulness, gentleness, self-control; against such things there is no law." Similarly, he teaches the churches in Ephesus the importance of moving beyond verbal confession of faith to a realized expression of faith in everyday life. He writes to them from prison, "Walk in a manner worthy of the calling to which you have been called, with all humility and gentleness, with patience, bearing with one another in love, eager to maintain the unity of the Spirit in the bond of peace" (Eph 4:1–3).

Paul is affirming the relationship between God's calling and the fruitful lifestyle that maximizes the potential of that calling in their lives. Six key concepts emerge to summarize what it means to live a fruitful life: humility, gentleness, patience, love, unity, and peace. These are the essential elements of a fruitful life lived under the dictates of the divine call to holiness.

## Holiness as Humility and Gentleness

It suffices to draw attention to the Greek word used in both Galatians and Ephesians for "gentleness." *Prautetos* may be translated more clearly as self-control for the one who is strong-willed. Gentleness does not equal weakness, but rather exemplifies the application of intentional self-control or controlled strength. A gentle person gives room for the strength of the Spirit. The realization that true emotional, psychological, and spiritual strength comes from the Lord becomes central to life in the Spirit.

26. As quoted in Searle, "Music," 91.

## Holiness as Patience

We have heard it said many times, "Patience is a virtue." More importantly, patience is a fruit of the Spirit. Holiness requires time. It cannot be imposed nor rushed. God calls. We answer. Then, God waits with us as we pursue the journey of holiness. Indeed, faith is a journey. Like an infant, we can only undertake the journey after we have first learned to walk. Then, we must exercise what we have learned.

## Holiness as Love

Love as holiness and holiness as love is also an Old Testament concept that is expanded in the teachings of Jesus. In John's gospel, Jesus requires his followers to possess love—it is essential to their faith. He challenges them, "A new commandment I give unto you, that ye love one another; even as I have loved you, that ye also love one another. By this shall all men know that ye are my disciples, if ye have love one to another" (John 13:34–35 ASV). The discipline to obey God's Word includes love as its foundation. Jesus expects that love becomes the church's virtue and reputation.

Paul extends the Christological emphasis on love to a pneumatological prominence, as well. In his discussion on the fruit of the Spirit in Galations 5, the first fruit is love. There is no other fruit available unless love exists first. In Matthew 22:34–40, Luke 10:25–28, and Mark 12:28–34, Jesus stands in the center of the traditional vertical Hebrew Shema (Deut 6:4–5) and provides the apex for a horizontal connection to it:

> [One of the scribes] asked him, "Which commandment is the most important of all?" Jesus answered, "The most important is, 'Hear, O Israel: The Lord our God, the Lord is one. And you shall love the Lord your God with all your heart and with all your soul and with all your mind and with all your strength.' The second is this: 'You shall love your neighbor as yourself.' There is no other commandment greater than these." And the scribe said to him, "You are right, Teacher. You have truly said that he is one, and there is no other besides him. And to love him with all the heart and with all the understanding and with all the strength, and to love one's neighbor as oneself, is much more than all whole burnt offerings and sacrifices." And when Jesus saw that he answered wisely, he said to him, "You are not far from the kingdom of God." And after that no one dared to ask him any more questions.[27]

27. Mark 12:28–34.

God's instructions are rooted in love because God is love. They are spoken in love because Jesus, as the Word of God, is the chief exemplar of that love. Christ calls all to love as he does; there is no greater holiness than to love like Jesus. All other elements of holiness must be aligned under the rubric of love. With love of God and others as its foundation, truth moves beyond purely cognitive dimensions to practical faith. Second-century apologist Aristides wrote this to the Roman emperor Hadrian concerning the exemplary love of believers:

> But the Christians, O King, while they went about and made search, have found the truth; and . . . have come nearer to truth and genuine knowledge than the rest of the nations. For they know and trust in God, the Creator of heaven and of earth, in whom and from whom are all things, to whom there is no other god as companion, from whom they received commandments which they engraved upon their minds and observe in hope and expectation of the world which is to come. Wherefore they do not commit adultery nor fornication, nor bear false witness, nor embezzle what is held in pledge, nor covet what is not theirs. They honor father and mother, and show kindness to those near to them; and whenever they are judges, they judge uprightly. They do not worship idols (made) in the image of man; and whatsoever they would not that others should do unto them, they do not to others; and of the food which is consecrated to idols they do not eat, for they are pure. And their oppressors they appease (lit: comfort) and make them their friends; they do good to their enemies; and their women, O King, are pure as virgins, and their daughters are modest; and their men keep themselves from every unlawful union and from all uncleanness, in the hope of a recompense to come in the other world. Further, if one or other of them have bondmen and bondwomen or children, *through love toward them they persuade them to become Christians,* and when they have done so, they call them brethren without distinction. They do not worship strange gods, and they go their way in all modesty and cheerfulness. Falsehood is not found among them; and *they love one another,* and from widows they do not turn away their esteem; and they deliver the orphan from him who treats him harshly. And he, who has, gives to him who has not, without boasting. And when they see a stranger, they take him in to their homes and rejoice over him as a very brother; for they do not call them brethren after the flesh, but brethren after the spirit and in God.[28]

---

28. Aristides, "Apology."

## Holiness as Unity and Peace

Notice that in the New Testament, all Christians are part of God's royal priesthood, regardless of whether they were from Thessalonica, Corinth, Ephesus, Rome, or Jerusalem. The New Testament (particularly Acts 1) celebrates diversity insofar as there is unity. Diversity, however, collapses into division when there is no objective premise that maintains unity with diversity. Diversity is a buzzword in contemporary society. Tertullian seems to weigh unity as primal among the four principles of concern—holiness, unity, catholicity, and apostolicity.[29] Unity, for Tertullian, was the common denominator for holiness and the other tenets of concern.

Eighteenth-century Moravian leader Count Zinzendorf offers helpful insight on the premium relationship between love and unity in holiness.[30] For Zinzendorf, the Holy Spirit at Pentecost was the endowing of an existential spirituality that overwhelms the heart and is best expressed through Christian love. Moravian historian John Greenfield recounts the following experience among the Moravians:

> The thirteenth of August 1727 was a day of the outpouring of the Holy Spirit. We saw the hand of God and His wonders, and we were all under the cloud of our fathers baptized with their Spirit. The Holy Ghost came upon us and in those days great signs and wonders took place in our midst. From that time scarcely a day passed but what we beheld His almighty workings amongst us. A great hunger after the Word of God took possession of us so that we had to have three services every day, viz. 5.00 and 7.30 a.m. and 9.00 p.m. Everyone desired above everything else that the Holy Spirit might have full control. Self-love and self-will, as well as all

---

29. The Council of Constantinople (381 CE) rendered holiness, unity, catholicity, and apostolicity as foundational tenets of the church. Yet, the weight of each tenet has not always been consistent. Which carries the most weight—the unity of Acts 2, the role of the apostle in Ephesians 2:20, the holiness of the church in Ephesians 5:26–27, or the universality of the church in Revelation 7:9? Throughout history, much ink has been spilled and much blood has been shed as church leaders have clamored and fought over the issue of the foundation of the church.

30. The Lutheran preacher and Pietist may have been one of the key voices in the history of the holiness movement. Yet, he is not credited as such. Vinson Synan argues that John Wesley is the founder of all modern holiness, Pentecostal, and charismatic movements. While Synan makes a compelling argument, given Wesley's emphasis on grace, the second blessing, and holiness, Zinzendorf and the Moravians deserve credit for their emphasis on the baptism of the Spirit and biblical holiness. Their influence on the Wesley brothers was paramount in John Wesley's leadership in the holiness movement.

disobedience disappeared and an overwhelming flood of graces swept us all out into the great ocean of Divine Love.[31]

Formally a Lutheran priest who later became a leader among the Moravians, Zinzendorf resolved that practicing love in unity has ecumenical implications. Theological differences and traditional trajectories should not impede the power of love as expressed in unity. God's love unifies people who come from different places and think conflicting thoughts. The only resolution to the inevitable kaleidoscope of human diversity is the power of love. Christians, moreover, are compelled to unity above the common denominator of faith in Christ. It is through this unity in love that we best express the power of Christian holiness.

For Zinzendorf, holiness (piety or sanctification) does not represent a unilateral claim on truth by any person or group, and neither is holiness the assimilation of the faithful to worldly ideals. Holiness is the divine Spirit of unity that selflessly draws together the body of Christ in "faith and humility." Contemporary scholar Christopher B. Barnett points out that Zinzendorf downplayed much of Christianity's propositional content in favor of a rigorous existential ethic. Love of Christ and neighbor trumps indifference among Christians.[32]

Undoubtedly, Zinzendorf's emphasis on love heavily influenced Wesley's theology of holiness. However, Wesley departs from the Moravian interpretation of holiness that placed a premium on personal piety at the expense and neglect of the role of unity in community. Yet, Zinzendorf's focus on personal piety is notable. Holiness must first transform the mind and soul. Personal piety speaks to our consciousness of God's love and its work in transforming our lives from the inside out.

We are one body of believers. Our diversity of beliefs is due in part to the reality that as fallen human beings we have only partial knowledge. First Corinthians 13:9–10 states, "For we know in part and we prophesy in part, but when the perfect comes, the partial will pass away." In another place, Paul adds to his theology of perfection stating, "And above all these

31. Adapted from Greenfield, *When the Spirit*, 10. "The Rev John Greenfield, an American Moravian evangelist, published his book 'Power from on High' in 1927 on the 200th anniversary of the Moravian revival. . . . The Moravians, a refugee colony from Bohemia, settled on the estates of Count Nicholas Zinzendorf in Herrnhut, Germany, where a powerful revival began in 1727. It launched 100 years of continuous prayer and within 25 years 100 Moravians were missionaries, more than the rest of the Protestant church had sent out in two centuries."

32. Barnett, *Kierkegaard*, 29.

put on love, which binds everything together in perfect harmony" (Col 3:14). The heart inscription of love produces a love ethic. This love ethic is the unifier of the body of Christ. Moreover, from a biblical perspective, as Christians, we are called to live in love and faith together in Christian unity (ecumenism), and community is at the core of true Christian holiness.

Wesley emphasized perfection as the practical application of holiness in the everyday life. At the root of his theology of holiness, or "sanctification," is love. Runyon points out that in Wesley's notion, holiness is love. There is a continual streaming forth of love directly to humanity from the divine Source. Love then reflects back to God and outward to all of God's creation.[33] Importantly, the essential qualities of the image of God are to be found in God, whom humanity is called to reflect. Our efforts alone are insufficient. As my dad used to sing, "Without Him I can do nothing; without Him I would surely fail; without Him I would be drifting; like a ship without a sail."[34]

Life is fullest when we know what it means to love God and others. Within the framework of Wesley's notion of the "image of God," holiness "reflects love back to God, the love called forth by receiving God's love and it reflects God's grace, justice, mercy, and love to the neighbors God has given us." Runyon reasons that, as Christians, we are "partakers of the divine nature" (2 Pet 1:4). Therefore, we are made agents of God's redeeming power, that power by means of which, according to God's "great and precious promise, we assist God in lifting up fallen humanity."[35]

A few centuries beyond Wesley, William Seymour, leader of the 1906 Azusa Street Revival, proffered a theology of the Holy Spirit grounded in a love that breaks down walls of racial segregation. For Seymour, the racial divide was "washed away in the blood" through the baptism of the Holy Spirit. For him, life in the Spirit overcomes hate, bigotry, and prejudice. Like Zinzendorf, Seymour interpreted the sanctifying work of the Spirit as unifying believers amid a world of religious, racial, and political divisions. Similarly, Christian mystic Howard Thurman summarizes the message of Christ in one word—love.[36] If we want to become like Christ we must love like Christ. Christ's love is unconditional and nonviolent.

33. Runyon, "Holiness," 80.

34 "Without Him," hymn by Mylon R. LeFevre, 1963.

35. Runyon, "Holiness," 80.

36. Howard Thurman was the philosopher whose theological insights heavily influenced Martin Luther King Jr. and became the philosophical platform upon which the

Pentecostal theologians have noted that love is the Spirit. In his *Spirit of Love,* Amos Yong explains that the Spirit poured out at Pentecost may be defined as a baptism into the Spirit of holy love.[37] He derives this interpretation of the Spirit through the lenses of twenty-first-century pentecostal beliefs and practices. Yong points out that this baptism of holy love "in turn has had important performative implications both for the life of holiness and the pentecostal witness."[38] He posits that interpreting Spirit baptism as baptism in this way heavily impacted twentieth-century pentecostal outlooks on life. Yong further explains, "Pentecostal spirituality can be understood as tapping into . . . 'divine love energy,' which members of the Azusa Street Mission understood simply as the transformative power of the 'baptism of love.'"[39]

The transcendent love of God is not just from God, but the very essence of God. The Holy Spirit is neither reduced to energy, a force, a feeling, or a thing from God. The Holy Spirit is a divine person—the fullness of God. The human longing for God, moreover, is satisfied through divine self-outpouring. When the believer longs for holiness, God's transcendence fills the emptiness of the soul. In short, this gift from God is God. This means that a life of holiness expressed in love is impossible without the gift of the Holy Spirit. What an amazing gift!

## HOLINESS AS GOD'S GRACE

At first glance, holiness and grace seem antithetical. While some Christians are attracted to a biblical concept of grace because it seems to get the perpetual sinner off the hook, holiness holds our feet to the fire. So, while legalism becomes hinged on conversations about appropriate Christian activities, appropriate entertainments for Christians, and appropriate Christian speech and thinking, as well as where Christians should go or not go, the mishandling of grace makes it easy to be cavalier about freedom in Christ. Chapell insightfully notes that with comments like "'nobody's perfect,' we can quickly say, that's why we serve a God of grace!"[40] Grace

---

nonviolent Civil Rights Movement was built.

37. Yong, *Spirit,* 60.

38. Ibid.

39. Ibid. Yong explains that his use of "energy of love" calls attention not to the causal features of the Spirit's empowering activity but to its transformative impact.

40. Chapell, *Holiness,* 112.

should not be an excuse for either avoiding Christian responsibility or for making the issue of behavior and attitudes off limits.

Furthermore, grace does not release us from our obligation to God and to each other.[41] Grace does not prohibit us from correcting others and facing the consequences of our actions. God's calling on our lives does not translate into tolerating every way of living. Neither is it necessary for believers to accommodate our understanding of the Christian faith to include those who choose to live contrary to biblical standards. God's unchanging requirements of holiness transmit a beautiful picture with God's unconditional love.[42] According to Psalm 85:9–10, God's holiness and his love "kiss" each other. They form a marriage that produces the life that God intends. For Chapell, grace does not preclude holiness. Rather, it makes it possible. For him, holiness springs from the fountain of grace.[43] He further points out that Colossians 2 and 3 reveal that there is a way to drink from this fountain of grace to strengthen our obedience to God's holiness.[44]

Grace, by definition, is a gift freely given. The term derives from the Greek term *charismata*, meaning "gift." There is no other way to think about grace than as an unearned gift from God. So holiness is a beautiful grace from God. God freely gives this beautiful gift to the believer. Our only duty is to live out the beauty of holiness in our daily lives. Holiness can neither be defined by imposed practices nor by resistant attitudes toward the spiritual discipline, which result in lifestyles with no revealed differences between Christians and non-Christians.

Despite our sins, grace invites us to divine communion through faith. No one is deserving of God's holiness. Again, the longing of the human soul is a longing for holiness. Yet, the fulfillment of that longing is a work of grace. Julian of Norwich explains the Holy Spirit's work as "rewarding" and "giving," in which "rewarding is a gift of our confidence which the Lord makes to those who have labored; and giving is a courteous act which [the Lord] does freely, by grace fulfilling and surpassing all that creatures deserve."[45] Thus, there are rewards associated with some divine matters. The more we give, the more God gives to us. When it comes to holiness, however, we cannot give nor earn holiness. God's grace initiates divine self-

41. Ibid.
42. Ibid.
43. Ibid.
44. Ibid., 113.
45. Julian of Norwich, *Showings*, 295.

disclosure of holiness, thereby making God's likeness available to all who choose to receive it. Holiness by grace fulfils our internal desire to walk in God-likeness. Luther's words seem appropriate here:

> This despair and search for grace should not last only for an hour and then cease. Rather, all our work and words and thoughts as long as we live should be directed solely toward despairing of ourselves and abiding in God's grace, longing and yearning for it, as the prophet says in Ps 42, 'As a [deer] longs for flowing streams, so longs my soul for [you], O God.' This yearning for God and yearning to be good is initiated by grace and it continues."[46]

Not only is this yearning for holiness initiated by God, but God also fulfills it in us by the power of the Holy Spirit. Our hard work to please God without the Spirit fails to accomplish the goal.

## DON'T LEAVE IT ON THE TABLE

When I was a child, as I was seeking the infilling of the Holy Spirit, my parents would encourage me to surrender to God and to open my heart to the Lord. My father regularly preached sermons on the importance of receiving the baptism of the Spirit by faith reflected in the willingness to accept the gift from God.

Often, we miss out on what God has for us because we do not recognize God's gift comes to us despite of our worthlessness. While it is true that God's holiness exposes our unholiness, with its redemptive power, God's holiness is also ready to fill our lives with righteousness, peace, and joy according to the holiness of God's Spirit.[47] If we want righteousness, we must not lean to our own ideas of what is right. Divine righteousness comes to us solely by God's Spirit. If we want peace, we must not depend on our own abilities to experience peace. Divine peace comes to us solely by God's Spirit. If we want joy, it also comes to us by God's Spirit.

Some Christians, however, profess the infilling of the Holy Spirit, but leave the assets of that infilling on the table. They do not behave according to God's righteousness. They are jealous of others, hate themselves, and feel insignificant. Some live in fear on several levels—economic fear, fear of others, fear of death, fear of life, fear of failure, fear of success. Their

---

46. Luther, *Works*, 51:58.

47. See Rom 14:17.

happiness is determined by what happens to them. They cannot seem to discover joy during hard times.

Most secular jobs come with some type of employee benefits. Sometimes we are required to make choices about which benefit we will choose. When we are uninformed, however, we could make a choice that would limit our resources. For example, we could choose a health care benefit that would limit our resources in the event we become ill and need to see a physician or purchase prescriptions. Some choices require us to make greater sacrifice on the front end, but yield a larger benefit in the long run. There are some choices, however, wherein we, in essence, leave money on the table. But it's up to you. We can make the choice that requires sacrifice on the front end, but renders the greater benefits when we need them.

The same is true with righteousness, peace, and joy. If we do not choose to make the necessary sacrifice on the front end, in essence, we leave righteousness, peace, and joy on the table. My charge, moreover, is that Christians get all of what the Holy Spirit has to offer. Don't leave the ultimate Gift from God on the table!

The Holy Spirit is God's gift to transfer God's Word from the believer's hearing to the believer's living. Romans 8:14 states, "For all who are led by the Spirit of God are [sons and daughters] of God." Therefore, there must be a greater emphasis on the power of the Holy Spirit and the role of the Holy Spirit to make the believer holy. Scripture misappropriated becomes a legalistic rod on the backs of untransformed people. Scripture correctly appropriated becomes a guide that points us to the power of the Holy Spirit to transform the heart and thereby transform our lifestyle.

Growing up in the rural South, I thought everyone who claimed to be "Spirit-filled" also pursued a holy lifestyle. I experienced something like a culture shock when I entered seminary. Several of my colleagues claimed to be Spirit-filled. They exercised free and vibrant worship, danced in the Spirit, and spoke with tongues. But their commitment to what I had learned to be the lifestyle of holiness seemed to be shallow. They regularly engaged in behaviors that I had come to view as worldly: they got drunk, smoked cigarettes, engaged in premarital sexual relations, and partied on a regular basis.

It is critical that believers include the language of "holy" in the conversation of being Spirit-filled. Scripture calls the Spirit of God the *Holy* Spirit. Exuberant spiritual experience that is related to Holy Spirit baptism should never supersede the critical element of holiness that is also related to life in the Spirit. To be truly Spirit-filled means more than the freeing of the tongue to the Spirit to speak incomprehensible words. To be filled with God's Spirit means allowing God's Spirit to cause us to live a life of holiness. Galatians 5:16–25 states:

> Walk by the Spirit, and ye shall not fulfill the lust of the flesh. For the flesh lusts against the Spirit, and the Spirit against the flesh; for these are contrary the one to the other; that you may not do the things that you would. But if you are led by the Spirit, you are not under the law. Now the works of the flesh are manifest, which are these, fornication, uncleanness, lasciviousness, idolatry, sorcery, enmities, strife, jealousies, wraths, factions, divisions, heresies, envying, drunkenness, revellings, and such like . . . even as I did forewarn you, that they which practice such things shall not inherit the kingdom of God. . . . And they that are of Christ Jesus have crucified the flesh with the passions and the lusts thereof. If we live by the Spirit, by the Spirit let us also walk.

When we receive the Holy Spirit—the Spirit of love, power and self-control—God endows the individual with the power to crucify the flesh and live according to God's plan. At the end of the day, it is the power within us that fosters self-control.

## LIVING IN THE SPIRIT

God's love comes in power. When the believer receives the Spirit of love, that same Spirit is a Spirit of power. In 2 Timothy 1:7, Paul explains that God's Spirit is the Spirit of love, power, and self-control. The Spirit of God's love, which transforms our will into a willingness to obey God, is not absent of God's power. As undergraduates, my brother and I enjoyed gathering students together and talking about the Lord. Once, an unlikely young student came to our discussions. Given her partying lifestyle and reputation on campus, we were surprised to learn of her knowledge of Scripture. When we would reference a biblical principle or story, she would quote the verse or finish the story. She would conclude by saying, "I know you think I don't know the Bible. But I do!" While we felt some guilt for having gone to the movies on occasion, this Bible-quoting young woman lived however she chose.[48]

---

48. Our home pentecostal church and many other classical Pentecostal churches traditionally preached against going to movies. It was considered a worldly activity.

My brother and I pondered our role in helping a person who knows Scripture to do what Scripture says. In a way, she undermined our Bible-thumping approach to Bible study. It became clear to us that just knowing and even believing what the Bible says is not powerful enough to compel us to live it. There must be another step in the process.

A few years later, the same young woman, Sarah (not her real name), developed a desire to change her ways. She started attending church with us. One night I preached a sermon on the power of the Holy Spirit. She opened up her heart to the Lord and received the baptism of the Spirit. She developed a yearning in her heart to do what God is calling her to do. Today, she is traveling the world as a missionary. Her story exemplifies the reality that doing the right thing is not merely achieved by knowing the right thing. Knowledge is only the first step in the process. It takes God's power. The Holy Spirit is that power that brings about a deep yearning to live out the principles of Christ.

The "Spirit of power" that Paul speaks of enables us to overcome carnal desires and execute our willingness to follow God. In the contemporary church, there is a greater need for emphasis on the Holy Spirit's power to bring about self-control than on doctrinal requirements and confessional statements. Scripture teaches that the Holy Spirit is the primary guide for everyday living. While Bible thumping only leaves a bad taste in people's mouths—it takes the Holy Spirit, the transforming nature of God, to sanctify the life of the believer.

Yet, the Bible is the compass for the church, and through it the church is able to discern the voice of God. A biblical worldview is sustained by the power of the Holy Spirit through changing times, perverted cultural climates, and increasingly secularized ideologies. The Holy Spirit, as God's transcendent nature, transforms human hearts and empowers believers to live out a biblical lifestyle in contexts that are adverse to holiness.


## REFLECTION

Holiness constitutes the fruit of the Spirit. It is impossible to live holy from the heart if we have not accepted Christ as Savior. We cannot live what we have not received. The fruit of the Spirit flows from the heart that is regenerated by God's Spirit. Salvation is where it starts. When we received what Christ has done for us, we posture ourselves for holiness. It is a lifelong journey of faith. Each day we grow in grace—the sanctification process.

## PRAYER

If this chapter has helped you understand more clearly what holiness is all about, and you sense the calling of God to be holy, let's pray this prayer together:

> How can I be holy? How can I be pure? Only by Your Spirit can I win this war. Greater is He who lives in me, doing His will and good pleasure. So take me, and make me, like Your holy Son. Thy will, not my will, be done. Dear Potter, I pray, please mold me like clay. Finish the work you've begun. Finish the work you've begun. How can I be holy? How can I be pure? Only by devotion will I love you more; learning the truth, setting me free; walking in works You've prepared. How can I be holy? How can I be pure? Walking with You Lord, my way is sure; Your law, a delight; Your word is my sight. Lead me in Your righteous paths.[49]

49. Servant, "Prayer for Holiness."

# PART TWO

Practicing Holiness

# 5

## Central Tenets of Holiness: The Four Ds

God is calling [God's] people to true holiness in these days.

—William Seymour

THERE ARE MORE THAN six hundred million Spirit-filled Christians in the world today. Luke 11:13b explains that the Holy Spirit is God's sanctifying Spirit. The life we live is the most profound evidence that we are filled with the Spirit. The Holy Spirit, moreover, empowers us to live holy or walk in the fruit of the Spirit. Often pentecostal and charismatic Christians associate the baptism of the Spirit with speaking in tongues and other charismatic gifts, such as prophecy and miraculous healings. While I do value these biblical gifts as part of the experience of the contemporary church, parallel ecstatic expressions are indigenous to many spiritualist religions around the world. Furthermore, the devil can mimic *glossolalia,* but the devil cannot live holy nor can the devil enable human beings to live holy. It is prudent, moreover, to note the Apostle's words in 1 John 4:1: "Beloved, do not believe every spirit, but test the spirits to see whether they are from God, for many false prophets have gone out into the world." The Spirit of God is holy and compels us to live holy.

Kevin DeYoung is correct to suggest that the sum of holiness involves a million little things. This includes avoiding little evils and the little faults, the setting aside of little bits of worldliness and simple acts of compromise, ending minuscule inconsistencies and indiscretions, attending to little duties and dealings, the hard work of little self-denials and little self-restraints, as well as the cultivation of small benevolences and forbearances.[50] Accompanying questions include the following: Are you trustworthy? Are you kind? Are you patient? Are you joyful? Do you love?[51] Examining ourselves through a microscope would undoubtedly discourage us from trying. But true holiness says that we can neither produce this kind of life on our own nor should we spend too much time judging our every move. We need God to help us and only God can judge our utmost intents. This chapter explains that holiness requires a devoted life of prayer, a disciplined lifestyle with determination to live God's ways despite the odds, and commitment to developing a life of service to and on behalf of others.

## DEVOTED ENTIRELY TO GOD

### A Life of Prayer

Prayer is central to life in the Spirit. Throughout Scripture, prayer is shown to be a medicine that heals the fractured relationship between God and God's people. It is the healing balm of a nation. Prayer is the force of change in the hands of the powerless. As leader of the Civil Rights Movement, Martin Luther King Jr. learned the power of prayer. He once said, "To be a Christian without prayer is no more possible than to be alive without breathing." With similar conviction about prayer, my mom used to sing with confidence, "I know prayer changes things. I know prayer changes things. We must always pray and never faint. I know prayer changes things." The power of prayer is essential in the life of the church and the church's mission in society. Second Chronicles 7:14–16 states, "If my people who are called by my name will humble themselves, and pray and seek my face and turn from their wicked ways, then I will hear from heaven and will forgive their sin and heal their land. Now my eyes will be open and my ears attentive to the prayer that is made in this place. For now I have chosen and consecrated this house that my name may be there forever. My eyes and my heart will be there for all time." Translating the Old Testament notion of the "people of God" into the New Testament notion that the "people of God" are those of the "household of faith"—the church—this passage has profound implications for the church in regards to prayer. If the church humbles herself, prays, and seeks God's face, if she turns from her wicked

50. DeYoung, *Hole*, 145.
51. Ibid.

ways, then God will hear her prayers and will forgive her sins and heal the society wherever in the world the church finds herself.

The formula for society's transformation begins with (a) the church's humility, (b) seeking God's face through prayer, and (c) the church's repentance. Ironically, prayer meetings in our churches are often poorly attended. Christians are often more interested in concerts and celebrity preaching than prayer meetings. Whether sex scandals and abuse in the Catholic churches and many Protestant ones as well, squabbles among churches over whose doctrine is right and whose is wrong, political fights, tugs-of-war over membership, hard feelings about the building projects, or greedy and power-stricken preachers who build their services around fundraising, the church must humble herself, pray, and repent.

Prayer is essential to the call for the church to regain reverence for God, to recommit to the life of the Spirit, and to impact society. Barth explains that through prayer the church shares in the common interests with society and its task to give resolute practical expression for this community of interest.[52] He points out the importance for the church collectively and Christians individually to pray for society. Prayers from the Christian community are needed all the more since society on its own is not in the habit of praying. But by praying for society, the church before God acknowledges her responsibility in regards to society. Barth further posits that the Christian community would not be taking this responsibility seriously enough if it did no more than pray. In his view, God absolutely requires that the Christian community work actively on behalf of society.[53]

Charles G. Finney lectured on the power and effectiveness of prayer in the mission of the church to influence an unbelieving society.

> Prayer is an essential link in the chain of causes that lead to a revival; as much so as truth is. Some have zealously used truth to convert men, and laid very little stress on prayer. They have preached, and talked, and distributed tracts with great zeal, and then wondered that they had so little success. And the reason was, that they forgot to use the other branch of the means, effectual prayer. They overlooked the fact, that truth by itself will never produce the effect, without the Spirit of God, and that Spirit is given in answer to earnest prayer.[54]

52. Barth, *Karl Barth*, 273.

53. Ibid.

54. Finney, "Prevailing Prayer," n.p.

When we make prayer our standard, society watches as God responds with answers to our prayers. Exemplified through Finney, God releases vision as a result of prayer. Prayer was the impetus for Finney's practical and prophetic approach to ministry. An abolitionist and a believer in education as a vehicle to transform society for Christ, Finney in 1852 led Oberlin College to impact society for Jesus Christ. His prophetic leadership impacted social reform as relating to morality, the issue of women's rights, the abolition of slavery, anti-prostitution, Sabbath observance on Sundays, how society treated prisoners, the psychologically impaired, and physically disabled people. Finney's standards were distinctively related to his understanding of the biblical church and the divine call for her to stand with distinction in society, even against society when necessary, to impact it by virtue of merely being the church that God intends.

Let's think of holiness as a journey with God. The believer encounters many challenges along the way. The path seems harder when we remove our eyes from God to explore worldly temptations. In simple terms, DeYoung correctly admits, "There's the reality that holiness is plain hard work, and we're often lazy. We like our sins, and dying to them is painful. Almost everything is easier than growing in godliness. . . . It's one thing to graduate from college ready to change the world. It is another to be resolute in praying that God would change you."[55] Yet, prayer is the power that transforms our will and empowers us in the continuous and progressive pathway of holiness with God. John Wesley aptly comments, "The neglect of prayer is a grand hindrance to holiness."[56] Prayer becomes a spiritual discipline to refuel us for a continued pursuit of holiness. I have heard it said, "More prayer, more power; less prayer, less power and no prayer, no power." Sincere prayer is two-way communication. We speak to God; God speaks back to us. Attempting to live holy without a heartfelt emphasis on prayer leads to a slippery slope of self-righteousness.

Self-righteousness says, "I am right and others need to see that I am right." Though a controversial figure in his time, David B. Berg correctly notes that "self-righteousness is very closely related to pride, and stems directly from it. And though we all have the besetting sin of pride and a love and concern for ourselves, the enemy of our soul can often play on that natural human weakness and blow it up into the worst of all problems." He adds, "Pride is the root of all sin, and was the cause of Satan's demise

55. Ibid.,19.
56. Wesley, *Works*, ed. Joseph Benson, 8:88.

(see Isa 14:12–15). Scripture teaches that the Lord hates pride (see Prov 6:16–17)."[57] Pride fosters rebellion and selfishness. A life of prayer, however, reminds the believer of a need for self-emptying. Self-emptying is something quite different than self-righteousness. Self-emptying says, "I am dependent on a righteousness that is bigger than me. I need God." The self-realization that we need God is the impetus for prayer and the foundation of a prayerful life.

## A Selfless Attitude

Self-emptying is significant to the life of holiness. In Floyd McClung's work he unearths a deep-seated connection between the practice of holiness and rebellion, pride and selfishness. He says, "Pride is an unwillingness to see ourselves as we really are, especially when we are rebellious or hurt. Pride is extreme self-centeredness."[58] McClung further explains that "self-centeredness grieves the Holy Spirit."[59] Christ is our chief exemplar of holiness. Like Him, we must empty ourselves before God. Self-emptying is the precursor for any attempt to follow Christ. Jesus said, "If anyone would come after me, let him [or her] deny himself [or herself] and take up his [or her] cross daily and follow me" (Luke 9:23). Self-emptying requires that we mortify the passions that pound against our human will.

Tertullian posits, "Daily, every moment, prayer is necessary to men; of course continence (is so) too, since prayer is necessary."[60] Constant self-emptying through prayer requires considerable self-restraint, because overwhelming persuasion often accompanies temptation. Moreover, while praying is critical, human will has a significant role in the pursuit of holiness. Jerry Bridges, former national president of the interdenominational Navigators ministry says, "The pursuit of holiness is a joint venture between God and the Christian. No one can attain any degree of holiness without God working in his life, but just as surely no one will attain it without effort on his own part. God has made it possible for us to walk in holiness. But He has given to us the responsibility of doing the walking; He does not do that for us."[61] We must consciously turn away from the ways, ideas,

57. Berg, "Overcoming," n.p.

58. McClung Jr., *Holiness*, 135.

59. Ibid., *Father*, 50.

60. Tertullian, "On Exhortation," n.p.

61. Bridges, *Pursuit*, 14.

and thought patterns of the world in pursuit of intense devotion to God. This is the moderation to which Tertullian refers. Our devotion comes as a continual process, lived out through prayer, coupled with self-restraint. We must walk in holiness to reach holiness. John White makes an important point that "there are no shortcuts to holiness. . . . It must always begin with the renewed thankfulness for the never-ending grace of God, and a sense of being set free repeatedly to a life of holiness."[62]

Devoted pursuit of the "holy" requires self-recognition that we were born in sin and from our birth we have mastered nothing other than sin. Moreover, God's grace beckons for us. Part of the work of the Holy Spirit is to shape and reshape God's people until we conform into God's image. Isaiah 64:6–8 says,

> All of us have become like one who is unclean, and all our righteous acts are like filthy rags; we all shrivel up like a leaf, and like the wind our sins sweep us away. No one calls on your name or strives to lay hold of you; for you have hidden your face from us and made us waste away because of our sins. Yet, O LORD, you are our Father. We are the clay, you are the potter; we are all the work of your hand.

Devotion to God requires that we make moves toward God. Another adage comes to mind: "If you make one step, God will make two. There is no limit to what God will do." When we advance toward God, God advances toward us. As we pursue God, we must let go of thoughts, behaviors, and involvements that are contrary to what God requires. In essence, the clay must cooperate with the potter to become truly the work of God's hand.

## DISCIPLINED EVERYDAY BEHAVIOR

God is a God of order. The beauty of creation is the result of divine order. Natural laws are set in place to maintain natural systems and forces. The solar system, the Milky Way galaxy, gravity, centripetal force, and aerodynamics, to name a few, hold things together and fortify the natural world, making it possible for us to live comfortable and adventurous lives. God forbid these natural phenomena resist divine instruction—it would become impossible for us to experience the splendor of the world around us.

---

62. White, *Flirting*, 131.

In like manner, when we fail to follow divine orders—instructions on how to live—we forfeit the splendor that God intends for every human life.

Moreover, God's affinity for order suggests that God expects a level of discipline from us, in order to align ourselves with the holiness of God's order. Max van Manen asserts, "A person's attitude toward discipline is the measure of that person's own orientation to order."[63] A lack of discipline produces lawlessness. Lawlessness may be the greatest temptation among humankind. It is the spirit of lawlessness that compels us to run from the guiding principles and instructions by which God intends us to live—what we should do and where we should go. To this end, Paul's first pastoral letter to Timothy teaches about the spiritual importance of self-discipline: "Discipline yourself for the purpose of godliness" (1 Tim 4:7b NASB). Often, when we hear the word *discipline*, we think of punishment, restriction, or coerced submission. Perhaps we associate discipline with our childrearing years. The word discipline communicates something punitive. However, *discipline* here means, "to teach or train." So, as opposed to castigatory implications, Paul exhorts Timothy pertaining to the value of spiritual training, or spiritual formation. This spiritual training is in the areas of divine reverence and personal piety and conformation to pure religion.

## Redeeming Religion from the Dumpster

A few years ago, I taught religion as an adjunct professor at Sacred Heart University in Fairfield, Connecticut. During introductions, I asked my students to tell us a little about their religious backgrounds. Time and time again, students would say, "I was raised Catholic but now I do not consider myself religious. But, I am spiritual"; or, "I have a relationship with God but not with institutional religion." You have heard similar statements as well. There are certainly many ways to interpret what they mean.

The main caution is when people erroneously imply a bifurcation between religion and spirituality. Such a distinction is mindboggling for anyone who understands the true meaning of religion. Etymologically, the term *religion* derives from the Latin word *religare*, which means "to bind." The term *religion* arrives in English as a term that speaks to "binding oneself to a set of beliefs and practices." Ideally, those beliefs and practices are passed on from the ultimate being to which the person or group of people submit in worship and admiration. It is, moreover, difficult to explain how

63. Van Manen, *Tact*, 198.

we could have an intimate relationship with God without binding ourselves to the beliefs and practices associated with that relationship. So then, spirituality and religion must remain bedfellows in true "spirituality" and in true "religion." To be spiritual is religious and to be religious is to be spiritual. Any attempt to divorce these faith tenets lends to lawlessness and the absence of a divine inner knowing. Both lawlessness and the lack of an inner connection with God are associated with pseudo spirituality and the enemy of true religion. The deficiency of guiding principles and behavior results in lawlessness.

## Ordering Our Steps in God's Word

As God is a God of order, God is a God of discipline. It is not surprising, therefore, that before institutional Christianity, Jesus' earliest followers were called "disciples." Christ commissioned them to "go into the entire world, making disciples" (Matt 28:19). So then, even today, Christ calls for disciples. The call to discipleship is a call to holiness. Drawing from the Wesleyan tradition, as Allan Coppedge explains it, discipleship begins when people are called to repent of their sins and believe on the gospel of Jesus Christ (Matt 4:17; Mark 1:14–15).[64] A person begins to follow Jesus when she or he turns away from disobedience or unholiness and embraces faith in Jesus Christ.[65]

Corné Bekker explains that as disciples, we cannot, by any self-discipline, transform our own hearts to be like Christ. Only Christ can transform the heart.[66] We must seek to understand Christ's ways and put forth effort to implement Christ's way of behaving. Christ transforms our hearts in a moment; yet, translating the transformed heart into transformed behavior involves intentionality on our part. This is a process. We must submit to listening to the Word of God to apply God's principles in everyday life.

Bekker explains that the goal of Christian spiritual formation is "Christ-in-charge."[67] We are not able to change ourselves. Yet, it is not enough to recognize this fact. It is necessary for believers to rely on the Spirit of Christ to bring about that transformation in us, for the purpose of following Christ. Spiritual practices such as reading Scripture and praying and

64. See Coppedge, "Holiness," 82.

65. Ibid.

66. Bekker, "Becoming," n.p.

67. Ibid.

healthy friendships with other Christians can help to clear space through the clutter of life for the Holy Spirit to enter and guide the believer into the life of God. The Holy Spirit is that transcendent power, fully God's presence, that transforms our lives into holiness. The Holy Spirit empowers the believer to live like Christ from a pure heart.[68] In *The Pursuit of Holiness,* Jerry Bridges points out that the only safe evidence that we are in Christ is not church membership or charismatic gifts but rather a holy life. He builds his argument from Scripture: 1 John 3:3 states, "And everyone who thus hopes in [Christ] purifies himself [or herself] as [Christ] is pure"; and Romans 8:14 states, "For all who are led by the Spirit of God are sons [and daughters] of God." Based on this biblical premise, Bridges concludes that it is a contradiction to claim to be a Christian but not to earnestly seek to live holy. He explains, "Everyone, then, who professes to be a Christian should ask himself [or herself], 'Is there evidence of practical holiness in my life? Do I desire and strive after holiness? Do I grieve over my lack of it and earnestly seek the help of God to be holy?'"[69]

Many Christians, however, become lackadaisical; we become satisfied with initiation into the Christian walk through quoting the sinner's prayer, or water baptism, or even the baptism of the Spirit. Sometimes we, as Christians—new or long-standing—do not avail ourselves to a lifelong process of discipleship, integrity, and personal faithfulness to the life of Christ. Using the words of J. I. Packer, our personal piety is often "three thousand miles wide and three inches deep."

## Classic Spiritual Disciplines

Popular Christian minister Joyce Meyer explains that discipline is really for self-improvement and for self-preservation. She says, "When discipline is sown, like a good seed, it yields a harvest of things that fulfill and satisfy us—things that make us happy and release peace and joy in our lives."[70] Classic spiritual disciplines are a wonderful starting point in Christian discipleship. These include reading Scripture, praying, fasting, regularly attending church services, and regular fellowship with believers. For the new believer, these classic spiritual disciplines pose challenges. Reading the

68. See Coppedge, "Holiness."

69. Bridges, *Pursuit*, 43.

70. Meyer, *Secret*, 240.

Bible could be intimidating—Where should I start? How do I know what it means? These are just some of the questions that come to mind.

Let me offer a few tips for Bible reading. First of all, do not look at the Bible and think, "*All* of this?" Consider when you were learning to swim. You did not look at the pool and say, "All of that water?" Rather, you focused on the lesson from the trainer to develop the skills to float and then to paddle one stroke at a time. Similarly, when it comes to Bible study, don't say, "This *entire* book?" We glean the most from Scripture when we focus on developing tools for Bible study and then by reading a little at a time. Before we know it, over time, we have read and gleaned much valuable instruction and inspiration for everyday lives of holiness.

## Smart Choices

When we come to faith in Christ, it is important that we posture ourselves for the life of holiness. A new life requires a new lifestyle. A new lifestyle requires making smart choices and developing godly habits.[71] Faith in Christ means that Christ becomes the center of one's universe. No virtue can be reduced to a list of rules that the church pressures us to follow. Holiness is an essential Christian virtue. In Wesley's sermon "Circumcision of the Heart," he aptly states, "It is that habitual disposition of soul which . . . is termed 'holiness', and which directly implies the being cleansed from sin, 'from all filthiness both of flesh and spirit', and by consequence the being endued with those virtues which were also in Christ Jesus, the being so 'renewed in the image of our mind' as to be 'perfect, as our Father in heaven is perfect.'"[72] Holiness is not a natural consequence of salvation. The Holy Spirit empowers the believer. Yet, a holy lifestyle requires disciplined behavior in pursuit of a renewed life that is only possible after we accept what Christ has done for us. Believers, moreover, must habituate certain practices as a lifestyle in pursuit of holiness.

There are several habits that one must develop as part of a lifestyle of holiness. Therefore, the most essential decision in the life of a believer is the decision daily to position our thoughts and behaviors by making smart choices. There are many Christians who (to use colloquial language)

71. By "habits" I do not mean ostentation. Ostentation means living only for others to see. Habits imply living life on purpose and should not include an expectation of accolades or praise for good deeds, moral or ethical behavior, or acts of kindness.

72. Wesley, "Circumcision," 25.

straddle the fence. When called upon to make difficult decisions within the daily walk of faith, ambivalence strangles faith, and even the believer falls into demonic snares. Moses and Joshua observed the spirit of ambivalence among the Hebrew people as well. Joshua echoed Moses' sentiment that making important choices is indispensable to the holy walk. Moses said, "Who is on the Lord's side? Come to me" (Exod 32:26). Similarly, Joshua said, "Now therefore fear the Lord and serve him in sincerity and in faithfulness. Put away the gods that your fathers served beyond the River and in Egypt, and serve the Lord. And if it is evil in your eyes to serve the Lord, choose this day whom you will serve, whether the gods your fathers served in the region beyond the River, or the gods of the Amorites in whose land you dwell. But as for me and my house, we will serve the Lord" (Josh 24:14–15). Herein lies the smartest decision the believer can make: to publically profess God's side over against the world's. All other habits should flow out of that decision.

For example, when brothers and sisters in Christ are blessed with a car or a house, those of us with developed habits of holiness would rejoice. Contrariwise, those of us who are not habituated in holiness become jealous because we do not have a house or have been struggling and praying for a long time, but have not gotten our desire. Furthermore, when those of us who possess developed habits of holiness see someone in need, we offer help and do not expect anything in return; neither would we sound the alarm nor make a report to the church for a pat on our backs. However, Christians who are not habituated in holiness might help others with the intent of drawing attention for self-glorification. Holiness is a way of life— it's just what Christians do, or are supposed to do. One cannot legislate habituated smart choices. One cannot be taught habits of the heart through classroom pedagogical methods that inform only cognitive development. These habits flow from a heart disposed to Christ-like behavior.

To truly be habituated toward holiness, the believer needs to develop devotional disciplines. These are intentional devotional disciplines that orient the heart in Christ-like behavior. Bekker calls devotional disciplines "habits of the heart."[73] Habits of the heart bring forth change in how we understand God and how we understand ourselves in relation to God and God's will for us.

Paul teaches the Corinthian church a valuable lesson pertaining to the spiritual process of Christian formation (2 Cor 3:18): "And we all, with

73. Bekker, "Becoming," n.p.

unveiled face, beholding the glory of the Lord, are being transformed into the same image from one degree of glory to another. For this comes from the Lord who is the Spirit." Episcopal priest James C. Fenhagen points out that when the believer is open to the Spirit of God to be reformed in Christ, an environment is created that opens us to the leading of the Spirit. Like formerly blind Bartimaeus (Mark 10:46–52) when he pursued Jesus, explains Fenhagen, we begin to see the glory of the Lord.[74] God's glory is transformational, in that we are changed from one state of awareness to a greater awareness of Christ. It is conformational as it forms the believer into the likeness of Christ. Christ's likeness includes participation in the body of Christ—the church; but also, Christ's likeness is a way of thinking and living in the world. Advancing from *transformational* to *conformational* expresses Paul's point in 2 Corinthians 3:18. When we are transformed into the image of Christ, we are then able to embrace his character and way of being in the world.

Building on Paul's teachings in this verse, Bekker offers three practical suggestions toward forming into Christ's likeness. All of Bekker's propositions include a sense of presence: "communal presence," "intrapersonal presence," and "devotional presence." The language of "presence" is an effort to overcome exhibitionistic behavior. So often, when I preach or teach and look people straight in the eyes, they nod, smile, or even say, "Amen"—yet, they have no clue of what I am talking about. They respond out of habit or because they think I want them to. But, in fact, they are not "fully present." Their bodies are in the room but their minds are not. Their minds are at the mall shopping, trying to figure out finances, planning for the week, or something else. It is not always apparent when one is not fully present. However, sometimes it is. It becomes clearer when I ask a question that they cannot answer because they have not been listening. I know this behavior all too well. Sometimes the same is true for me when I am talking to my wife, or when I am the audience member at a conference.

When we are guilty of being in the room but not listening to what is being said, we are not fully present. In Isaiah, God points out a similar experience between God and the Hebrew people: "And the Lord said: 'Because this people draw near with their mouth and honor me with their lips, while their hearts are far from me, and their fear of me is a commandment taught by [people]'" (Isa 29:13). Jesus echoes a similar observation among the religious sects of the day: "Well did Isaiah prophesy of you hypocrites,

74. Fenhagen, *Invitation*, 9.

as it is written, 'This people honors me with their lips, but their heart is far from me'" (Mark 7:6). Notwithstanding the harsh words, Jesus sends out a strong message pertaining to divine expectation: that students of the faith practice full presence. Moreover, Bekker's emphasis on "presence" as spiritual discipline or habit toward the formation into the likeness of Christ is not only critical but also imperative. To be "fully present" means that one brings all of oneself to bear on the process of spiritual formation.

## Self-Awareness

Bekker is helpful in understanding the value of making smart choices in the Christian walk. What he calls "dimensions of presence" are essentially what I call "smart choices" to advance the process of Christian formation. Using as a base 2 Corinthians 3:18a, Bekker reflects on Paul's phrase "we all, with unveiled faces," pointing out the need for what he calls "self-exposure." By self-exposure he means that it is a smart choice for believers to be honest with themselves. This "intrapersonal presence" (à la Bekker) is helpful for Christian development into the image of Christ, to which the believer is called. Drawing upon American author Thomas Merton's comment that "we make ourselves real by telling the truth," Bekker explains that one can only confess the Word of the Lord when one confesses what is wrong with her or him.[75]

For the purpose of spiritual formation or discipleship, we must practice honesty in all things. Telling the truth (period) is part of what it means to be holy. However, confronting the truth about ourselves is a significant part of our own spiritual development. Pretense has no place in holiness. Holiness is, rather, a call to authentic conformation into the likeness of Christ. Fenhagen poses an important challenge on the issue of self-awareness. He says, "I believe we have to ask ourselves in all honesty why, for so many Christians (including the one posing the question), it is so hard to act on those aspects of our faith that challenge the status quo. In response to the critical issues that face the world, we seem to be better at talking than acting—and as a result, much of what people see and hear of the Christian faith is often a religion of narrow focus and brittle edges."[76] Having a good feeling and a heart that supports faith are important components of self-awareness. Yet, there is a need for a deeper self-awareness. The Christian

75. Bekker, "Becoming," n.p.
76. Fenhagen, *Invitation*, 9.

faith, in the words of Fenhagen, "is incredibly realistic about the power of human sin and affirms that until there is a basic reorientation in the way we think and the way we see and the way we live, the incredible destructiveness we see in the world will continue. Christianity is not a religion that sees the human journey primarily in terms of growth, but in terms of transformation. [In this way], Christianity is not fundamentally about wholeness but holiness."[77] The needed reorientation is made possible as the Christian recognizes the sovereignty of God and who the person is called to be in relation to God's sovereignty.

## Christ-Focus

Bekker, furthermore, explains the devotional presence as a smart habit of positioning on divine matters, even Christ himself. It is easy to become distracted by people and the events of everyday life. It is critical, moreover, for the Christian to be intentional with her or his gazing. Always ask, where is Christ in this or that? John Calvin insightfully comments,

> It is evident that man never attains to a true self-knowledge until he has previously contemplated the face of God, and come down after such contemplation to look into himself. For (such is our innate pride) we always seem to ourselves just, and upright, and wise, and holy, until we are convinced, by clear evidence, of our injustice, vileness, folly, and impurity. Convinced, however, we are not, if we look to ourselves only, and not to the Lord also—He being the only standard by the application of which this conviction can be produced . . . the knowledge of God and the knowledge of ourselves are mutually connected.[78]

Discovering Christ not only gives us a sense of direction, but also brings self-discovery. On several levels, therefore, it is a smart habit to look for Christ in every situation. If Christ is not evident in our life experiences, we need to redirect our attention until we see him clearly.

Distancing from distractions and focusing on Jesus is critical to discipleship or spiritual formation. Hebrews 12:1b–2a says, "Let us also lay aside every weight, and sin which clings so closely, and let us run with endurance the race that is set before us, *looking to Jesus,* the founder and perfector of our faith" (italics added). Several songs echo the purpose and

77. Ibid.

78. Calvin, *Institutes*, 44–45.

power of devotional presence. For example, the slaves understood the value of habitual concentration on Jesus. They often sang the song "Woke Up This Morning," the lyrics of which are:

> Woke up this morning with my mind stayed on Jesus / Woke up this morning with my mind stayed on Jesus / Woke up this Morning with my mind stayed on Jesus / Hallelulu, Hallelu, Hallelujah; Singing and praying with my mind stayed on Jesus / Singing and praying with my mind stayed on Jesus / Singing and praying with my mind stayed on Jesus / Hallelulu, Hallelu, Hallelujah / Ain't no harm to keep my mind stayed on Jesus / Ain't no harm to keep my mind stayed on Jesus / Ain't no harm to keep my mind stayed on Jesus / Hallelulu, Hallelu, Hallelujah.

Also, the refrain in Helen H. Lemmel's "Turn Your Eyes Upon Jesus" is fitting. The lyrics of the refrain are:

> Turn your eyes upon Jesus / Look full in his wonderful face / And the things of earth will grow strangely dim / In the light of his glory and grace.

The primary way to turn one's eyes upon Jesus is through continual prayer. In the gospels, Jesus teaches that we should always pray (Luke 18:1). Paul also teaches, "Pray without ceasing" (1 Thess 5:17).

## DETERMINE TO LIVE GOD'S WAY

### Individual Decision

The skeptical reader might say, "It is easy to say, 'Make smart choices.'" I concur. The power of smart choices is rooted in a pre-commitment of determination. It is easy to be sidetracked or lured into ideologies and behaviors that compete with a holy life when one deals casually with choices. In the Old Testament, Joshua understood the power of determination. He jolts the minds of the Hebrew people into the seriousness associated with divine holiness. It is nothing to deal with casually. Each believer must be determined to live on the Lord's side; we must consciously live out that indomitable decision even in the face of adversity.

Unlike certain countries—like Morocco, parts of India, North Korea, China, Afghanistan, Northern Sudan, and Iran—in the United States of America, we have freedom of religion. In the "Free World," it becomes easy to take what should be serious faith decisions casually. When the preacher makes an altar call after a moving sermon, it is not uncommon for the altar to be flooded with people whose emotions are running over with guilt or even with people who feel that others expect them to go to the altar.

Regularly, Evangelicals invite the unsaved to confess a sinner's prayer that goes something like: "Dear Lord, I believe that you died and rose again for me. I acknowledge my sins and ask you to forgive me. I will live for you from this day forward, Amen." Most of us, who come from Evangelical and pentecostal traditions, have said this prayer hundreds of times. Yet, the deeper question is whether this prayer has become pretentious rhetoric or truly a moment of deep commitment and unyielding determination to serve the Lord. In the Free World, our confession of faith is untested by our government. However, beyond the mere confession of faith, our value system seems to be constantly under scrutiny. The company we keep often impacts the values that we live by.

## Impact of Community

Yong draws attention to the role of community through his theology of hospitality, based on Luke. In a broad-stroked interpretation, Yong's theology of hospitality emphasizes the centrality of the Spirit in community formation.[79] As such, the Spirit is hospitable, inviting others to share in the community of faith. Thereby, the Spirit affirms the communal nature of the church. Being holy, the Spirit's chief distinction is holiness, which is God's nature.

The African proverb "It takes a village" is appropriate for a discussion of communal formation in holiness. The community of the Spirit fosters the life of holiness. Regardless of how "holy" one thinks she or he is, no single person will be the only person in heaven. Also, there is no special seat in heaven reserved for a single person. John the evangelist says, "I saw a number that no one can number." The biblical record implies that the citizens of heaven are a collective body—the body of Christ. As it will be in heaven, so it is on earth. The church is a community of believers in Christ. Believers must give up the "self" concept to be part of a collective body—the church of Jesus Christ. It is in this way that the Holy Spirit uses community as a mechanism of spiritual formation. When we submit the

79. Yong, *Hospitality*, 105–7. The main thrust of Yong's theology, on a macro level, is "Hospitality in a pluralistic world." His argument from Luke's gospel also speaks to the nature and role of a Spirit-filled community in developing lives of holiness.

"self" to the work of the Spirit in community, we are positioned for being shaped into the fullness of the image and likeness of God—the *Imago Dei*.

Bekker sheds helpful light on the issue of the habitual assembly of believers. The communal assembly should not be an ostentatious act but a type of communal positioning; or, as Hauerwas seems to imply, the forming of habits that determine unavoidable worship of God.[80] Although in the history of Christianity there have been some who thought otherwise (i.e., some of the desert fathers, some of the Moravians, and others), biblical Christianity is not a faith for isolated hermits. God birthed the "church" as a community of faith for a reason.

Connecting his doctrine of holiness with ecclesiology, Wesley sees the role of community as extremely vital to the Christian life. Runyon points out that Wesley lists the issue of community among his various "means of grace."[81] Wesley explains, "Christianity is essentially a social religion, and that to turn it into a solitary religion is indeed to destroy it. When I say [Christianity] is essentially a social religion, I mean not only that it cannot subsist so well, but that it cannot subsist at all without society, without living and conversing with [others]."[82] By "social," Wesley is referring to community. God's grace both appears to humanity, drawing people to faith in Christ through community, and nurtures the believer's faith through community. Thus, community is a critical component to the holy life. Building upon his strong belief that communities help to form the holy life, Wesley set up societies, classes, and bands. Runyon explains that through these various expressions of community, Wesley "provided the necessary communal setting within which faith could not only be generated but enriched and sustained."[83] Runyon further points out, "Together (i.e. Conferring together) they sought the meaning of Scripture, prayed, and shared life experiences that both challenged and confirmed their faith. Wesley could not imagine Christians not benefiting from this kind of exchange and mutual support." And Wesley observed, notes Runyon, that "where this kind of [communal] support was not available, although the seed sowed in preaching might quickly spring up, it withered away just as quickly."[84]

---

80. Hauerwas, "Sanctified," 22.

81. Runyon, "Holiness," 81.

82. Wesley, "Upon," 195–96.

83. Runyon, "Holiness," 81.

84. Ibid., 81–82.

Furthermore, Wesley cautions that rest, reflection, prayer, and devotional time in a private space to "converse with God; to commune more freely with our Father which is in secret" are significant to holy living.[85] Yet, the fullness of Christian discipleship is not a privatized process. Community is essential to living a sanctified life. As mentioned earlier, the Christian lifestyle of holiness requires associating with people who are struggling to move in the same direction that the believer is going. This means that our choice of friends, who we choose to marry, and the company we choose to keep are all critical choices in the formation into the image of Christ. Additionally, Wesley emphasizes the role of congregational life is fostering a "means of grace" through which the Holy Spirit fortifies faith and nurtures the believer in a life of holiness.

There are several other means by which community forms one into the image of Christ. Regular church attendance, Bible study, table fellowship, and routine outings with people of the faith are all examples of ways that community attendance contributes to the formation of holiness in the life of the believer. Hebrews 10:25 admonishes Christians not to neglect to meet together, but to encourage one another. The writer of Hebrews sees a connection between the habituation of community and spiritual formation within Christ's church. The persecution that lay ahead of them then and for us today requires communal habituated practices to endure. Isolation and individualism breeds defeat. The pliability of communal spirituality and faith forms a crucial element of holiness, as they fortify a common bond of the faithful, fostering the victory of Christian living. The community bonding that happens during frequent assemblies helps us make it, together, through tough times.

## DEVELOP A LIFE OF ADVOCACY AND SERVICE

At first glance there appears to be tension between holiness and love. Practically speaking, if holiness demands that we be separate from the world, or that we "love not the world," how then do we express love for "worldly" people? It is important to note that loving worldly ways of thinking and being is different from loving people who subscribe to non-Christian ways of thinking and being. Christ-like love is able to love people authentically regardless of their way of being and living in the world. It follows that when this Christ-like love is the foundation of holiness, service to and on behalf

85. Wesley, "Upon," 196.

of others becomes its chief expression. Yong comments that "to love is to allow the love of God that has been poured out in our hearts through the Holy Spirit to flow out into the lives of others."[86] Thus, holiness flows from the Spirit of holiness to impact the world for Christ.

David Kinnaman, president of the Barna Group, reports some positive facts from his research of twenty-first-century young Christians. He explains that young Christians are not as expressive about their faith as generations of the past; however, among those who are willing to share their faith, they consistently and clearly state that they do not believe evangelism can be separated from action.[87] Kinnaman further posits, "This generation doesn't want to be merely hearers of faith but also doers."[88] Their desire explains this generation's focus on social justice. The crux of faith is connected to action on behalf of others. Although concerned that social justice replaces the emphasis on Christ's redemptive work on the cross, Kinnaman sees the emphasis on a life of service as an important lesson for the broader church.[89] For years, Christians have focused too heavily on getting the message of the cross out and "winning souls," such that the practical dimensions of the Christians' faith have been overshadowed. It is important to note that before the cross, there was a loving Christ who helped people and advocated for those who could not help themselves. I believe that, in this order, the contemporary Christ will redeem a world that is lost through practical expressions of faith.

We bring people to Christ by giving them a hand up, speaking out on their behalf, and communicating to them love in action. We extend a hand up when we advocate success through education more than through acts of kindness. It has been said, "If we give someone a fish, they will eat one time; but if we teach them how to fish, they will eat whenever they are hungry." In emergencies such as hurricanes, earthquakes, the aftermath of war, and other such times, a handout for relief is appropriate. But, for the long run, a hand up seems to reflect Christ's love the best. We speak out on behalf of those who cannot speak for themselves when we use our platforms of privilege to speak against injustice and on behalf of the violated and muted people of all ages, from the womb to the tomb. We communicate love in action when we sacrifice our time, talents, and resources to extend

86. Yong, *Theology*, 250.
87. Kinnaman, *You*, 177.
88. Ibid.
89. Ibid.

opportunities for everyone's common good. At times a hand up, speaking out, and love in action demand radical measures. The prince of darkness often expresses oppression through the oppressors with severity and great hostility. The call to service requires a response to injustice and oppression that is both genuinely loving, but also radically and urgently active.

I am not surprised when Boyd reminds us that holiness, as a radical way of *being*, has preeminence over a way of *acting* against injustice and oppression. First, it is about *living* in love, as Christ loves us and gave his life for us. Then, it is about *acting* in a loving manner that will improve the world.[90] Yet, the primary step of *being* does not undercut the necessary next step—*acting*. We will never be able to do the latter unless we have cultivated the former. And the latter is necessarily the outcome of the former. Slave abolitionist Frederick Douglass insightfully commented, "Power concedes nothing without a demand. It never did and it never will."[91] Holiness as acting in love on behalf of the powerless sometimes requires radically bold and often unpopular action. Such advocacy must flow from something more than genuineness. The strength and courage that helping others often requires must flow from one's *being*.

Christ-like love upsets any system of hate as expressed through injustice and oppression. This fact is not only evidenced throughout history, but also at the pinnacle of Christian history—the cross of Christ. At Calvary, the King of love has upset a system of injustice and oppression. As a result, love at its best suffers the worst and most embarrassing torture that injustice could inflict. Indeed, the kingdom of God suffered severe violence (see Matt 11:12). Yet, Christ's holiness was greater than the suffering. His holiness is expressed through his relentless commitment to act on behalf of a world that could not, and in many ways refused to, understand his love, even those who were committing the violence toward him.

In a practical sense, Kinnaman's research findings seem very much in line with an important lesson about the public life of faith-in-action that Wesley teaches in his eighteenth-century sermon "Upon Our Lord's Sermon on the Mount." He suitably points out, "Your holiness makes you as conspicuous as the sun in the midst of heaven. As ye cannot go out of the world, so neither can ye stay in it without appearing to all [humankind]."[92] Underscore "appearing." Notably, Wesley expresses that there is a visible ar-

---

90. Boyd, *Myth*, 183

91. Douglass, *Frederick Douglass*, 367.

92. Wesley, "Upon," 200.

ticulation of holiness that the world notices when Christians live according to the biblical distinction to which God calls all believers. "[You] may not flee from [people], and while you are among them," Wesley argues, "it is impossible to hide your lowliness and meekness, and those other dispositions whereby [you] aspire to be perfect."[93] By engaging other Christians, as well as those who are not Christians, with tangible expressions of love through acts of kindness and service, we bear witness to Christ in the world. For Wesley, that is the deepest expression of divine holiness.

I fondly remember that, as a child, my home church was a church with maximal emphasis on holiness; love was the vitality of faith and community. It was also the fabric of evangelism—the drawing card for many people who were attracted to faith and even joined our local congregation in Manchester, Georgia. One wonders what drew so many young people to a church that emphasized the importance of holiness. I remember that when I was a young boy a man commented to my dad that my dad's church was the church of "butt-to-butt saints." My dad asked him what he meant. He explained that there is nothing that could happen to one of the members without the others getting involved.

Practical expressions of love were second nature to the church's understanding of holiness. Although a small congregation, love compelled the church to support, assist, and even prod each other toward success. For example, if there were financial difficulties, my dad would lead the church to bail out the struggling brother or sister. No one was left without food, clothing, or shelter. Much like the second-century report from Aristides mentioned earlier, in my home church, the ones who had resources gave to the ones who did not have; they did it without boasting.

Other examples include when a young person expressed interest in pursuing higher education, the pastor took upon himself the responsibility of leading the congregation to helping that young woman or man to get into college. Also, once the church was planning a trip to Six Flags Over Georgia, and a young couple could not afford the trip. The "saints" rallied together to help them to go on the trip. The community's love ethic was rooted in an understanding of the biblical love ethic in Acts 2:44: "And all who believed were together and had all things in common." Love makes a way for others. In this small congregation, no sister or brother went lacking.

Moreover, their love compelled them to extend their hands and homes to strangers; often, they took them into their homes, and treated them like brothers or sisters. Certainly, people abused their love at times. There were

93. Ibid.

people without authentic interest in the faith; they were attracted to the expressions of kindness that characterized the church. But, the congregation's love was as authentic and as strong as their faith, and as their commitment to rigid doctrinal practices pertaining to dress codes and the prohibition of alcohol, television, movies, and the like. In this way, their love extended beyond the walls of the church in tangible ways to help people.

Wesley emphasizes that the life of service is essential to holiness, whether service is rendered to others who are believers or those who are unbelievers. The close association of holiness and service is greatly expressed in "Upon Our Lord's Sermon on the Mount." Wesley explains that while the root of holiness lies in the heart, in the inmost soul, "if this root be really in the heart it cannot but put forth branches. And these are the several instances of outward obedience, which partake of the same nature with the root, and consequently are not only marks or signs, but substantial parts of [the Christian faith]."[94] From a Wesleyan perspective, no expression of kindness, community outreach, or service to others can replace the fundamental mark of holiness. The mark of holiness involves the transformation of the heart. Nonetheless, Wesley explains that "[God] is also pleased with all that outward service which arises from the heart . . . with sacrifice of our goods, humbly devoted to [God] and employed wholly to [God's] glory."[95]

Outward service or acts of kindness that stem from a heart of holiness often are met with abuse and misuse. As a pastor's kid, I cannot count the times that I saw my mom and dad bend over backward to help others. Sometimes, the ones they helped the most by paying their bills, helping them get in and out of high school and through college, and assisting them in getting jobs, were the very ones who got their "goods" but disappeared with no expression of gratitude. As a result of this observation, I have learned that the weight of holiness rides not on the ones who return to say "thank you," but on the believers' power to love—even when the ones to whom love is expressed do not express love or appreciation in return. Many believers have a great start in their walk of faith. They feel like they could change the world. Then reality hits that the world does not respond to love with the measure of love that the believer is excited to give. Without awareness, the believer might grow frustrated and even wounded at heart.

It is important that the believer understands ahead of time that God's love flows through us to a world that does not understand God's love. Often

94. Ibid., 201.
95. Ibid.

the world rejects love out of fear. We must not allow rejection to determine our love. We must love even when love is rejected. Recognizing the common reaction to rejection, Jesus says, "You have heard that it was said, 'You shall love your neighbor and hate your enemy'" (Matt 5:43). Yet, promoting the ethic of love, Jesus says, "But I say to you, Love your enemies and pray for those who persecute you" (Matt 5:44 NRSV). Paul expounds the practical application of the love ethic: "Beloved, never avenge yourselves, but leave it to the wrath of God, for it is written, 'Vengeance is mine, I will repay, says the Lord.' To the contrary, 'if your enemy is hungry, feed him; if he is thirsty, give him something to drink; for by so doing you will heap burning coals on his head.' Do not be overcome by evil, but overcome evil with good" (Rom 12:19–21; see also Prov 25:21).

Walking in holiness means to walk out love daily. Love insists on being kind and expresses acts of kindness even when (in some cases) love is rejected. Where love grows cold, the believer loses the power of holiness in their lives, because the power of love is inseparable from holiness.

## REFLECTION

Living holy is more than a notion. It requires commitment to Christ and the infilling of the Holy Spirit. The Spirit is an enabler, freeing us to walk in the fruit of the Spirit amid a world that cannot know God on their own terms. We must deny the world, and even ourselves, to pursue a life of holiness. Have you found it challenging to live holy? Have you given up on trying? This is not the time to give up. This is the time to seek God more for the grace to walk in holiness. It is through holiness that we discern God in an ungodly world.

## PRAYER

If you have heard the voice of God speak to you through the pages of this book, pause and pray this prayer:

> Lord, prepare me for service that flows from a heart that is holy, tried, and true. Purify my heart so that I may serve you by serving others. May my lifestyle of holiness engulf me such that I serve as to an audience of one, with no dictates from either the ones who appreciate my love or reject my love. My life is yours. Sanctify me and use me according to your glory and for the sake of the gospel. Amen.

# 6

## Hindrances to Holiness: The Four Cs

The church needs not worry about where to be in the world. The church's only concern is *how* to be in the world, in what form, for what purpose.

—STANLEY HAUERWAS AND WILLIAM WILLIMON

THE GREATEST CONCERN ABOUT holiness is the question of perfection. Jesus says, "You therefore must be perfect, as your heavenly Father is perfect" (Matt 5:48). Merriam-Webster defines the word *perfect* as: "being entirely without fault or defect, satisfying all requirements, or lacking in no essential detail." In our contemporary ears, the language of perfection rings as that which appears flawless. We exclaim, who could really ever be flawless but God! So why would Jesus require us to be perfect? If we view biblical perfection through the lens of Webster's definition, we would remain confused about holiness. The Greek word used in the Gospel (quoted above) for perfection is *teleos*. *Teleos* suggests acting responsibly with matured love, finishing the journey of faith well. Biblical perfection does not suggest flawlessness. It suggests that serious pursuit of righteousness requires perseverance and tenacity to finish well.

I observe four key obstacles to finishing the Christian race well. They are (1) confusion about the definition of holiness; (2) distractions of culture (society); (3) misrepresentations of holiness perpetuated by churches; and (4) personal weaknesses and sinful cravings. We must deal with the realities of these four Cs (confusion, culture, churches, and cravings) with humility and prayer as we seek to walk in divine holiness with integrity.

## CONFUSION ABOUT THE DEFINITION OF HOLINESS

### Holiness Is the Way I Look?

Furthermore, the essence of perfect holiness cannot be grounded in superficiality but must proceed from the heart. In 1 Samuel 16:7, the Lord has a conversation with Samuel concerning who should be the second king of Israel after Saul: "But the LORD said to Samuel, 'Do not look on his appearance or on the height of his stature, because I have rejected him; for the LORD does not see as mortals see; they look on the outward appearance, but the LORD looks on the heart" (NRSV). Looking "good," looking "deep," looking like a "Catholic bishop" or a "saint" who dresses in long garments, covering their arms and legs[1]—all of these have their place, but these images mean more to human beings than to God. None of them scratch the surface of what it means to be holy. Being holy is a condition of the heart.

### Holiness: How Many Scriptures I Can Quote?

Recently, I read a quote from a friend on Facebook that said, "Being in a garage doesn't make you a car and being in the church doesn't make you a Christian." Similarly, reading and memorizing Scriptures are smart choices but do not make us holy. In chapter 4, I shared the story of Sarah, a friend from college. Sarah could quote Scripture very well. However, her partying and promiscuous lifestyle was not consistent with her knowledge of Scripture. As a young child, I also knew the Scriptures from Sunday school. Later, my dad founded a Christian school. Based on the School of Tomorrow curriculum, by the time we finished high school, we would have studied and memorized nearly the entire sixty-six books of the Bible. Yet, as with Sarah, knowing and studying Scripture were not enough to satisfy the deep yearning for God. One day I made a conscious decision to bow before the cross of Christ in total submission to God's gift of salvation and the subsequent life of holiness.

---

1. By "looking like a Catholic bishop," I mean wearing the pontifical vestments and carrying a crosier.

Life is full of temptation. No matter how many Scriptures we know, cognitive elements of salvation must be translated to the knowledge of the heart. Salvation is of the heart. Holiness is of the heart. The heart is the center of all of life—physical and spiritual. Proverbs 4:23 (NLT) reads, "Guard your heart above all else, for it determines the course of your life." Guarding the heart includes, but is not limited to, being careful about what one sees, hears, and gets involved in, maintaining a steady diet of godly conversation, and bible reading. Yet, guarding a heart that is not convicted to live holy creates a life of boredom and frustration. The heart must be sanctified and willing to do God's will. Only then will Bible reading and healthy spiritual practices become spiritual support in the stride toward holiness, rather than a burden.

## Can A Christian Do This or That?

In a previous chapter, I mentioned that a traditional emphasis among holiness-pentecostal churches has been that "we are in the world but not of it." Although this sounds old fashioned in a young person's ears, it is a theologically profound concept. To be in the world but not of it suggests that there is a different system of beliefs and practices by which the believer abides than the ones in society. A more appropriate question for the believer than "Can I do this or that?" is "How must I live to please the Lord?" Christian life is not governed by a list of rules.

Believers note a difference between Old Testament and New Testament religious life. In the Old Testament, God's people measured their status with God based largely on how much of the law they could keep. This approach fostered a castigatory outlook on God's relationship with God's people. The first three chapters of Genesis suggest that God did not intend a punitive relationship from the beginning. Yet, the fall in the garden of Eden initiated constant dissonance between God and human beings, despite God's love and intended relationship with them. So then, the New Testament aims to roll back the negative tenor associated with the divine relationship with God's people.

In Jesus, God extends God's love to humankind. From the story of Christ's birth to his resurrection and beyond, God invites human beings into the loving relationship that God always intended. God invites humankind to a loving relationship with a holy God. That divine love comes to us through Christ. That love compels us to love God as God has loved us.

When the Christian's behavior flows from a deep love for God, she or he is compelled to obey God, because God's love teaches us that God has our best interest at heart. So then, the Christian does not ask, "Can I do this or can I do that?" Rather, the Christian asks, "What is God's will for me in this situation or that?" Such questions should be rooted in a divine love affair, not by a legalistic requirement. The fact is, God does have dos and don'ts. One cannot simply live as one pleases or as society dictates and lay claim to a divine love affair. There is holy and unholy thinking and behavior that God defines as such.

## CULTURE (SOCIETY) MIGHT GET IN THE WAY

There are many temptations in the world. Even the strongest Christian is one step away from immoral behavior. Especially in the United States of America, where society claims to be Christian, or at least more open to Christianity than other societies in the world, the ethical line of demarcation between the church and society, the holy and profane, is often faded. It is easy to slip into temptation without even realizing it. While in conversation with a Christian musician, he said, "Man, I was at the gas station pumping gas. I looked around and everywhere I looked there were sexual innuendos." For example, suggestive photos on billboards or in advertisements, sexually explicit music, and the like are common distractions. At that moment, my friend said, it became clear why even Christians are so easily deceived into the traps of sexual sins. Besides the human desire for sexuality, society has glorified it so much that even Christians are often distracted by a society that is infatuated with sexual licentiousness.

As a son of a very rural community in Georgia, climbing trees, roaming wooded areas, fishing, and playing with dogs were common leisure activities for boys. Our parents were protective of my siblings and me. Dad and mom advised us not to go far into the woods. And they warned my brothers and me not to roam the paths and alleys near our house in Manchester, Georgia. You can imagine that the temptation to roam those forbidden places grew stronger for young adventurous brothers who absolutely loved the outdoors.

As a young ten-year-old boy who (at times) listened to his friends more than his parents, I roamed one of the forbidden alleyways with two of my young buddies. My friends, who were older than me, found a catalogue in the thickets. They rushed to grab the book. The pages were stuck together. I was not sure why. My friends huddled to look through the tearing pages. Knowing that my parents were pastors and that I was a tattletale, my friends made me promise that I would not tell. That day, my ten-year-old eyes were introduced to images that I had never seen before—pornography. My friends seemed familiar with these types of photos. I do not know for sure. Their intense interest made me more curious. It was not until I was an adult that I realized the mental impression that those images made. As a young virgin getting older and older but trying to hold on to my teenaged promise of abstinence before marriage, I had to pray that God would wash my mind from those erotic images that constantly resurfaced in my mind.

Sex is holy when correctly appropriated within marriage. Sexual purity is an attitude of the mind and desire of the heart. It comes from an understanding of divine holiness that is manifest in our thoughts, speech, and behavior.[2] Impurity, sexual immorality, fornication, pornography, homosexuality, and extramarital affairs constitute sexual immorality; but they have gained widespread acceptance as norms in society.

Many Christian singles have a limited understanding of sexual indiscretion. They think of improper sexual behavior as sexual intercourse with another person. Moreover, as Edward S. Williams has put it, "All immorality, impurity, and uncontrolled passion are out of place for Christians."[3] Paul warns the Christians at Ephesus, "Sexual immorality and all impurity or covetousness must not even be named among you, as is proper among saints" (Eph 5:3).

Psychologists Alex W. Kwee, Amy W. Dominguez, and Donald Ferrell point out that Christian sexual misbehavior, which conventionally assumes "partnered sex," creates a dilemma when young, unmarried Christian men, such as those seen at Christian college counseling centers, avoid "partnered sex" because of religious teachings but are silently addicted to solo sex behavior such as masturbation and pornography. These Christian psychologists argue, however, that one also experiences sexual misbehavior when one depends on solo sex behaviors "to regulate their emotional state."[4] Solo sexual behavior plants seeds that often grow to full-blown sexual misbehavior. Mary Anne Layden, codirector of the Sexual Trauma and Psychopathology Program at the University of Pennsylvania's Center for Cognitive Therapy, says that "pornography is extremely harmful to

2. Williams, "Sexual Conduct," n.p.

3. Ibid.

4. Kwee, et al., "Sexual Addiction," 3–13.

those who consume it on a regular basis. Layden said there is a correlation between viewing porn and sexual behavior among individuals."[5]

Paul, moreover, teaches the Christians at Thessalonica to shun the appearance of evil in any form: "Abstain from every form of evil. Now may the God of peace himself sanctify you completely, and may your whole spirit and soul and body be kept blameless at the coming of our Lord Jesus Christ" (1 Thess 5:22–23). Pornography and masturbation appear to safeguard one from sexual immorality when in fact they create a false sense of escape. The only true escape happens when the believer invites God to sanctify every aspect of one's life, including one's sex life. God wants us to be pure and holy in every aspect of our lives—even the hidden iniquities that people do not know.

Later, I will discuss the issue of personal lust as a hindrance to holiness. For now, there are two critical and common issues that emerge from the aforementioned situation that speak to this issue of cultural hindrances to holiness.[6] The first issue of interest is the role of peer pressure. In 1 Corinthians 15:33, Paul teaches that bad company corrupts good behavior. It is amazing that we (children and adults alike) would rather adhere to the influence of people who do not have our best interests at heart. Society teaches us that trends and the majority rule. Yet, Paul is correct. Ungodly friendships negatively affect us—not only in the moment, but also in the long run.

Other vices, such as greed, anger, vindictiveness, abuse, pride, and jealousy are the silent diseases of the heart. A defense attorney called me to serve as an expert witness in the case of a well-known bishop who was found guilty of tax evasion. The bishop lived lavishly and had cheated the government of millions. His greed caught up with him. He was now looking at lengthy jail time. His defense team offered me whatever price I desired to help them defend the bishop in this case. They requested that I help them explain to the courts the concept of love offerings to the bishop in the

5. As quoted in Lewis, "Porn," n.p.

6. See Harris, *For Such a Time as This*. I proffer a theological paradigm that values culture. It is important to note that my critique of culture in this book does not contradict my appraisal of culture. Theologically speaking, my treatment recognizes culture as paradoxical. On the one hand, there is redeemable substance to culture. The gospel embraces culture as a viable tenet in theological discourse and in the development of church doctrine. On the other hand, the gospel critiques culture where it violates the norms of the gospel. When culture facilitates ungodly behavior, lifestyles inconsistent with biblical teachings, those characteristics of culture are unredeemable. In such cases, culture stands to be critiqued in theological discourse.

African American pentecostal church tradition. After praying about it, I declined the offer to participate in the case. In this particular case, I felt that if I participated, I would be as guilty of greed as the bishop.

All churches must come to terms with the truth about greed in society. When dollar signs blind the believer from honesty and integrity, holiness is compromised. Greed crashed Wall Street and landed Bernie Madoff in prison. But more importantly, greed angers God and will also destroy churches and disease the spiritual life of believers. It is a travesty when the church seeks to sanctify greed with theologies of materialism. Materialism is an original sin of American society. American history bears record that the fiber with which this country was manufactured is plagued with greed. From the purchase of slaves from Africa to the emancipation of slaves, the root was money. With evil at its core, America has always hustled the vulnerable for the advantage of the powerful. Churches often syncretize capitalistic materialism into church practice. Some preachers (like the bishop referenced above) hustle their congregations in the name of God to create their own wealth and personal empires.

Conversely, in Colossians 3:5 (NLT) Paul teaches, "Put to death the sinful, earthly things lurking within you. Have nothing to do with sexual immorality, impurity, lust, and evil desires. Don't be greedy, for a greedy person is an idolater, worshiping the things of this world." Christians are, moreover, called to guard their hearts from the weight of culture that presses so hard from the smorgasbord of temptations that lure the mind to damage the believer's heart.

So, while the gospel is indeed translatable to cultural vernacular, it maintains holiness as its internal norm; thus the gospel remains distinctive even when it enters culture. The point is that the gospel is translatable to people groups around the world, from people of different nationalities to "Pookie and them" in the hood. A uniqueness of the gospel is that in this way it affirms culture; yet, the gospel critiques culture by its own terms. On the one hand, there is something redeemable about ethnic culture; on the other hand, we must not be defined by systems of belief within society that are contrary to God's worldview. In this sense, Christians must be culturally conscious without being culturally controlled. As Hauerwas and Willimon put it, "There is no other place for the church to be than here. . . . The church needs not worry about where to be in the world. The church's only concern is *how* to be in the world, in what form, for what purpose."[7]

7. Hauerwas and Willimon, *Resident Aliens*, 43.

In 1 Peter 5:8, the apostle instructs the Christian, "Be sober-minded; be watchful. Your adversary the devil prowls around like a roaring lion, seeking someone to devour." Christians must, moreover, be diligent in discerning satanic distractions within society and maintain a consciousness of identity in Christ. Although not entirely appropriate contextually speaking, the famous language from W. E. B. DuBois's *Souls of Black Folk* remains on my mind as I ponder the life of the Christian in America—the language of "double-consciousness." He was speaking of African Americans' awareness as both African and American, or the self-understanding and the awareness for their identity that formed them or was imposed upon them by the American situation at the time. Similarly to DuBois's "double-consciousness," the Christian must see herself or himself as having two consciousnesses. One is the awareness of the world in which the believer lives. The other is consciousness that this world is not home for the believer.

As citizens within society, Christians must negotiate responsibility as citizens with a biblical worldview. The questions of righteousness and justice remain in tension. By the term righteousness, I am speaking of the vertical relationship between Christians and God. This relationship requires a horizontal dimension to holiness. The term justice describes the horizontal dimension. The language of justice has become a buzzword in our society for social advocacy. However, my usage of the term is general, simply speaking to the horizontal life and the responsibility of the Christian within the church and the church in relationship to society.

This two-dimensional life of the Christians creates a "double-conscious" lifestyle: vertical and horizontal. Moreover, if we factor in the relationship between the church and society, we may even consider a "tertiary-consciousness." Christians are always aware of the *earthly house*, but Christians are *not at home* on earth. God calls for Christians to enjoy the abundance of life on earth; yet that abundance is not complete on earth. Christians are called to possess the land but store up treasure in heavenly places. Christians are called to engage the world but refrain from loving the world. Everyday Christians struggle to live in society as cultured beings, discerning and deciphering the "human self" from the "worldly self." As a result, cultural dominance threatens to control the Christian agenda, thus posing a hindrance to holiness. Often, when Christians find ourselves in compromising situations or when we violate biblical principles, we say, "I'm just human." But holiness challenges us to exist as fully human while still living distinctively from the lifestyle of the dominant culture.

## CHURCH MIGHT GET IN THE WAY

Ironically, local churches often become their own hindrance to the life of holiness to which they are called. I will explain ecclesial hindrances to holiness in two ways: the first speaks to human-generated codes of holiness and the second speaks to deception in the church that drives people away from the church.

### Burdensome Rules or Holiness?

God calls the church of Jesus Christ to be holy. As a spiritual conditioning of the heart, spirituality can neither be legislated in society nor in churches. People who try to subscribe to church doctrine without a spiritual transformation of the heart find religion to be a mechanism of oppression. As a result, such persons are vulnerable in one of two ways: (1) becoming faithful to the local church as an institution, with little or no faithfulness to communion with Christ through a personal relationship with the Spirit; or (2) becoming frustrated with the local church for feeling trapped into bondage rather than being free in Christ. Neither of these is good.

Believers who make church rules their litmus test for holiness become idolatrous. They make their own church the kingdom of God and judge others who do not share their measuring rod, regardless of how God may be using them to propagate the gospel throughout the world. When one feels the weight of rules over a relationship with God, holiness becomes arduous.

It is true that much of our association with the term holiness is tainted by a list of dos and don'ts. These are off-putting; they foster a hostile environment rather than an inviting place of love, hope, and peace that God intends the church to be. Legalistic notions of holiness satisfy the devil's mission to slander holiness, using churches to do it.

True holiness is both beautiful and liberating. The beauty of holiness is not limited, however, to physical aesthetics; also, the liberation of holiness does not mean freedom to do as one pleases. Rather, the beauty of holiness has to do with the Christian's communion with God that empowers one to find fulfillment in God's instructions for life. Theologian Cheryl Bridges Johns explains, "A holy person is beautiful. Such a person seems to have an inner light that radiates through her [or his] countenance."[8] Holi-

8. Johns, "Can I Live," 24.

ness is beautiful when understood and embraced as the product of a life of intimacy with God.

Historically, biblical holiness has been construed as being the purview of certain church traditions and/or denominations. Thwarted by negative tones, the biblical notion of the "beauty of holiness" is overshadowed by legalistic holiness. Yet, a close read of Scripture reveals that such claims are misleading—Scripture seems clear that holiness is not a negative topic to shun but a topic to pursue, as it is valuable to the quality of life that Christ intends for us to experience. Several traditions contribute significantly to our understanding of holiness; but no one tradition, to the exclusion of others, possesses holiness as its own distinction. All authentically Christian traditions have valuable insights on the subject, because holiness is the divine ideal for all Christians. Furthermore, it is not the private possession of those who formally call themselves by that title.

Scripture declares that holiness is part of God's enduring nature. And, God invites God's people to unite with God through holiness. God, not us, moreover, defines and sets the standard(s) for holiness. It is our responsibility to seek to understand and appropriate God's ideals and standards.

In attempting to recover the biblical holiness that seems lost within contemporary churches and in the everyday life of Christians, legalism cannot replace internal transformation. And rigid rules are never strong enough to enforce the true spirit of holiness. Spiritual empowerment is essential to the healthy life of believers and the future of a holy church.

Oswald Chambers suggested that holiness, not happiness, is the chief end of man.[9] Personal fulfillment in holiness supersedes any happiness that one could imagine. Chamber's insight might be summed up in the words of another old gospel song: "This joy I have, and the world didn't give it to me / The world didn't give it and the world can't take it away." When we submit to God's standard of holiness, we experience a satisfaction that nothing else can give. Submission to the biblical standard of holiness aligns us with God's beauty.[10]

Regent University Theologian Dale Coulter notes a connection between holiness, beauty, and happiness, pointing out that God's holiness is God's own beauty that gives rise to a God-defined happiness.[11] Most people

---

9. As quoted in Akers, *Enriching*, 53.

10. Psalms 29:2 states, "Ascribe to the Lord the glory due God's name. Worship the Lord in the splendor of holiness."

11. Coulter, *Holiness*, 81.

want to be happy, and when people understand the connection between a happy life and holiness, everyone should want to live holy. When we have a clear understanding of who God is and how God loves people, our actions transition from gestures in search of merit to celebratory gestures—we seek to please God because God loves us immeasurably. We follow God not because we feel that we have to win over God, we realize that God is already in love with us. The rhetorical question in Romans 8:31—"What then shall we say to these things? If God is for us, who can be against us?"—persuades us that God is for us more than the world could ever be against us.

Deep relationship with God orients the mind and soul toward God-related things. Legislation cannot encode such beautiful holiness. Only a deep embrace of God's love produces the beauty of holiness. Such divine intimacy is liberating—not to follow the flesh but to follow the Spirit.

The liberation that holiness brings is freedom from the nature of the fall in the garden of Eden, so that the believer may obey God's Word. Thus, a person's attitude frees one to pursue God's will for one's life. The soul loses the ability to be the eternal determinate. The hole, the gap, the emptiness is in the soul. The soul, moreover, must be filled, healed, and redirected. The spirit is, therefore, sanctified to heal the soul and determine its divine destiny. In short, the spirit is made holy and thereby liberates the soul to pursue God. This is why growing up, Holy Spirit–filled Christians would sing, "My soul loves Jesus, bless His name."

## Indiscretion Among Church Leadership

Second, among several impediments, the church must deal with the problem of indiscretion within leadership. Holiness calls for accountability. Neither church leadership nor any Christian should use their influence or power or leadership to inflict psychological, emotional, or sexual abuse. This problem impedes holiness in both Catholic and Protestant churches around the world. Often clergy use the power of their positions to manipulate people to serve their own interests, build their own careers, or even their own religious empires. Worse, some clergy make aggressive sexual advances toward men, women, and even children. These crises have become a deeply-rooted hindrance to the message of holiness for many churches.

On the issue of the abuse of power among Catholic priests, John Allen, CNN's Vatican analyst and senior correspondent for the National Catholic Reporter, comments, "Now we have obvious confirmation that this is a global crisis."[12] The Associated Press reports that the three companies that insure a majority of Protestant churches say they typically receive upward of 260 reports a year of children younger than eighteen being sexually abused by members of the clergy, church staff members, volunteers, or congregants.

The figures released to the Associated Press offer a glimpse into what has long been a difficult phenomenon to detail: the frequency of sexual abuse in Protestant congregations.[13] In response to this observation, Catholic Father Jonathan Morris says,

> This bad news for Protestant churches is sad news for all of us. . . . I would prefer the problem be limited to any one church—even if that church were my own—because it would mean more kids would be safe. But as I have said repeatedly over the last few years, the problem of sexual abuse of minors is not an issue of religious affiliation because there is nothing religious about abusing children. The phenomenon of sexual abuse of minors in church settings is the story of sick human beings taking advantage of their position of moral authority to prey on the weak and vulnerable. If Catholic clergy were to be faithful to their church's teaching, there would be no abuse in the Catholic Church. The same goes for Protestant clergy. The problem, then, is not one of corrupt doctrine, but of individuals being unfaithful to the most basic precepts of their own religious belief.[14]

Abusive clergy stand in serious guilt before God, who said, "Feed my sheep; feed my lambs." Divine food is the Word of God. When clergy sexually or otherwise violate those whom God has committed to their spiritual care, they (like all of us) are responsible for their actions. Importantly, incendiary acts and scandals among clergy impact their victims, but also many others whom they are called to serve. The visage of an abusive, sexually perverted church in the media is off-putting, both to those who are seeking refuge from the world and those who are directly affected by it. God intends for the church to serve as a beacon in the night, a symbol of hope. Her holiness is her distinction *from* the world but even more importantly *in* the world. When church leaders represent hostility and perversion, one becomes cynical of the church. Where can one go to discover God and learn about holiness if they can't go to the church?

12. Gilgoff, "Catholic," n.p.
13. Associated Press, "Data," n.p.
14. Jonathan Morris, as quoted in Allen, "Insurance," n.p.

## CRAVINGS (LUST) GET IN THE WAY

Another distraction to holiness is one's own lust. Lust produces apathy. It's not always an external attraction (a friend, a movie, a person dressed provocatively, a commercial that we just happen to stumble upon) that distracts us from God. Romans 1 explains how personal cravings diverge us from the urgency to even care much about pursuing God. New Testament scholar Luke Timothy Johnson interprets lust as a "desiring disease."[15] This disease eats away at godly desires. Spiritual stagnation occurs, and inner starvation becomes the precursor to spiritual death.

New Testament scholar James Dunn offers another perspective on the issues of lust in the life of the believer. He terms lust in Romans as "self-indulgence."[16] Lust becomes the impetus for doing what we want, how we want to do it. Self-indulgence disregards the ramifications of one's behavior. It also shows no consideration for what one's actions might mean or do to others. As the Isley Brothers put it: "It's your thing / Do what you want to do / I can't tell you who to sock it to." From a Jewish perspective, "self-indulgence" means lawlessness.

Coulter adds that this "disease", or "self-indulgence," is an "inborn disease" that affects our desires from birth. At the moment of birth, babies are unconscious of their deceptive and manipulative behavior. As they grow, this inborn disease only matures and expresses itself in unpredictable ways. Over time, this "inborn disease" turns our desires away from their natural courses to unnatural ones. In so doing, we often become (although unconsciously) proactive in a search for sin.

The soul's natural desire to pursue God, moreover, is interrupted by this inborn lustful spirit to do our own thing. As a result, the soul experiences what is best described as a gap, a hole (mentioned earlier). The soul yearns for the gap to be filled, the hole to be closed. Yet, we often adhere to the voices in our heads that tell us that holiness is hard, undesirable, and unattainable. Second-century bishop of Lyons, in Gaul (France), Irenaeus writes, "By the effusion of the Spirit the spiritual and perfect [person] is made: and this is [the one] who was made after the *image* and *likeness* of God."[17] Both the image and likeness of God fill the gap of the soul. Irenaeus explains that if our souls are not filled with the Spirit, our lives are incom-

15. Johnson, *Reading*, 113–15.

16. Dunn, *Theology*, 119–23.

17. Irenaeus, *Five Books*, 461 (italics added).

plete. This is how we fall into all sorts of sensuality and self-indulgence. In such a case, we maintain the *image* of God's fleshly form (i.e., Jesus Christ) but we lack the *likeness* of Christ by the Spirit.[18] Some Christians, particularly pentecostals/charismatics, tend to speak of the infilling of the Spirit in emotive terms (i.e., dancing, shouting, speaking in tongues, prophesying, preaching, and giving words of knowledge) more than as that infilling being a pathway to holiness. The hindering, carnal voices in our heads and from those around us that discourage the pursuit of divine holiness scream so loudly at times. Yet, the Word of the Lord comes tenderly to remind us of the Spirit's role to empower us to live out God's will.

## THEOLOGICAL REFLECTIONS: PERSONAL AND BIBLICAL

For nearly a week, Micah and I came home to a kitchen floor with a sporadic deposit of winged ants. After days of repeatedly spraying and killing them, Micah and I grew deeply concerned that these flying ants were coming from a nest of eggs. We set out to find their secret source. We spent our romantic Friday evening with bug spray in hand, determined to find where the ants were coming from.

We trailed the ants one by one and discovered a nest in an unlikely corner of our dining room. We felt resolved that we had found the root of the problem. We killed the nest. But Micah saw a few more ants in the kitchen that seemed to be coming from a different location. I then pulled the refrigerator from the wall. We discovered a huge nest behind it. Immediately, we destroyed that nest also. This means that even when we did not see the ants on the kitchen floor, there was a nest of them.

The situation of the flying ants reminds me that often we spend time trying to eradicate the symptoms of issues that have a hidden source. Not until we go after the root cause of the sin in our lives will we be able to destroy its nest in our lives. Holiness that focuses on that which is most obvious to the naked eye is not true holiness. When we try to create a holy life by creating rules for ourselves, it is like killing the ants on the kitchen floor rather than going after the source.

Holiness goes beyond that which is in immediate sight. A great hindrance to holiness is a focus on superficial things that does not get at the more important thing(s). To use Jesus' words, when we "strain at gnats,

18. Ibid.

we swallow camels."[19] By this I mean that it is easy to focus on the insignificant and omit the core issue of the heart. The human heart is central to physical vitality. It is important for us to eat foods with nutrients that take good care of the heart. Certainly, I want to do what I can to prolong my heart health. So I have increased my omega 3 intake and closely monitor my blood pressure levels. In the same way, it is important that we purify the spiritual dynamics of the heart. What are we letting into our hearts? Envy? Jealousy? Malice? Anger? Hate? Or, are we entertaining pure thoughts? Lovely thoughts? Holiness speaks to the thoughts of the heart. To this end, the Bible teaches us that above everything else, we must guard our hearts, because out of the heart flows the wealth of life.[20]

God charged the prophet Samuel to select the second king of Israel from among the patriarch Jesse's sons. The prophet was certain that one of Jesse's eldest sons, with military experience and flattering physiques, would surely be God's chosen successor to the throne. However, 1 Samuel 16: 7 records that the Lord's interest was beyond experience and external appearances. The Lord cautioned the prophet, "Do not look on his appearance or on the height of his stature, because I have rejected him. For the LORD sees not as man sees: man looks on the outward appearance, but the LORD looks on the heart."[21] Seeing that the heart is of divine interest, it is important, moreover, that Christians are concerned about the heart—each about our own heart. We must search our hearts to discover the root of the problem. It is quite probable that beyond the superficial, outward expressions of church attendance and religious jargon, there is a heart that proves the depth of our faith. Living a holy life is more than throwing away secular music, refraining from watching television, and adhering to a list of strict dress codes. Holiness is purity at the core—the state of a pure heart. When a person's heart is after God, the quest of the heart is for divine purity beyond what the eyes can see.

The psalmist understands holiness as a state of the heart. In Psalm 139:1–6, the psalmist writes:

> O LORD, you have searched me and known me! You know when
> I sit down and when I rise up; you discern my thoughts from afar.
> You search out my path and my lying down and are acquainted
> with all my ways. Even before a word is on my tongue, behold,

19. See Matt 23:24.

20. Prov 4:23: "Keep your heart with all vigilance, for from it flow the springs of life."

21. See 1 Sam 16:7.

O LORD, you know it altogether. You hem me in, behind and before, and lay your hand upon me. Such knowledge is too wonderful for me; it is high; I cannot attain it.

This is a psalm that in a sense gets at the heart of holiness. Holiness is God's
sanctifying investigation of the heart. Only God's eternal knowledge can
know the root source of anything. That knowledge is beyond human capacity to fully attain. So then, God's holiness transcends human capacity and
deposits a divine, sapient knowledge within the Christian about oneself. In
verses 23–24, David resolves: "Search me, O God, and know my heart! Try
me and know my thoughts! And see if there be any grievous way in me,
and lead me in the way everlasting!" I am convinced that every human being yearns for self-understanding and divine leadership. The challenge for
most of us lies in the details in achieving it. We must undergo self-denial, a
type of crucifixion of the flesh.

Consider Adolph Rosa's testimony. Rosa attended the early twentieth-
century Azusa Street Revival. "The power of God came upon me until I
dropped to the floor," said Rosa. He continued, "I was under the power of
God for about an hour and a half, and it was there that all pride, and self,
and conceit disappeared and I was really dead to the world, for I had Christ
within in His fullness."[22] Rosa understood that there is a moment in which
the believer must begin a journey of self-denial, which is a type of crucifixion of self-will, to truly know what it means for God to be Lord of our lives.

This notion of self-crucifixion is reminiscent of one aspect of the
late-nineteenth-century Wesleyan tradition that emerged from Keswick in
England, called Keswick spirituality. Keswick spirituality was also called
"higher life spirituality."[23] Like the desert fathers, they took seriously the
need to dethrone the self. Steven Fanning in part describes Keswick spirituality in the following manner: "Saying 'No' to self leads to sanctification,
which in turn unites the believer with Christ."[24]

---

22. Quoted from Johns, "Can I Live," 21. See also Seymour, "Pentecostal."
23. Fanning, *Mystics*, 199.
24. Ibid.

## REFLECTION

There are many hindrances to the pursuit of holiness—namely, character flaws. Arrogance and unwise dependence on self-will create key hindrances to holiness. When we depend on ourselves or veer our dependence and focus away from God, we fail in the pursuit of holiness. We become discouraged and start to believe that holy living is impossible in the twenty-first century. Yet, God beckons for us to live holy. God not only expects for us to live holy, but also continues to remind us that, by the power of the Holy Spirit, we are empowered to live in a way that we could never imagine on our own terms.

## PRAYER

If you have heard the voice of God speak to you through the pages of this chapter, pause, and pray this prayer:

> Dear Lord, in my life I have experienced hindrances to your holiness. I sincerely seek your will for me. I repent for allowing Satan's strategies to impede my journey. Please, restore my focus and strengthen me so that I might do your will, in Jesus' name, Amen.

# 7

# Let the Church Cry, "Holy!": The Four Rs

God meant to impress [people] by the contrast of the unworldliness
of His people; but, on the whole, the witness of a separate
and sanctified life is gone, and the witness of the tongue of fire
is gone with it. The worldliness of the church is a fact
to which we cannot with impunity shut our eyes.

—A. T. Pearson

The modern church is, quite simply,
just the world with a Christian T-shirt on!

—Nicky Cruz

The famous nineteenth-century preacher Charles Haddon Spurgeon
once commented, "Great attempts have been made of late to make the
church receive the world and wherever it has succeeded it has come to this
result—the world has swallowed up the church. It must be so. The greater
is sure to swamp the lesser. They say, 'Do not let us draw any hard and fast
lines.'"[1] In essence, Spurgeon observed a dilemma within the church. This
problem had to do with the relationship between the church and society's
ideological systems. Although more than a hundred years old, a similar

1. Spurgeon, "Lord's Own," 5.

quandary between the church and the world in many ways has only grown more complex.

What does it really mean to be the church anymore? How do we know the difference between the church and the world when Christians seem more interested in defending a so-called "Christian Society"? Does God want a Christian society or a church? Is there more than one church?

Over the past fifty years or more, American Evangelical and later pentecostal/charismatic Christians have been attracted to Dominion theology's "possess the land" approach to Christianity. In some ways Dominion theology seems reminiscent of Constantine's "Christianity as religion of the Empire." I went into greater depth on Constantinian Christianity in chapter 2. The two main strands of Dominion theology are Rousas John Rushdoony's and Gary North's Christian Reconstructionism theology[2] and the later Kingdom Now theology. Rooted in a Reformed perspective, Christian Reconstructionism imagines a world made Christian through an emphasis on the "New Covenant." Basing his theology on Galatians 6:16, Rushdoony explains that Christians are the New Israel of God; thus, we have a duty to "occupy the whole world" just as Israel of the "Old Covenant" was called to possess the land.[3] Rushdoony's theonomic approach to Christian Reconstructionism has considerably influenced the Evangelical way of engaging the world, both ideologically and theologically. For example, this is especially evident in his call for Christian political involvement.[4]

In the late 1980s, pentecostal/charismatic Christians became attracted to Dominion theological ideals through what became known as Kingdom Now theology.[5] With Christian Reconstructionism as its antecedent, Kingdom Now theology also interprets Christianity as the "New Israel" sent to possess the land. An emphasis on gifts of the Spirit and the five-fold ministry gifts (Eph 4:11) distinguishes Kingdom Now theology from Christian Reconstructionism. Kingdom Now theology asserts that God assigns roles and responsibilities to local church leaders for the purpose of leading the church in a charge to possess the nations.[6] As pentecostal theologian Simon

---

2. See Rushdoony, *Institutes*.

3. Ibid. See also Rushdoony, "Second," n.p.

4. See Martin, *With God*.

5. Kingdom Now theology teaches that God will send a revival in these end times that will establish God's kingdom on earth before the second coming of Christ. See footnotes in Tramel, "Beauty," 243.

6. See Griffin, "Kingdom," and Anderson, "Kingdom."

Chan puts it, the Kingdom Now theology approach has become an uncritical assimilation of modern culture.[7] It assumes that those who subscribe to it are God's gift to America. The country is "ours and not theirs." In this view, the Christian's chief role is to defend the country against its own people, those who do not share certain theological and ideological perspectives. Such an outlook breeds arrogance, hostility, and bigotry. All of which are antithetical to the essence of the gospel. A serious read of Scripture juxtaposed against American history must conclude that Jesus did not leave the promise of a country—a sweet land of liberty. Rather, he left the church to influence the world by virtue of a Christian presence. Christian presence is summarized in one word, holiness.

There is no denying that the world is rapidly changing. Any one area of the developed world experiences the impact of rampant ideological, theological, and cultural diversity. Undoubtedly, advanced technology contributes to how small the world is becoming in terms of coexisting diverse thoughts and practices. Like never before, the church as a whole, but even more so local congregations, are experiencing an identity crisis. By identity crisis, I mean that the situation of churches, particularly in North America, is challenged by cultural shifts in society. What is the relationship between the church and culture? Should the church resist culture? Or should the church assimilate to it?

Theologian Conrad Wethmar points out, "Whenever the church is confronted by a substantial change in cultural context the question regarding the identity of Christianity becomes urgent."[8] At the turn of the century, the question of Christian identity and the relationship between the church and society has become a significant query for pentecostal/charismatic Christians. Within several historical, cultural contexts, Western Christianity has endured the mingling of belief systems encoded in society's cultural shifting. Reflecting on these changes, prominent twentieth-century theologian Jurgen Moltmann refers to this trend as "identity-involvement dilemma."[9] He explains, "The more theology tries to be relevant to the social crises of its society, the more deeply it is itself drawn into the crisis of its own Christian identity."[10] Stated differently, the ideology encoded into culture presents a dilemma for how Christians understand God. It also raises

7. Chan, *Pentecostal*, 85.

8. Wethmar, "Confessionality," 135.

9. Moltmann, *Crucified*, 12–33. See also Moltmann, "My Theological Career," 182.

10. Moltmann, "My Theological Career," 182.

questions about God's expectations for our relationship with the culture in which we find ourselves. Therefore, it is not surprising that the church, amid a plethora of cultural trends, has encountered an identity crisis. In the last fifty years or so, the Evangelical and pentecostal/charismatic church dilemma rests in churches' close alignment with political parties.

In previous chapters, I dealt more with personal holiness. This chapter serves primarily as an appeal to the church on four levels as pertaining to her situation of urgency in society: corporate repentance for areas of weakness; corporate recommitment and total submission to Christ; recovery of her identity in Christ; and renewal of emphasis on standards for holiness.[11] I call these the four Rs (repentance, recommitment, recovery, and renewal).

## THE RELIGIOUS FIRESTORM: CHURCH VERSUS SOCIETY—BARACK OBAMA

The influence of Dominion theology thought continues to trouble the church's identity as Christians grapple with the relationship between the church and society. Like never in history, the country, including churches, was divided over the Obama versus Romney election. Prominent preachers endorsed the Mormon leader Mitt Romney for president, primarily on the bases of protecting marriage between male and female, certain pro-Israel ideals, economic advantages for the wealthiest Americans, and confessional statements as pertaining to pro-life. Some other prominent preachers either endorsed or continued to support Barack Obama for a second term.[12]

Some of Obama's supporters believed that Obama's Health Care Act came as an answer to many prayers and even to voices that cry out from the graveyard. There are those who believe that his plans for economic recovery had promising advantages, particularly for poor and middle-class

11. This chapter addresses the need for the Western church to repent; yet, it should be noted that corporate repentance is of no consequence so long as personal repentance is lacking or nonexistent. Both corporate and personal holiness are essential to the life and vitality of the faith.

12. It's interesting that most of the pastors who publically endorsed or supported Barack Obama were not from American Evangelical or pentecostal denominations. Many of them were African American pastors from mainline African American churches. Although not pentecostal, most are charismatic in their worship. In general, African American pentecostal preachers have tended to stay away from public political endorsements, except for a few who follow the trends of European American pentecostal preachers who align themselves with political parties.

Americans. Others believe that Obama's presidency is best for moving the country forward despite (or in addition to) his endorsement of same sex marriage and far-left advocacy for women's rights. Still others were convinced that a "nominal" Christian is a better fit for leading America than Romney, a Mormon cult leader.

These and other theological and ideological contentions contributed to the uproar in many of our churches—within churches and between churches. There were competing prayer vigils, praying that either Romney would win the election or that Obama would win. There were few prayers that were truly open to whomever God chose. People's minds were already made up before praying. On Election Day, very few people went to the ballot box, closed their eyes, and said, "Lord, take control of my hands and touch whichever name on the ballot you choose." The fact is that we often want God to do what we have already decided to be the right thing. Usually, such judgments are grounded in systems of thought grounded in worldviews coded within corrupted systems more than authentic communion with God.

Just after the 2012 election, I had breakfast with a group of pastors. One of the pastors commented, "I have come to the conclusion that [party] politics are America's religion". Rather than continuing God's reign as Dominion theology claims, politics have co-opted American Evangelical, pentecostal/charismatic theology to support certain political agendas. In this way, American politics have hijacked American Christian thinking.

There may be a parallel between Barth's analysis of "systems" and "theology" and the current discussion of "politics" and "theology." Barth emphasizes the misleading notion of "systematic theology" by insightfully drawing the following line between the two. He says,

> A 'system' is an edifice of thought, constructed on certain fundamental conceptions, which are selected in accordance with a certain philosophy by a method, which corresponds to these conceptions. Theology cannot be carried on in confinement or under the pressure of such a construction. The subject of theology is the history of the communion of God with man and of man with God.[13]

The biblical church is a theological organism and not a political party organization—American or otherwise. While there are some basic moral teachings such as love and peace, which are both biblical and normative in

13. Barth, *Dogmatics*, 5.

a civilized society, philosophical and political systems wherein Scripture is not foundational will eventually reveal their impermeability to holiness. The church, moreover, must subscribe to what Barth calls "theology . . . [that is] based on and determined by kingly freedom of the Word of God."[14] These enduring truths both critique and confirm the rightness and wrongness of worldly systems and practices.

As American party politics are not grounded in the Word of God, but are grounded in systems with a range of philosophical influences, the church should not be in the business of (implicitly or explicitly) endorsing national party politics. Rather, she must engage in the following manner: expound upon biblical principles, speak prophetically to a world in need of God's love and grace, and distinguish herself as the body of Christ in a way that both persuades unbelievers to faith in Christ and distances herself from the ideological trappings of society.

## PRESIDENT OR PASTOR—DOES IT MATTER?

During President Obama's first term, in the summer of 2012, he announced his support for same-sex marriage. Having previously favored same-sex unions but not same-sex marriages, President Obama admitted that his position "had been evolving because of the powerful traditions and religious beliefs attached to the word marriage."[15] He explained his "evolved position" to be according to the adjudication of American freedom as granted by the founding documents of the United States. This announcement stirred a heated debate among pastors, as well as ordinary Christians. The salient question relates to the presidential allegiance to traditional Christian beliefs or according to the precepts of the country's founding documents. The challenge at hand is that God expects pastors to lead churches according to the holiness of Christ. But the origins of this country demand that the president govern according to legislation, with commitment not to Scripture, but to the founding documents.

14. Ibid.
15. Gast, "Obama," n.p.

## WHO IS AMERICA?

From the philosophical outlook of democracy, America promotes freedom. The Declaration of Independence extends equal rights for all citizens:

> We hold these truths to be self-evident, that all men are created equal, that they are endowed by their Creator with certain un-alienable Rights, that among these are Life, Liberty and the pursuit of Happiness.

"All" means "all," including people from a wide range of ethnic heritages, diverse religious traditions, education backgrounds, varying economic statuses, both genders, and yes—straight, gay, lesbian, bi-sexual, transgendered persons.

## Founded on Liberal Ideals or the Bible?

Forming the famous "Committee of Five," Thomas Jefferson (the leader), Benjamin Franklin, John Adams, Roger Sherman, and Robert Livingston drafted the Declaration of Independence. Thomas Paine's popular pamphlet *Common Sense* somewhat influenced John Adams and Thomas Jefferson's philosophy of independence from Great Britain. It should be noted that Adams disagreed with some of his methods and even criticized his strong anti-Christian ideals in Paine's *Age of Reasoning.* Yet, Paine's general sentiment of human freedom as expressed in his *Common Sense,* although radical, laid somewhat of an intellectual foundation for persuasion against colonization and for the Declaration of Independence.[16] Adams once commented on the indelible impression of Paine's work on the propagation of American Independence from Great Britain saying, "Without the pen of Paine, the sword of Washington would have been wielded in vain."[17] Paine's influence continues to echo in American philosophy and politics today.

Additionally, although hotly debated, Benjamin Franklin's own admiration for John Locke's work, coupled with the comparable language of the document, suggests that the Declaration of Independence includes elements of an experiment in Locke's liberal democratic philosophy. Locke's idea of government includes the emancipation from British tyrannical rule

---

16. See Paine. *Thomas Paine Reader,* 65.
17. "Thomas Paine Library," n.p.

in pursuit of human liberty.[18] It freed Christians to worship God as they chose, but also freed others to worship and make personal decisions independent of the government's dictates. Looking one way—toward the west—a liberal government set the stage for the emancipation of slaves. I am sure, furthermore, that they did not think through all of the other possibilities that could follow this worldview. Yet, their work of freedom opened up for society a myriad of freedoms—both biblical and otherwise.

Moreover, as much as some Christians would like to align the freedom of the Declaration of Independence with Scripture, this document is not a commentary on biblical freedom. At times there are elements of comparison or even apparent alignment with biblical freedom; yet this is not always the case. Scripture speaks of freedom within the framework of God's holiness. Holiness does satisfy the soul and helps us pursue our deep-seated desire to please God and to succeed on God's terms. However, the Declaration of Independence speaks of freedom from the standpoint of opportunity for human beings to pursue life, liberty, and happiness. These pursuits may be achieved on human terms. And it is within this latter framework that the president of the United States must govern the country.

## The Pursuit of Happiness—Not Holiness

Notably, the United States of America was established on ideologies that pertain to freedom and the pursuit of happiness—not the pursuit of holiness. Although Christian values have been mixed in the history of the country, the country is not and has never been the church of Jesus Christ. Moreover, the president is not the pastor of a church. He is the leader of a free society that bears the identity of the founding documents and its citizens. Such a society is neither inherently Christian nor the church of which Scripture speaks. By inherently Christian, I mean that the United States Constitution does not establish any religion for the country. One could argue that, at the level of culture, the United States has been deeply impacted by Christianity. Notwithstanding, the president of the country has responsibilities as a leader in a free world; thus, his stance on issues might well be in keeping with the American claim on equality for all. The following might be a salient theological question for another book or article: what is the role of a Christian leader in a free world?

18. See Locke, *Two Treatises*.

In light of Obama's comments in support of same-sex marriage, a question emerges concerning Christian identity and the church amid a plethora of ideas and beliefs. The American church increasingly exists in a pluralistic world, similar to the earliest history of the church in other parts of the world. Currently, the advantage is that Christians are free to disagree with discussions within broader society without severe persecution. Perhaps, the future will present more hostility toward the church of Jesus Christ.

## WHO IS THE CHURCH?

The church is called to be the community of believers who faithfully pursue God through the life of the Spirit. Part of that pursuit is through reverencing God. Yet, another part of that pursuit is through an attitude, lifestyle, and disposition that reflect God's will for God's people. An ecclesial stance that calls for God's people to live like Christ sets Christians at odds with the rest of society. Spurgeon said, "The church is not formed to be a social club to produce society for itself! [She] is not to be a political association to be a power in politics! Nor is [she] a religious confederacy promoting [her] own opinions! [She] is a body created of the Lord to answer His own ends and purposes."[19] Holiness sums up the peculiarity that defines God's agenda in the church. It is, moreover, increasingly prudent within a world of religious and ideological plurality that the church comes to terms with the call to holiness.

Scripture warrants that holiness is the essence of God (Lev 11:26, 44; 1 Pet 1:16) transcendent to humankind through the power of the *Holy* Spirit. The church is God's gift to the world to escape the polluted ideologies and to exist as a community of believers, empowered by the Holy Spirit to live out God's holiness in the world. Therefore, a more poignant discussion strikes at the heart of identity—a discussion that draws attention to potential weaknesses within divided, unconscious denominations or nondenominations—religious institutions that call themselves "the church." What has happened to the church's identity?

In Spurgeon's words, Christ says, "Ye are not of the world, even as I am not of the world."[20] He is calling for a church that is called out of the world (mainstream society)—a peculiar people who bear witness to

19. Spurgeon, "Lord's Own," 6.
20. Ibid.

the "out of this world" identity of Christ. To be "called out of the world" certainly speaks to the divine invitation to publicly profess faith in Christ, but it also speaks to God's call for us to remove ourselves from ideological and philosophical alignment with systems that are antithetical to the ways and thinking of Christ.

Peter addresses Christians' distinctiveness in the world. He says, "As you come to him [Jesus], a living stone rejected by [people] but in the sight of God chosen and precious, you yourselves like living stones are being built up as a spiritual house [the church], to be a holy priesthood, to offer spiritual sacrifices acceptable to God through Jesus Christ" (1 Pet 2:4–5). New Testament scholar Karen Jobes points out that this section of 1 Peter describes to the believers the nature of the community into which they have been born (again). Here, notes Jobes, "Peter emphasizes the community of believers . . . in terms of that community's relationship to God, to redemptive history, and to those outside the community."[21] In Peter's view, the church is not called to "take over" the world, but rather to be at odds with the world's systems of belief. In other words, there is a church and there is a world that can never become Christian. The world's systems of thought are adversative to the spiritual and holy priesthood to which believers are called.

## THE CHURCH: RECOVER LOST IDENTITY

The church must rediscover her biblical identity in Christ. Her biblical identity is inevitably independent of national identity. The church by definition is the global community of "called-out ones" for the purpose of identity in Christ. In this sense, the church is called to be countercultural. *Countercultural*, as used here, suggests that Christians abide by systems of beliefs that are likely to be antithetical to systems of belief developed and propagated by the broader society. In this sense, while the church exists within broader society, she consists of people with dual citizenship. At one level, the laws of a country tell us how to define our citizenship—that is, citizenship within the kingdoms of the world. Yet, as Christians, we are citizens of heaven. Our confession of faith in Christ makes us his ambassadors on earth. Because of the Christian's newfound reality in Christ, our loyalty must be to Christ as Master. Luke 16:13 teaches us that we cannot serve two masters. Gregory A. Boyd explains: "Our allegiance, therefore,

21. Jobes, 1 *Peter*, 142.

can never be to any version of the kingdom-of-the-world, however much better we may think it is than other versions of the kingdom-of-the-world. Our allegiance is to our heavenly Father, whose country we belong to and into whose family we've been adopted."[22] God calls the church and those who are a part of the church (believers) to live out God's will, even when the broader society (the kingdoms-of-the-world) in which she finds herself proffers belief systems that are contrary to God's way.

Christians must live according to principles and teachings of the church of Jesus Christ that are grounded in divine holiness as expressed in Scripture. American Christians must come to terms with the fact that an earthly society or nation is not and can never replace the church of Jesus Christ. Upon this resolve, American Christians will become more conscious of the divine calling for a church whose foundation and practices are grounded within biblical teachings.

## Christians, the Church, Holiness, and a Free Society

There is no denying that Christians have advantages within a free society. Like other people from other religions, we are free to express our religious beliefs. Christians and people from diverse religious backgrounds were granted freedom to live and believe according to their faith traditions. However, freedom to live and believe as one chooses is not a definitively "Christian" position.

The holiness into which we, as believers, are called is not a "free religion" or "free spirituality" as defined by personal choice. John 8:36 has become the Christian anthem of true freedom: "So if the Son sets you free, you will be free indeed." Thus, Christian freedom should not be confused with human free will or even with American freedom. Human free will has to do with the divine self-constraint that permits human beings to choose to accept God's gift in Christ or not. American freedom coincides with human free will in that it offers freedom of religion. Yet, human free will as a gift from God does not imply God's ideal choice, or as Scripture puts it, *ontos eleutheroi esesthe*—"you will be free indeed."

Luke Timothy Johnson posits, "Jesus is speaking less to his opponents than to the Christian readers of the Fourth Gospel."[23] Johnson explains that the principle of freedom in this passage speaks against an illusion of

22. Boyd, *Myth*, 71. Boyd goes on to cite Rom 8:29; Gal 1:2; 6:10; Eph 1:4–5.

23. Johnson, *Writings*, 546.

freedom when we are slaves to sin. Only the truth can make one free (John 8:31–32); that is to say, only the free Son (Jesus) can liberate us from our sins (John 8:36).[24] Pentecostals define that freedom in pneumatological categories: "Now the Lord is the Spirit, and where the Spirit of the Lord is, there is freedom" (2 Cor 3:17). True liberation in Christ is freedom to live holy and not to live according to fleshly passions.

The church that God intends is called to be holy amid a world that is not. Paul states in Romans 12:1–2: "I appeal to you therefore, brothers, by the mercies of God, to present your bodies as a living sacrifice, holy and acceptable to God, which is your spiritual worship. Do not be conformed to this world, but be transformed by the renewal of your mind, that by testing you may discern what is the will of God, what is good and acceptable and perfect." Paul explains that the only acceptable life in God's eyes is a life lived counterculturally—not conforming to logic and principles established by the larger society. As indicated in the quote from Paul above, this life is the holy one that God accepts. It is this lifestyle with which the church of Jesus Christ must identify. In his sermon "The Lord's Own View of His Church and People," Spurgeon comments, "The church is a separate and distinct thing from the world. I suppose there is such a thing as 'the Christian world;' but I do not know what it is, or where it can be found. It must be a singular mixture. I know what is meant by a worldly Christian; and I suppose the Christian world must be an aggregate of worldly Christians. But the church of Christ is not of the world. 'You are not of the world,' says Christ, 'even as I am not of the world.'"[25] The church, as "otherworldly," is in the world, engaged with the world, but distinct from the world. Spurgeon is correct to suggest that Christ never expected that this world would be entirely Christian. But, Christ does expect for the church to be Christian. This means that the church is not of this world. Christ empowers the church by the power of the Holy Spirit to influence the world by simply being and doing the work of Christ in the world. Part of the church's witness is her countercultural approach in moments when culture resists the teachings of Christ.

24. Ibid.

25. Spurgeon, "Lord's Own," 5.

## The Church: An Otherworldly Community of Holiness

From the start of the church in Acts 2, the church has always consisted of a countercultural community of believers who live out their faith in Christ at odds with the rest of society. Although the earliest Christians were primarily Jewish, their worldview and behavior set them at odds with the other Jews. Then, as the gospel went west and became more and more ethnically diverse, the distinctive nature of the church carved out its identity in whatever society it found itself. This otherworldly nature of the church that mirrored the peculiar life of Christ merited them the label of "little Christs" or "Christians." Although the term "Christian" may have been a label of mockery for believers, the validity of the term was marked by an intentional lifestyle to carry out the life, teachings, and message of Jesus Christ in a world that was indifferent to it. In other words, the early Christians aimed to transform society by being a distinctive community before a watching world. That distinctiveness was recognizable because it was marked by the thought and lifestyle of Christ.

From the history of the early church we learn that the Christian's thinking, living, and behaving must be according to principles and ethics that God defines. Such a lifestyle was exemplified in Christ, is discernible in Scripture, and becomes transcendent by the Holy Spirit. This life of Christ is lived in community through the lives of the faithful—members of Christ's church. There is no holiness outside of the church. It is a charade for the faithful to impose holiness upon those who are not part of the church. The line of distinction between the church and the world must be accented through lifestyle and behavior. When the church, or the faithful, imposes itself upon society to force laws that are indeed biblical but antithetical to trends and behaviors of the world, the church loses its witness. Peter explains, "You [the called out ones—the church] are a chosen race, a royal priesthood, a holy nation, a people for God's own possession" (1 Pet 2:9). The church is chosen to bear witness of God's holiness amid a world that is contrary to it.

Paul's theology of holiness is consistent with that of Peter. Romans 8:7 states, "For the mind that is set on the flesh is hostile to God, for it does not submit to God's law; indeed, it cannot." Hence, God provides free will. According to divine order, people are allowed to behave as they please. Those who are not part of Christ's church, born again, and filled with the Holy Spirit have no power to submit to God's will. A local church, therefore, that pits itself against society in hostility, such as by advocating hate toward homosexuals, burning Qur'ans, and posting hate signs toward those whose ideas and behaviors are not according to biblical teachings, weaken their own witness. We must speak strongly to those within the church who subscribe to ideas, practices, and lifestyles that are contrary to biblical teachings. A Christian should disassociate with a brother in Christ who chooses and insists to walk contrary to godly principles (see 2 Thess 3:6). However, lashing out at mainstream media and at people who are not in the church fosters a mean religion; as a result, the loving nature of holiness is compromised.

## THE CHURCH: REPENT FOR AREAS OF WEAKNESS

Amid a wide array of philosophical and theological perspectives, many churches lose their theological distinctiveness in the world. Consequently, the witness of the American church, particularly, seems weakened at several levels. In 1984, A. M. Hills characterized the weakening of the Christian witness as a disease, eating away at the image of the church that God intends. This continues to be observable today. As Hills puts it, "We have established institutions and organizations and all needed facilities, the Bible printed [in many] languages and a Christian literature in abundance, like the leaves of the forest. We have everything desirable for doing Christian work but the general enduement of the Holy Spirit power. But without that, alas how feeble, comparatively, when measured by that first century, are our Christian triumphs!"[26] In Hills' view, the abundance of contemporary resources has clouded the church's understanding that nothing can replace the power and life of the Spirit. Accordingly, American churches continue to relish in the history of American society that has been bent toward freedom of religious expression. This legacy of freedom has provided opportunities for what is often called "the American dream," and other perceived assets in being a part of a democratic republic in the West.

However, a Christian view of freedom is rooted in a spiritual freedom that transcends political categories. It is a spiritual freedom that emancipates the mind, soul, and spirit. As such, people of all nations need God. In recent years, the United States of America has endured several national atrocities: the bombing of the twin towers in New York on 9/11, destroyed levees in New Orleans during Katrina, the worst economic crisis since the Great Depression, multiple destructive hurricanes and tornadoes, increased

26. Hills, *Holiness*, 19.

joblessness, unexpected earthquake of 2011, unprecedented violence, the killing of children and the unborn, and more. If America does not see that we desperately need God's hope and help, Christians should definitely see this need.

When there are laws that are contrary to biblical standards, believers should not lash out at America. Rather, the wake-up call is for believers to rise up and share Christ's love and hope in a world of desperation.

## The Church Versus Society's Systems

The church is called to operate differently from the world's systems. If the church is not the first to admit it, society is certainly willing to denounce holiness for fleshly passions. Churches must not become too closely aligned with political, philosophical, and theological agendas that are rooted in non-biblical ideologies and promoted by mainstream society. In doing so, society sets the agenda for the church—drawing attention to certain matters and leaving others untouched. The grip of political polarities appears strong in the American consciousness. In a search for correcting what has gone wrong in America's finances and the social inequalities, American politics have taken the stage. American people are too obsessed with political parties and depend too heavily on the next politician in leadership, as if a human being has the answers to remedy American political, economic, and social debauchery.

Many Christians subscribe to triumphalism. By triumphalism, I am referring to Christian movements that historically have not only held stridently to their own beliefs, but also championed certain propositions as superior to others. These Christians interpret Christ's call to bear witness in the world as a charge to impose their beliefs on people. They often believe that their duty is to advance particular biblical worldviews through avenues like media, education, and party politics, to name a few. For example, several presidential candidates over the past forty years have run for office with a religious agenda to sanctify what is "wrong" in America. There are varying assumptions—depending on political interests and religious formations—that Christian identity is encoded into one side or the other.

A student shared with me that most of her family are registered Democrats. She also resonated with many of the ideals of the Democrats. So, with her family, she tended to vote along the Democratic party lines. But, when she became a Christian, her Christian friends advised her that

Christians should vote for Republican candidates. The student was baffled but was willing to do whatever God wanted her to do. Despite her affinity toward the Democratic party's ideals, she was willing to part with her family to vote—in no uncertain terms—"God's way."

Similarly, a colleague shared with me that a prominent African American bishop once included in his sermon that "the best thing a Christian could do is vote Republican." My colleague—a theologian—was highly offended, as her political position was that of a long-standing Democrat. She did not see how voting Democrat could be contrary to her biblical worldview. Even so, there are many Christians who are Democrats with attitudes that the Democratic party is the "Christian Party."

Accordingly, many Christians have allowed party politics to create factions, similar to how theological differences divided Christianity in the Western world during the sixteenth-century Reformation, when Luther, Zwingli, Calvin, John Knox, and others led groups of Western Christians in theological schisms. Politics have become the mark of demarcation in popular Christianity that separates so-called liberals from conservatives. If one subscribes to progressive politics that believe that government should extend economic policies, health care advantages, and other programs to help the poor, and social policies that privilege the voices of the marginalized to the same opportunities of the majority groups, the politically conservative Evangelicals would judge that person as having a liberal theology, defining all so-called liberal theologies as anti-biblical. The same is true the other way around. Christians have mingled politics too closely. They often legitimize certain political ideals as leading Christian principles when political ideologies, and not the Bible, often frame the conversations of interest.

Similarly, since the days of Franklin Delano Roosevelt, the majority of African American voters in America have tended to vote for leaders in the Democratic party. The affinity of the black church toward helping the poor and toward civil rights for African Americans and women in America has created a natural alignment with the Democratic party. The Republican party's recent resistance toward immigration reform has alienated Latin Americans from their party. But, with the African Americans, the Democrats' affinity toward helping those in need and advocacy for immigration reform has garnered the Hispanic support in the elections of recent years. To this end, many African and Latin American pastors have aligned their message with political party expediency just as many Evangelical conservatives and mostly White Americans have done on the Republican side. These religious and political alignments often seem antithetical to the morality of Christian holiness. For example, on the one hand, concerning the issue of abortion, the Democratic party struggles to find balance between women's rights and the protection of the unborn. On the other hand, concerning the problem of murder, Republicans seem to value constitutional rights for easy access to guns over the reduction of gun violence. The point here is that flawed political systems and convoluted moral integrity have polluted systems of power. Christians and the church must refocus on holiness more than moral principles framed by American party politics.

## The Call for Christianity to Divorce from Party Politics

Exclusively aligning Christian identity with American political parties is unhelpful for the identity to which the church is called. Unity in Christ must be based on an "other worldly" system of beliefs and practices rather than any national politics. Stated plainly, whether one is "pro-life" or "pro-choice"—language encoded with political definition—is confusing. The usage of the terms is rooted in political interests and not biblical love. So as political parties, political terms are polarizing, and ultimately neither protects children nor their mothers; thus, they are irrelevant to Christian identity. More edifying conversation for the Christian should pertain to sanctification and holiness—how these terms define the church in the world.

Within a political context, Samuel Rodriguez, president of the National Hispanic Leadership Conference, offers an alternate perspective. He professes, "I'm not committed to the donkey or the elephant. I'm committed to the agenda of the Lamb."[27] It should be clear, however, that the agenda of the Lamb does not fit alongside existing party politics. The agenda of the Lamb is not of this world. We must not create another political party called "the Party of the Lamb" alongside the "Tea Party." Barth is helpful here. He explains that just because the church has a responsibility to society does not suggest that the church has an exclusive theory of her own to advocate in the face of various forms and realities of political life.[28] The church is not in a position to establish one particular doctrine as *the* Christian doctrine of the just state.[29] In Barth's own words, "There is but one body of Christ,

27. Newhouse, "Voice," n.p.
28. Barth, *Karl Barth*, 274.
29. Ibid.

born of the Word of God, which is heard in faith. There is therefore no such thing as a Christian state corresponding to the Christian church; there is no duplicate of the church in the political sphere."[30]

Properly understood, the "Lamb's agenda" is God's plan ascribed to the church of Jesus Christ. Revelation 5:12 asserts that the Lamb is worthy (holy). So then, everyone who names the name of the Lamb must forsake the world and live holy unto the Lamb. The lifestyle of holiness is one defined on the Lamb's terms. As pertaining to politics and other matters, moreover, there is a need for the church to engage an alternative discussion that is initiated and grounded within a biblical worldview. John Yoder calls attention to the fact that the church has her own body politics (broadly speaking)—a separate way of being and doing in the world.[31]

On the other hand, there are churches that spend their time lashing out at mainstream society with hostility and condemnation because the rest of the world has chosen to live as they please. Both sides present a travesty against the church God intends. The holiness of God is both separate from the world and loving toward the world. To this end, it is essential to the vitality of the church that the church purifies herself.

Hills reflects on Oberlin University professor Henry Cowles' warning pertaining to the trajectory of a depressed standard of holiness among the churches and the need for repentance:

> Plainly, there is no remedy but for the church to come back to the very elements of piety. She must return to God and Holy Communion. The standard of piety must be raised. What can the church do for the conversion of the world, for her own existence even, without personal holiness—much deep, pure, personal holiness? No wonder that a conviction of this truth should have fastened upon discerning minds with painful strength. The standard of piety throughout the American church is extremely and deplorably low. It is low compared with that of the primitive church, compared with the provisions of the gospel, with the obligations of redeemed sinners, or with the requisite qualifications for the work to be done. The spirit of the world has deeply pervaded and exceedingly engrossed the heart of the church. . . . The responsibilities and privileges of Christians in this life must be clearly exhibited, and urged upon the conscience of the church.[32]

30. Ibid.
31. See Yoder, *Body Politics*, vi–xi.
32. Hills, *Holiness*, 19.

Hills' thesis is relevant today. The pursuit of power and control in the world's systems and the loss of emphasis on personal piety have negatively affected the church's distinctiveness and collective witness in the world. In the words of Jesus to John the evangelist concerning the church at Ephesus, "But I have this against you, that you have abandoned the love you had at first" (Rev 2:4).

## THE CHURCH: RECOMMIT TO LIFE
## OF TOTAL SUBMISSION TO CHRIST

Southern Baptist preacher Henry Blackaby writes, "If there is anything that characterizes God's people in America today, it is the loss of the [reverence] of God."[33] Although he is not pentecostal, Blackaby's analysis seems appropriate cross denominationally. When we do not reverence God, our everyday decisions are governed by systems of belief that may be antithetical to biblical teachings. Identity in Christ and reverence for God must govern the Christian's self-awareness and decisions in everyday life. "True revival can only come," notes Blackaby, "when the people of God return to a healthy, holy reverence of God."[34] Identity in Christ and reverence for God must govern the Christian's decisions on all issues, irrespective of societal belief systems that may or may not be consistent with Christ's teachings.

## Scripture

In the Old Testament, God's Word was inscribed into stones and sent through the voice of the prophets. Yet, other matriarchs and patriarchs of Hebrew history testify to have heard God's voice audibly with instructions and promises. These witnesses established an overarching tenor and revelatory depiction for the trajectory of the biblical worldview.

According to the New Testament, the last written letters—the Johannine literature—bear clear record that Jesus is the incarnate Word of God (John 1:1, 14). Jesus' emissaries experienced, intermingled, and touched the physical presence of the life-giving Word (1 John 1:1–4). God's Word continues to live today through the Spirit of Christ (or the Holy Spirit).

---

33. Blackaby, *Holiness*, 2.
34. Ibid., 3.

## Holy Spirit

We can posture ourselves for holiness of our own desire and commitment to Christ, but we cannot live holiness with our own power. We need the Holy Spirit. Late second-century Christian theologian and minister Clement of Alexandria characterizes the Holy Spirit as "Instructor." "[God] formed [humanity] out of the dust; regenerates [them] by water; causes [them] to grow by the Spirit; instructs [them] by the Word, directing [them] by holy precepts."[35] Eastern priest Tadros Y. Malaty points out that when Clement of Alexandria says, "The Instructor nurses [humanity] by the Spirit," he means that the Divine Instructor, Jesus Christ, sent his Spirit to the church not only to grant adoption to God, but to nurse us continuously by the divine life, or by 'holiness in Jesus Christ that we might become holy as our God is Holy'" (Lev 11:44, 45; 1 Pet 1:16).[36]

Today, some Christians fail to emphasize the importance of the Holy Spirit for holy living. Even pentecostal/charismatic Christians who underscore the embodiment of the Spirit fall short on the issue of Spirit-filled living. As practical theologian Mark Cartlege puts it, "Charismatic power and its manifestations are linked to an ethical community in a covenant with God. This means that the charismatic life is authenticated by holiness and not by spiritual power" (Matt 7:21–3).[37] To borrow language from Cheryl Sanders, we need more than "ecstatic" gifts. We need "static" fruit.[38] The *Holy* Spirit produces power and courage both to *be* holy and to *practice* holiness. That's the static fruit!

Holiness is only possible by the work of the Holy Spirit in the life of the believer. In the words of Wesley, "We are convinced that we are not sufficient of ourselves to help ourselves; that without the Spirit of God we can do nothing but add sin to sin; that is [the Holy Spirit] alone 'who worketh in us' by [God's] almighty power."[39] Jones's son-in-law, another Wesleyan scholar and preacher, James K. Mathews, posits that everything in Christianity is not only possible, but actual, where the Spirit has free course.[40]

---

35. Kaye, *Some Account*, 65.

36. Malaty, *Gift*, 51.

37. Cartledge, *Encountering*, 98.

38. Sanders, *Saints*, 133.

39. Wesley, "Circumcision," 25.

40. Mathews, "Spirit," 137.

Believers should live every day as informed by Scripture and as empowered by a life in the Spirit. The study of Scripture cannot be realized in the life of the believer without the powerful insight of the Holy Spirit. Scripture teaches that the Holy Spirit is the guide. Jesus promises in John 16:13a: "When the Spirit of truth comes, [the Holy Spirit] will guide you into all the truth." The Holy Spirit is the helper. Jesus also promises in John 15:26: "But when the Helper comes, whom I will send to you from the Father, the Spirit of truth, who proceeds from the Father, [the Spirit of truth] will bear witness about me."[41] Paul adds that the Holy Spirit is also a protector. Second Timothy 1:14 states, "By the Holy Spirit who dwells within us, guard the good deposit entrusted to you." When the church emphasizes the life of the Spirit more than the emotion of the Spirit, the Spirit captures the people's hearts and governs their lives.

## THE CHURCH: RAISE UP A STANDARD

My dad has often preached, "Raise up a standard of holiness!" As I consider the trajectory of our world today and the observable concessions among Christians to be as close to the world as possible and still profess to be Christians, I am convinced that my dad was right. There has been an earthquake in the church's spirituality, and biblical standards are crumbling into its cleavage. I have a deep concern that the church is becoming a country club or mate-meeting grounds. Neither of these metaphors is bad in and of itself. Christians need social gatherings and places to meet and greet. But, when the local church becomes more identifiable as a country club or as merely mate-meeting grounds, the spiritual significance and biblical image of the church as the body of Christ becomes something else other than what God intends. It follows that the church's sound moral platform of holiness is weakened.

For example, as a former youth pastor, I would teach the youth those old worn-out clichés—"no wed no bed" and "worth the wait"—as pertaining to pre-marital virginity or celibacy. Many young people and adults alike boast in their virginity or celibacy; yet, they engage in oral sex, heavy petting, even same-gender fondling. Often, the assumption is that as long as one does not have heterosexual intercourse, she or he is in good standing

---

41. Also, see John 14:26: "But the Helper, the Holy Spirit, whom the Father will send in my name, he will teach you all things and bring to your remembrance all that I have said to you."

with the "no wed no bed" and "worth the wait" Bible lesson. The same is true in some cases concerning babies out of wedlock.

There is a certain cultural taboo concerning getting pregnant before marriage—even among the churches. Churches reinforce this taboo when they suspend ladies from the choir or from ushering when they get pregnant out of wedlock. The emphasis is on pregnancy as a sin. I have observed that when "pregnancy as the sin" becomes the focus of church doctrine rather than abstinence, the message of sexual purity becomes secondary. As a result, many unmarried, sexually active believers land in the abortion clinics to rid themselves of the "sin"—the pregnancy. It has been heartbreaking to hear several stories where even pastors advised young ladies to abort babies! When Christians compromise holiness and participate in the abortion epidemic—wherein millions of babies are aborted every year—the church's witness becomes weakened. There is a sense of urgency for the church of Jesus Christ to lift up a prevailing light of holiness.

The light of holiness is not merely conceptual or theological, but practical and institutional. Raising a standard of holiness includes building parochial schools, Christian universities, hospitals, crisis pregnancy centers, adoption agencies, Christian homeless shelters, and other ministries that extend Christ's love to the communities of the world. These institutions are under supported. As a result, many of them are struggling to remain open and others are closing down. Christians should fully support these institutional arms of the church. They represent practical witness of God's love in a world that desperately needs it. God calls the Christians to lead in expressions of help in the world, but not as followers of ideological trends and standards of living that are defined by the world.

In a very real sense, raising up a standard has potential for intense conflict. At times, the church endures pressures from society to compromise her beliefs. Looking to the early church for guidance, the church must resist society's pressures, even if it brings persecution upon the church. When society pressures the church to act differently than to her identity in Christ, the church must not compromise her standards.

God is not pleased when God's people compromise holiness, regardless of the source of pressure. In Exodus 32, Moses descends from a forty-day retreat with the Lord in Mount Horeb. God gave him the Word for the people of Israel. God chose them to be a peculiar people. But when Moses came off of the mountain, Israel was engaged in fleshly lusts. They were running wild, doing as they pleased—characteristic of a societal worldview that was antithetical to God's worldview. Having just experienced a retreat with God, Moses was terrified at the people's behavior. He threw the tablets of stone with the commandments of God on them and they crumbled into pieces. Moses forcefully declared among the people, "Who is on the Lord's side? Come to me" (Exod 32:26). It is impossible for people to be holy according to God's commandments when they have not made an important choice to follow God with sincerity. Following God with sincerity requires an intentional demarcation in the sand with a decision to stand on the Lord's side.

As explained earlier, the church bears the name of God, similarly to how Israel bore God's name in the Old Testament. While there are many expressions of ecclesiastical and theological traditions within the church, it is imperative that the church stakes a claim toward God's worldview of holiness. From that worldview, Christians must live according to biblical standards. One example that has been an object of discussion in this chapter has been the issue of marriage. A significant question is how does God understand marriage as explained in Scripture? This query cuts to the chase of many issues pertaining to marriage beyond the issue of same-sex marriage. The church must not take positions based on what's popular. The church must lift up a standard on marriage that also addresses heterosexual marriage, abuse in marriage, adultery, infidelity, and so on. God's standard does not side with some wrong while condemning other wrong. The standard of holiness asks, "Who is on the Lord's side?"

Columnist and blogger at the *Washington Post* Rahiel Tesfamariam responds to the firestorm among (especially African American) pastors and bishops pertaining to Obama's support for same-sex marriage in America:

> As marriage equality has elicited such a polarizing effect in black religious communities, some black religious leaders believe that the church has entered the fight of its life. What both clergy and congregants seem to be vigorously debating is love – love for neighbor (loving your neighbor as you love yourself) and, of course, love for God (loving nothing over and above your maker). . . . I am reminded here of Christ's own warning to his followers against mixing governance with God. Rather than give in to this tendency, I hope that the black church will be able to "give back to [Obama] what is [Obama's] and to God what is God's."[42]

42. Tesfamariam, "Is Gay Marriage," n.p.

Agreeing with Tesfamariam, the church's standards shape the identity of the church and the government's standards exist within a society of ideological freedom. Even if a society assumes the Constantinian model, wherein the ruler decrees Christianity as the official religion of the nation, no national ruler, prime minister, or president has divine authority to decree norms for the church. The church must submit to Christ. Moreover, the church must raise up God's standard of holiness amid a world of ideological plurality.

A quote on the issue of the holy church from early-twentieth-century German Catholic priest and commentator Constantine Kempf seems appropriate here: "Be the times as morally degenerate as they may, the church knows no other chastity than that which gave to martyr-heroes [and heroines] their supernatural strength and she yields not her position, although it has often been her sorrowful experience that it was the very severity of her moral demands which estranged so many from her or deterred them from acceptance of her doctrine."[43] In the twenty-first century, I hope that civility prevails over hostility. Yet, as martyrdom has been part of church history, it is not beyond the scope of modern faith, in America, that some will endure severe persecution when the believer holds high a standard of holiness—even in a free society.

Moreover, I want to discuss two points about God's standard of holiness. The first is that God's standard of holiness is unwavering in the face of fleshly passions. The second is that God's standard of holiness is not condemning of others. It is rooted and grounded in a divinely-compelling love.


## Peculiarity

God's standard of love violates neither a divine requirement of a holy life nor human freewill. God does not approve of sin. Sin is contrary to the essence of God. Holiness is pure. A life that ascribes to lustful passions is an offense to God's grace. Such living shortchanges us from God's glorious desire for humankind.[44] Additionally, sin is destructive to human peace and joy. Yet, God is not concerned that sin would desecrate God's holiness. God's holiness remains perfect amid a world of sin.

The church seeks to maintain its countercultural reality with Christ's love in a world that increasingly defines itself in contrast to the church's

---

43. Kempf, *Holiness*, 15.

44. See Rom 3:23: "For all have sinned and fall short of the glory of God."

identity. To this end, it must be clearer that America is best described as a free society and not a Christian society. Efforts to bear witness to Christ through condemning society when it pursues decisions contrary to biblical teachings ironically reduces the Christian witness from a loving, holy one to an angry and mean one. Hostility is in stark contradiction to the attitude, lifestyle, and disposition of Christ's love and compassion to which the Christian is called.

Christ does not call the church to fight and force society to respect biblical teachings or Christ. We are called to fight *for* people in society to come to Jesus through our lived witness and loving invitation to join Christ's holy church. To put it succinctly, a life lived as public witness to Christ's transformation is a much stronger testimony that subverts others into faith in Christ, rather than mean and hostile statements to coerce others into faith. In this sense, the church is called to model attitudes, lifestyles, and dispositions as God intends before a watching world. Christian theological ethicist John Yoder's remark pertaining to the life of the church before a watching world is helpful here. He says, "The people of God are called to be today what the world is called to be ultimately."[45] Yet, the world must join the church to be holy. Other than through Christ's body, there is no other holiness for the world. So the life of the church must be distinct, reflecting divine holiness in every way. Love and grace are part of the Christian witness of holiness.

## Love and Grace

God's love is more powerful than hate, fleshly passion, and ideological differences. This love draws others to God in a subversive (not coercive) manner. The Old Testament prophet Jeremiah sheds light onto the power of God's love in a world of indifference. The prophet suggests that "the Lord appear[s] [to us] from afar, *saying*, 'I have loved you with an everlasting love; Therefore I have drawn you with lovingkindness'" (Jer 31:3 NASB).

When the church embodies God's love, love becomes the only appropriate Christian response to society's decisions, even when they are contrary to a biblical worldview. People from around the world envy the freedom and opportunities in America. American Christians have found a home in such a society—a certain type of escape from hostility that many Christians endure in countries like North Korea, China, Afghanistan, and Saudi

45. Yoder, *Body Politics*, ix.

Arabia. One might even conclude that Christian history has misconstrued the divine calling for Christians to be a light in the world. American history shows that Christians have tried to lay a strong hold on governance in society, assuming its mission to transform the world (itself) for Christ. This philosophical approach to ministry has been the motor behind much of world missions and Western colonization in many areas of the world. In the name of God, there has been blood on the hands of many Christian colonizers. However, contemporary mission critics have pointed out that the "Christian globalization" approach to missions has also stirred an unintended message of hostility toward people who resist them. Such hostility has advanced Western imperialism more than an authentic love of Jesus Christ.

As pertaining to missions around the world and in America, the foundational Christian tenet called love is easily lost through efforts to strong-arm people and societies into certain beliefs. Hostility and coercion seem contrary to a gospel that is so inviting, so full of love and grace. God's love in Christ is compelling but not coercive. Notably, in Scripture, Christ only scorns corrupted people who were part of the household of God in the temple.[46] He whips them out of the temple because they claimed the name of God but were making God's house a place of self-aggrandizement and selfish material gain. Moreover, in Peter's words, "For it is time for judgment to begin at the household of God" (1 Pet 4:17).

As explained earlier, there are two types of prophetic voices in the church. The first one is the voice that purifies the church. This voice confronts evil, sexism, racism, abuse, scandal, avarice, hate, and human neglect in the house of God. God's house must maintain holy distinctiveness in society. Moreover, Christ restrains punitive expressions toward those who are not a part of God's house or "the church." Christ beckons for them with love and compassion saying, "Whosoever will, let them come." "Come to me, all who labor and are heavy laden, and I will give you rest. Take my yoke upon you, and learn from me" (Matt 11:28–30). The church must teach God's worldview.

The second prophetic voice of the church has to do with the church's voice within society. This voice is a voice of love and grace. This prophetic voice is evangelical. By evangelical, I mean that the prophetic voice in society seeks to bear witness to the message of the gospel that frees people from

46. See Matt 21:12 and John 2:14–15.

the bondage of sin—whether it is sins that we commit or the systemic sins that oppress people from the fullness of life that God intends.

The church, first, becomes prophetic through its presence with distinction from society. Local churches regain the message of holiness and exemplify that message through an everyday life of love, grace, and service among themselves and toward others who may not be Christians. A holy church comprises herself of people who have had an encounter with God's love and are compelled to conform to that love. God's love flows into every dimension of life. It makes a difference in the way we see ourselves in the world and the way that we see others. When one understands God's love, one understands holiness. Holiness begins with a fundamental experience of God's love.[47] God's love invites us to holiness and forms us into the fullness of Christ. God's love in the Christian flows through with truth and compassion for a world desperate for the light of Christ.

Then, the church's prophetic voice expresses itself through acts of love and kindness. It speaks on behalf of those whose life experiences have landed them in desperation. Some of them are mistreated, sex-trafficked, abandoned, poor, disenfranchised, marginalized, oppressed, and dejected. God's love acts through the church on the behalf of those who cannot help themselves.

## CONCLUSION

As you embark on your journey of holiness, remember that that One who charges us to be holy is the only One who is able to secure our hearts and lives in holiness. Holiness is acquired through prayer and commitment to God. Let not our prayers be filled with our own voices. But let God speak to our spirits and hearts in prayer. It is prudent to spend time sitting in silence, just listening to God (Psalms 62:1). God speaks through multiple means: from the beauty and sounds of nature to other people, and yes, through the distant voice (not multiple confusing voices) where there is no human person, just the living God.

God's voice is holy as God is holy. The closer we get to God, the more holy we become. Prayer, Bible study, fellowship with believers, outreach to the broken, and commitment to an image and behavior that reflect God's character are central to what it means to be holy.

---

47. Orsuto, *Holiness*, 201.

The beauty of holiness speaks to the glory of God. Grace applies a splendor in our lives that raises us above our pasts. That same holiness gives us a promising future with God, in this life and in the life to come.

## REFLECTION

As our world defines itself more and more in contrast to biblical principles, Christians must become more and more intentional in our pursuit of Christ. It is easy to waver in our faith when our eyes veer into lusting after worldly enticements. However, if we are to continue in God's Word and Christ's work in the world, we must fix our eyes on God's Word. Let's study the principles of Scripture more closely and pray to adapt our lifestyle accordingly.

## PRAYER

If you have heard the voice of God speak to you through the chapter, pause and pray this prayer:

> Dear Lord, please help me to embrace your holiness. It is my gift from you. Yet, the forces of evil often weaken me with discouragement in the face of difficulties and doubts. I am hungry for your grace and mighty strength to endure life's challenges. I trust you and desire greatly to follow Jesus faithfully. I need the joy that flows from intimate union with you.

# 8

## Toward Practical Steps to Holiness:
## Four Moves

There will be no great Revival until the people of God
are deeply convicted of their need of holiness.

—MAJOR ALLISTAIRE SMITH

As I COME TO the close of this book on holiness, one might ask, "So what
are some practical steps toward holiness?" I do not assume that the walk of
holiness can be reduced to a few action items. I have argued that holiness
is more than a notion; it is more than lip service, and it is more than a list
of dos and don'ts. Holiness is all-encompassing—*being* and *acting* in a way
that reflects life in Christ and continued *renewal* in Christ by the power of
the Holy Spirit. Transformed behavior must be rooted in a heart of godly
love and a pure conscience toward God.

There are at least four principles related to holy living: 1) Put God first;
2) Love others; 3) Flee sin; and 4) Faithfully pursue God's will. These four
principles are not put in a particular order. In my view, one should pursue
all of them at once. If one of them should emerge as most essential, however, it would be the first—"put God first." Truthfully, it is impossible to put
God first without loving others, fleeing sin, and faithfully pursuing God's
will; yet, it is of utmost value to understand that pursuing love, trying to live
right, or even engaging in ministry are null and void without a central focus
on the God who empowers the Christian to live these goals.

## PUT GOD FIRST

The providential nature of God is key. Divine providence, however, does not trump human free will. Rather, God's sovereignty means that there is nothing that exists beyond God's reign. It is a recognition that we need God to live life to its fullest. Again, Wesley's *Image of God* theology is helpful here. If humanity is able to experience anything good, holy, and right, the beauty of life is a mere reflection of God's image. It is, moreover, critical that Christians shun arrogant attitudes such as "I am because I am so good;" "I have because I know the right people;" or "I know how to make it happen." In Paul's words, "But by the grace of God I am what I am" (1 Cor 15:10). The "put God first" attitude assumes a total reliance on God. If *I am* because of God, *I will be* because of God. Thus, a relationship with the sovereign God becomes a wise pursuit. The emphasis is on pursuing God.

Pursuing God implies worship. For pentecostal/charismatic Christians, worship is central to experiencing the work of the Spirit. Worship becomes integral to a transformed life because God's presence becomes tangible when we involve ourselves in expressions of worship—namely, during a worship service. The charismatic British Anglican practical theologian Mark J. Cartledge explains it well: "A worship service is the place where people seek the presence of God. . . . It is the place where the glory of the Lord is revealed in power and people are transformed for the sake of the kingdom of God."[1]

Theologically speaking, worship becomes spiritual union between God and the worshipper. Fourth-century bishop of Caesarea Basil the Great wrote a lot on worship and the Godhead.[2] In his prominent treatise *On the Holy Spirit,* Basil the Great says, "To worship in the Spirit implies that our intelligence has been enlightened."[3] Christian theologian Geoffrey Wainwright posits that for Basil the Great, all of God's work in creation, redemption, and sanctification takes place through the Son and in the Spirit.[4] It is, therefore, appropriate that our grateful response should be in the Spirit and reach the Father through the Son.

Our worship, moreover, corresponds to God's dealings in the world and sets the trajectory of our pursuit of holiness toward the fullness of

1. Cartledge, *Encountering*, 51.
2. See Basil the Great, *On the Holy Spirit.*
3. Ibid., 97.
4. Wainwright, *Worship*, 238.

God.[5] Historian Robert Atwell adds that for Basil the Great the pursuit of a holy life rests in the life of worship. Atwell explains that for Basil, the Holy Spirit needs to penetrate the Christian's life, as well as the corporate life of the church, to transform them and make them conform to the divine nature. This process of transfiguration occurs most powerfully as people participate in worship.[6] Basil conceived of our relationship with God as one of thanksgiving and praise.

Additionally, true worship requires sacrifice. In the Old Testament, offering up worship included material sacrifice. Similarly, Christians must bring a sacrifice of thanksgiving and praise. Hebrews 13:15 states, "Through him then let us continually offer up a sacrifice of praise to God, that is, the fruit of lips that acknowledge his name." The language of sacrifice suggests willingness. Legalism, conversely, suggests force. When we put God first through sacrificial worship, the posture of worship becomes, "I will do whatever it takes to live according to God's will." This attitude flows from a regenerated heart in search of God.

The state of worship is the deep cry of words like those of Saul on the road to Damascus, "Who are you, Lord?" The divine response comes as God's self-revelation. In other words, worship is the opening of the soul to a divine outpouring. To this end, as Aiden Wilson Tozer says, "Without doubt the emphasis in Christian teaching today should be on worship."[7]

## LOVE OTHERS

Earlier I explained that love is the foundation of holiness. There is no holiness without love at the core and it is exemplified through practice. This love supersedes reciprocity—a holy love requires nothing in return. It is a love that is greater than hate, overcomes adversity, and heals a world of bigotry. As twentieth-century Catholic theologian Thomas Merton puts it: "Corrupt forms of love wait for the neighbor to 'become a worthy object of love' before actually loving. This is not the way of Christ. . . . Our job is to love others without stopping to inquire whether or not they are worthy. That is not our business and, in fact, it is nobody's business. What we are asked to do is to love; and this love itself will render both ourselves and our neighbor worthy if anything can."[8]

5. Ibid.

6. Atwell, *Spiritual*, 70.

7. See Tozer, *Born*, 63.

8. Merton, *Disputed*, 125.

Jesus gave two commandments: (1) Love the Lord your God with all of your heart, soul and mind; and (2) Love your neighbor as yourself. These two commandments are indispensible. One cannot love God without loving the neighbor; and it is impossible to fathom the depth of a Godlike love for the neighbor without loving God. Martin Luther King Jr. explains that a God kind of love "is expressed in Jesus' words, 'Love your enemies . . . that ye may be children of the Father which is in heaven.' We are called to this difficult task in order to realize a unique relationship with God," says King. He further explains, "We are potential [children] of God. Through love that potentiality becomes actuality. We must love our enemies, because only by loving them can we know God and experience the beauty of holiness."[9] When we fall in love with God, we love others just as God loves. We love them without restraint—regardless of who they are or the choices they make. To love unconditionally as God loves is central to being like God in holiness. No alternative to love exists in holiness.

## FLEE SIN

It must be clear that God hates sin but loves people. Because of this, Paul teaches the believers to "abstain from every form of evil" (1 Thess 5:22). The single divine conundrum occurs when humans helplessly engage in and enjoy what God hates. Paul identifies with the human affinity toward sin. He explains his own bout with sin. Paul exclaims, "Wretched man that I am" (Rom 7:24)! Then, he powerlessly ponders the rhetorical question, "Who will deliver me from this body of death?" In Paul's resolve, he extends a theology of redemption, a glimmer of hope to the weak sinner: "Thanks be to God through Jesus Christ our Lord" (Rom 7:25a)! Paul's redemption theology in 1 Corinthians 10:13 teaches that "God is faithful, and he will not let you be tempted beyond your ability, but with the temptation he will also provide the way of escape, that you may be able to endure it."

Central to redemption theology is the faithfulness of God. Also, in the Christian's walk, one must rely on that same divine faithfulness as help to overcome bad habits and lustful passions. Seventeenth-century English theologian John Owen reasons, "If we do not abide in prayer, we will abide in temptation. Let this be one aspect of our daily intercession: 'God, preserve my soul, and keep my heart and all its ways so that I will not be entangled.' When this is true in our lives, a passing temptation will not

9. King. *Strength*, 55.

overcome us. We will remain free while others lie in bondage."[10] Owen is correct that Christians must rely on God's grace to escape from sin's attraction. Reformed theologian Bryan Chapell notes that the translation of the latter part of 1 Corinthians 10:13, "a way of escape," helps to capture a key concept of the original Greek text. He correctly explains the Christian bout with sin as an "Alamo" situation:

> This expression would have brought a military image to the mind of ancient people, the image of a small troop surrounded by a larger, more powerful enemy and with no way out. Paul describes this 'Alamo' situation to help us envision how powerful are the forces of temptation that surround us. But he says, 'There is a way out; God will always provide a way of escape.' Though our spiritual enemies surround us, the cavalry will come, a secret passage will be discovered, an overpowering weapon will be supplied, or a weakness in the enemy lines will form. Somehow, God will provide an escape from the temptation.[11]

## FAITHFULLY PURSUE GOD'S WILL

Escaping from sin is not enough. We must also run toward Christ, who is stronger than sin. We need divine counsel to live righteously before God. Good ideas are not good enough. Every way that seems *right* is not *righteous*. Proverbs 14:12 states, "There is a way that seems right to a [human], but its end is the way to death." It's the difference between systems of belief that are contrary to God and God's way. The question of *good ideas* is not always consistent with *God-ideas*. As Christians, our desire is for divine inspiration more than human aspirations.

God-discovery in worship becomes the beginning of a life of obedience and the pursuit of God's will for our lives. A worship that totally relies on God for help produces a life in pursuit of God's will. A. W. Tozer says, "There is little danger that we shall become merely worshipers and neglect the practical implications of the gospel. No one can long worship God in Spirit and in truth before the obligation to holy service becomes too strong to resist. Fellowship with God leads straight to obedience and good works. That is the divine order and it can never be reversed."[12] Holiness is a lifestyle

10. Owen, *Triumph*, 165.

11. Chapell, *Holiness*, 101.

12. Tozer, *Born*, 126.

that includes the three principles of *rest, being,* and *doing.* When we live a life in pursuit of God, all other selfish concerns are subsumed in that quest. Resting in God requires that we trust him even through life's struggles. Such trust compels our willing worship. And worship requires living, being, and doing God's will with a heart of thanksgiving.

## REFLECTION

It is God's will that all goes well with us, and that we be in good health, as it goes well with our souls (see 3 John 1:2). Holiness liberates us to serve God freely. Such liberation becomes God's intention for believers individually and the church collectively. Walking in holiness means to conform to the image of God. We discover that our lives experience maximum human potential when we rest in God, become like Christ in love and grace, and follow the leadership of the Holy Spirit in holy living.

## PRAYER

If you have heard the voice of God speak to you through the pages of this chapter, pause and pray these two prayers:

> Heavenly Father, I am a believer. I am Your child and You are my Father. Jesus is my Lord. I believe with all my heart that Your Word is true. Your Word says if I will ask, I will receive the Holy Spirit. So in the Name of Jesus Christ, my Lord, I am asking You to fill me to overflowing with Your precious Holy Spirit. Jesus, baptize me in the Holy Spirit. Because of Your Word, I believe that I now receive and I thank You for it. I believe the Holy Spirit is within me and, by faith, I accept it. (Kenneth Copeland)

I will conclude this volume with this prayer from Bishop Augustine of Hippo. Will you join me?

> Breathe in me O Holy Spirit, that my thoughts may all be holy. Act in me O Holy Spirit, that my work, too, may be holy. Draw my heart O Holy Spirit, that I love but what is holy. Strengthen me O Holy Spirit, to defend all that is holy. Guard me, then, O Holy Spirit, that I always may be holy. Amen.[13]

---

13. Augustine, "Prayer," n.p.

# Epilogue

"Lord, prepare me, to be a sanctuary, pure and holy, tried and true
and with thanksgiving, I'll be a living, sanctuary, oh for You."

—JOHN W. THOMPSON AND RANDY SCRUGGS

THE FORMER PAGES AIM to construct a practical theological treatment on
holiness. As a practical theology, this work draws upon several theological
disciplines, such as biblical studies, Christian theological ethics, philosophy, and others. As human subjects, we do not think of or read of faith in
disciplinary isolation. We think broadly. Therefore, this academic work
aims to assemble a theological treatment of holiness that draws from a va-
riety of theological disciplines in its stride towards a practical theology on
holiness for this century's Christian church.

Furthermore, there are some important disclaimers that have helped
me to structure this work. First, while I have tried to develop a practical
theology of holiness that is both academically sound and practically appropriate for everyday life, this book is not a "how-to" manual; it aims,
however, to provide tools to help one think more theologically about what
it means to live a godly life in an ungodly world.

Second, the critical reader would notice that the ideas I propose in
this book emerge from a theological framework that values Scripture as
the inspired, infallible, and authoritative source of Christian doctrine and
precept. Higher criticism has influenced a move in contemporary theological discourse to challenge the biblical text, thus devaluing its integrity as
the primary source for Christian theology. To this end, I have employed a
theological reading of Scripture in conversation with historical resources
and personal experiences.

Third, this biblical theology advances an ecclesiology that privileges
the church as a countercultural community of believers. The church has a

divine calling to continue the presence of Christ in the world. In the words of James Mathews, "The Spirit dwells in the Church and in the hearts of the faithful as in a temple. [The Spirit] guides, purifies, equips, endows, liberates, empowers, inspires, instructs, unifies; [the Spirit] propels [the Church] to mission."[1] Stated another way, the Holy Spirit is the transcendence of God that empowers this community of the faithful to live holy and witness holiness amid and to an unholy world.

Fourth, a theology that emphasizes the divine calling for Christians to be distinct and "set apart" from the world raises questions concerning divine expectations for Christian public engagement. Does an ecclesiology require the church to be "set apart" mean that the church should withdraw herself from society? Practically speaking, if the church is to be separated from the world, what is the Christian's role as it pertains to community transformation? I have wrestled with these questions because much of my own work involves social engagement and community transformation—speaking out on behalf of the weak and most vulnerable.

As I process the paradox of seclusion and involvement, or being set apart and engaging, my resolve is that Christian theology must be grounded within an ecclesiology. Simply stated, it is necessary that Christians understand God-related matters from within the context of a clear understanding of who the church is called to be. While public theological discourse has its place, what appears to be a contemporary obsession with public theology seems devoid of authentic Christian foundation without first grounding itself within ecclesiology. Without a strong ecclesiology as its framework, Christian theology loses its biblical context. Moreover, Christians first must understand who we are called to *be*—the body of Christ, a reflection of God's holiness. The divine calling to *do*, as in public involvement, social engagement, must necessarily flow out of the divine calling to *be*. My reading of Scripture and understanding of holiness is consistent with social holiness in John Wesley's theology of holiness. Expressing a heart of Christian love on behalf of others in tangible ways is central to a life of holiness.

Fifth, one might notice that the ideas that are advanced seem to presuppose a homogeneous interpretation of the Christian faith. While I acknowledge the challenge proposed by the manner in which the theological and ecclesiological framework is structured, I contend that (broadly speaking) a catholic vision of the church is necessary to understand a biblically defined notion of holiness. While there are various congregations and

1. Mathews, "Spirit," 129.

several nuances among biblical churches, there is a greater sense of unity among the congregations in Scripture than the splintered versions of the church today. As a result, contemporary splintered churches breed splintered theologies and ecclesiologies.

The sixteenth-century Reformation is the most notable but was in no way the beginning or the end of varying interpretations of the faith. While I acknowledge a kaleidoscope of theological and ecclesiological perspectives, God envisions the church as one universal body. The basic premise is that the church is called to be holy in the midst of an unholy world. Just as in the past, great challenges lie ahead of the church. God intends for God's ideal church to rise up and cry, "Holy!" Holiness is revealed not only in word but also, even more importantly, by virtue of our ontological way of being in the world and as expressed through the way we live our lives.

# Bibliography

Akers, Michael J. *Enriching Christian Doctrine and Character.* Bloomington, IN: AuthorHouse, 2009.

Allen, Bob. "Insurance Companies Shed Light on Extent of Sex Abuse in Protestant Churches." *Free Republic,* July 6, 2007. No pages. Online: http://www.freerepublic. com/focus/f-news/2707908/posts.

Anderson, Gordon. "Kingdom Now Theology: A Look at Its Roots and Branches." *Paraclete* 24, no. 3 (Summer 1990) 1–12.

Aristides. "The Apology of Aristides the Philosopher." Translated by D. M. Kay. In *Early Christian Writings.* No pages. Online: http://www.earlychristianwritings.com/text /aristides-kay.html.

Ashcroft, John. "Hymns and Scripture." Lecture presented at Regent University's President's Circle, Virginia Beach, VA, February 7, 2013.

Associated Press. "Data Shed Light on Child Sexual Abuse by Protestant Clergy." *New York Times,* June 16, 2007. No pages. Online: http://www.nytimes.com/2007/06/16 /us/16protestant.html.

Atwell, Robert. *Spiritual Classics from the Early Church: An Anthology.* London: National Society/Church House, 1995.

Augustine. *The Confessions of St. Augustine.* Translated by Edward D. Pusey. New York: Cosimo, 2006.

———. "Prayer to the Holy Spirit." Augustinian Spirituality: Prayers of St. Augustine. No pages. Online: http://www1.villanova.edu/villanova/mission/campusministry/ spirituality/resources/spirituality/restlesshearts/prayers.html.

Barnett, Christopher B. *Kierkegaard, Pietism and Holiness.* Burlington, VT: Ashgate, 2011.

Barth, Karl. *Dogmatics in Outline.* New York: Harper & Row, 1959.

———. *Karl Barth: Theologian of Freedom.* Edited by Clifford Green. Minneapolis: Fortress Press, 1991.

Basil the Great. *On the Holy Spirit.* Edited by David Anderson. Popular Patristic Series. Crestwood, NY: St. Vladimir's Seminary Press, 1980.

Bass, Dorothy C. "Keeping Sabbath." In *Practicing Our Faith: A Way of Life for a Searching People,* edited by Dorothy C. Bass, 75–88. San Francisco: Jossey-Bass, 1997.

Bekker, Corné. "Becoming Who God Says You Are." Habits of the Heart video, 54:01. Regent University. Online: http://www.regent.edu/admin/stusrv/student_dev /online_workshops/habits_of_the_heart/becoming.cfm.

Berg, David Brandt. "Overcoming Vices!" *Deep Truths.* No pages. Online: http: //deeptruths.com/treasures/overcoming-vices.html.

Bernard, David K. *Practical Holiness: A Second Look.* Hazelwood, MO: Word Aflame, 1985.

# Bibliography

Blackaby, Henry T. *Holiness: God's Plan for Fullness of Life*. Nashville: Thomas Nelson, 2003.

Boyd, Gregory A. *The Myth of a Christian Nation: How the Quest for Political Power is Destroying the Church*. Grand Rapids: Zondervan, 2005.

Bratcher, Dennis R. "Torah as Holiness: Old Testament 'Law' as Response to Divine." *The Voice: Biblical and Theological Resources for Growing Christians*. Paper presented to the Thirtieth Annual Meeting of the Wesleyan Theological Society, Dayton, OH, November 5, 1994. No pages. Online: http://www.crivoice.org/torahholiness.html.

Bridges, Jerry. *The Pursuit of Holiness*. Colorado Springs: Navpress, 1978.

Bromiley, Geoffrey W., ed. *The International Standard Bible Encyclopedia*. Vol. 2, *E–J*. Grand Rapids: Eerdmans, 1982.

Brooks, Noel. *Scriptural Holiness*. Franklin Springs, GA: Advocate, 1967.

Brown, Raymond E. *The Churches the Apostles Left Behind*. Mahwah, NJ: Paulist, 1984.

Brueggemann, Walter. "Bounded by Obedience and Praise: The Psalms as Canon." *JSOT* 16 (June 1991): 63–92.

———. *Prophetic Imagination*. 2nd ed. Minneapolis: Fortress, 2001.

Burton-Christie, Douglas. *The Word in the Desert: Scripture and the Quest for Holiness in Early Christian Monasticism*. New York: Oxford University Press, 1993.

Calvin, John. *Institutes of the Christian Religion*. Translated by Henry Beveridge. Grand Rapids: Christian Ethereal Library. Online: http://www.ccel.org/ccel/calvin/institutes.pdf, (Grand Rapids: Christian Classics Ethereal Library).

Carawan, Lea. "In God We Trust: Restoring the True Spirit of America." *Charisma*, October 2012. Magazine insert. No pages. Online: http://www.charismamag.com/life/politics/15580-in-god-we-trust.

Cartledge, Mark J. *Encountering the Spirit: The Charismatic Tradition*. Maryknoll, NY: Orbis, 2006.

Cassian, John. *Conferences*. Conference 19, chapter 12. No pages. Online: http://www.newadvent.org/fathers/350819.htm.

———. *Institutes*. Book 5, chapter 36. No pages. Online: http://www.newadvent.org/fathers/350705.htm.

Chan, Simon. *Pentecostal Theology and the Christian Spiritual Tradition*. New York: Sheffield Academic, 2003.

Chapell, Bryan. *Holiness by Grace: Delighting in the Joy that is Our Strength*. Wheaton, IL: Crossway, 2001.

Charles, Tyler. "The Secret Sexual Revolution." *Relevant Magazine.com*, February 20, 2012. Adapted from article in September/October 2011 print edition of *Relevant*. No pages. Online: http://www.relevantmagazine.com/life/relationship/features/28337-the-secret-sexual-revolution.

"Christmas." Catholic Encyclopedia. No pages. Online: http://www.newadvent.org/cathen/03724b.htm.

Chryssavgis, John. *In the Heart of the Desert: The Spirituality of the Desert Fathers and Mothers*. Rev. ed. Bloomington, IN: World Wisdom, 2008.

Cone, James H. "Sanctification and Liberation in the Black Religious Tradition." In *Sanctification and Liberation: Liberation Theologies in Light of the Wesleyan Tradition*, edited by Theodore Runyon, 174–92. Nashville: Abingdon, 1981.

———. *The Spirituals and the Blues*. Maryknoll, NY: Orbis, 1975.

Coppedge, Allan. "Holiness and Discipleship." *Wesleyan Theological Journal* 15, no. 2 (Spring 1980): 78–94. Online: http://wesley.nnu.edu/fileadmin/imported_site /wesleyjournal/1980-wtj-15-2.pdf.

Coulter, Dale M. *Holiness: The Beauty of Perfection.* Cleveland, TN: Pathway, 2004.

Daniels, David D. "By Sound Doctrine: The Theological Legacy of Bishop Charles Harrison Mason." *Whole Truth Magazine,* October/November/December 2003, 30.

———. "Forging A Theological Future for COGIC: Metaphors of Holiness and Models of Doctrine." *Advocate: COGIC Scholars Fellowship* 9, no 2 (August/ September 2011): 1–3.

DeYoung, Kevin. *The Hole in Our Holiness: Filling the Gap between Gospel Passion and the Pursuit of Godliness.* Wheaton, IL: Crossway, 2012.

Dieter, Melvin E., et al. *Five Views on Sanctification.* Grand Rapids: Zondervan, 1987.

Douglass, Frederick. *Frederick Douglass: Selected Speeches and Writings.* Edited by Philip Sheldon Foner and Yuval Taylor. Chicago: Lawrence Hill Books, 1999.

DuBois, W. E. B. *The Souls of Black Folk.* New York: Fawcett, 1968.

Dunn, James D. G. *The Theology of Paul the Apostle.* Grand Rapids: Eerdmans, 1998.

———. *Unity and Diversity in the New Testament: An Inquiry into the Character of Earliest Christianity.* 3rd ed. London: SCM, 2006.

Fanning, Steven. *Mystics of the Christian Tradition.* New York: Routledge, 2001.

Fee, Gordon D. *The First Epistle to the Corinthians.* Grand Rapids: Eerdmans, 1987.

Fenhagen, James C. *Invitation to Holiness.* Harrisburg, PA: Morehouse, 1985.

Finney, Charles. "Prevailing Prayer: Lecture IV." No date. No pages. Online: http://www. path2prayer.com/article/329/intercessory-prayer/charles-finney-prevailing-prayer.

Fletcher, John. *The Works of the Reverend John Fletcher.* New York: Lane & Scott, 1851.

Floyd-Thomas, Stacey, Juan Floyd-Thomas, Carol B. Duncan, Stephen G. Ray Jr., and Nancy Lynne Westfield. *Black Church Studies: An Introduction.* Nashville: Abingdon, 2007.

Fox, George. *The Journal of George Fox.* Edited by Rufus Jones. Richmond, IN: Friends United, 2006.

Gast, Phil. "Obama Announces He Supports Same-Sex Marriage." Politics. *CNN.com.* May 9, 2012. No pages. Online: http://www.cnn.com/2012/05/09/politics/obama-same-sex-marriage/index.html.

Gilgoff, Dan. "Catholic Church's Sex Abuse Scandal Goes Global." World. *CNN.com.* No pages. Online: http://articles.cnn.com/2010-03-19/world/catholic.church.abuse_1 _abusive-priests-church-abuse-archdiocese?_s=PM:WORLD.

Greenfield, John, *When the Spirit Came: The Story of the Moravian Revival of 1727.* Minneapolis: Bethany Fellowship, 1967.

Griffin, William A. "Kingdom Now: New Hope or New Heresy." *Eastern Journal of Practical Theology* 2 (Spring 1988) 6–36.

Haines, Lee M. "A Grander, Nobler Work, Wesleyan Methodism's Transition 1867-1901." In *Reformers and Revivalists: History of the Wesleyan Church,* edited by Wayne E. Caldwell, 118–51. Indianapolis: Wesley Press: 1992.

Harris, Antipas L. *For Such a Time as This: Re-Imaging Practical Theology for Independent Pentecostal Churches.* Lexington, KY: Emeth Press, 2010.

Harrison, Everett F. "Holiness." In *The International Standard Bible Encyclopedia.* Vol. 2, *E–J,* edited by Geoffry W. Bromiley, 725–28. Grand Rapids: Eerdmans, 1982.

Hauerwas, Stanley. "The Sanctified Body: Why Perfection Does Not Require a 'Self.'" In *Embodied Holiness: Toward a Corporate Theology of Spiritual Growth,* edited by

# Bibliography

Samuel M. Powell and Michael E. Lodahl, 19–38. Downers Grove, IL: InterVarsity, 1999.

Hauerwas, Stanley, and William H. Willimon. *Resident Aliens: Life in the Christian Colony.* Nashville: Abingdon, 1989.

Heisler, Greg. *Spirit-Led Preaching: The Holy Spirit's Role in Sermon Preparation and Delivery.* Nashville: B & H Academic, 2007.

Heschel, Abraham Joshua. *The Sabbath.* New York: Farrar, Straus and Giroux, 1951.

Hills, A. M. *Holiness and Power for the Church and the Ministry.* New York: Garland, 1984.

Hollenweger, Walter. *Pentecostalism: Origins and Developments Worldwide.* Peabody, MA: Hendrickson, 1997.

Horsley, Richard A., and James Tracy, eds. *Christmas Unwrapped: Consumerism, Christ, and Culture.* Harrisburg, PA: Trinity Press, 2001.

Hunter, Harold D. "Beniah at the Apostolic Crossroads: Little Noticed Crosscurrents of B. H. Irwin, Charles Fox Parham, Frank Sandford, A. J. Tomlinson." *Cyberjournal for Pentecostal-Charismatic Research* 1 (January 1997). No Pages. Online: http://www.pctii.org/cyberj/cyberj1/hunter.html.

Irenaeus. *Five Books of S. Irenaeus, Bishop of Lyons, Against Heresies.* Translated by John Keble. Oxford: James Parker, 1872.

Jamieson, Bobby. *Built Upon the Rock: The Church.* Wheaton, IL: Crossway, 2012.

Jobes, Karen H. *1 Peter.* Baker Exegetical Commentary on the New Testament. Grand Rapids: Baker Academic, 2005.

Johns, Cheryl Bridges. "Can I Live Holy in a Sinful World?" *Evangel* 102, no. 8 (August 2012): 12–13, 21.

Johnson, Luke Timothy. *Reading Romans: A Literary and Theological Commentary.* New York: Crossroad, 1997.

———. *Religious Experience in Earliest Christianity: A Missing Dimension in New Testament Studies.* Minneapolis: Fortress, 1998.

———. *The Writings of the New Testament: An Interpretation.* Minneapolis: Fortress, 1999.

Jones, Charles Edwin. *Black Holiness: A Guide to the Study of Black Participation in Wesleyan Perfectionist and Glossolalic Pentecostal Movements.* Metuchen, NJ: American Theological Library Association and Scarecrow Press, 1987.

Jones, Timothy. "A Christmas Tree, a Black President and a 'Christian Nation': Reflections from a Restless Mind." *Urban Cusp*, December 12, 2011. No pages. Online: http://www.urbancusp.com/newspost/a-christmas-tree-a-black-president-and-a-christian-nation/.

Julian of Norwich. *Showings.* Translated by Edmund Colledge and James Walsh. Mahway, New Jersey: Paulist, 1978.

Kaye, John. *Some Account of the Writings and Opinions of Clement of Alexandria.* London: Gilbert & Rivington, 1835.

Kempf, Konstantin. *The Holiness of the Church in the Nineteenth Century: Saintly Men and Women of Our Own Times.* New York: Benziger Brothers, 1916.

King, Martin Luther, Jr. *Strength to Love.* Minneapolis: Fortress, 1981.

———. *Why We Can't Wait.* New York: Penguin, 1964.

Kinnaman, David. *You Lost Me: Why Young Christians Are Leavening Church . . . and Rethinking Faith.* Grand Rapids: Baker, 2011.

Kwee, Alex W., et al. "Sexual Addiction and Christian College Men: Conceptual, Assessment, and Treatment Challenges." *Journal of Psychology and Christianity*

26, no. 1 (Spring 2007) 3–13. Online: http://www.alexkwee.com/uploads /kweedominguezferrello7.pdf.

LaMonica, Gabe. "A Christmastime Fight: Christmas Trees Vs. Holiday Trees." CNN Belief Blog, December 10, 2011. No pages. Online: http://religion.blogs.cnn.com /2011/12/10/the-christmas-tree-fight/.

Levine, Baruch A. *Leviticus.* JPS Torah Commentary. New York: Jewish Publication Society, 1989.

Lewis, C. S. *Mere Christianity.* New York: MacMillan, 1952.

Lewis, Gerrick. "Porn Leads to Aggressive Behavior." *The Lantern,* November 26, 2007 (updated June 16, 2012). No pages. Online: http://www.thelantern.com/2.1345 /porn-leads-to-aggressive-behavior-1.76531#.UUPYxo4QifQ.

Lincoln, C. Eric, and Lawrence H. Mamiya. *The Black Church in the African American Experience.* Durham, NC: Duke University Press, 1990.

Locke, John. *Two Treatises of Government.* Edited by Thomas Hollis. London: A. Millar, 1764.

Luther, Martin. *Works.* Edited by Jaroslav Pelikan et al. 55 vols. St. Louis: Concordia, 1959.

MacPhail, Bryn. "In Search of the Truth: A Christian Response to Postmodernity." Thinking Big: The Reflections of Bryn MacPhail in the Bahamas (blog). No pages. Online: http://www.reformedtheology.ca/pmodernity.html.

Malaty, Tadros Y. *The Gift of the Holy Spirit.* Cairo, Egypt: Anba Reuiss Press, 1991.

Martin, William C. *With God on Our Side: The Rise of the Religious Right in America.* New York: Broadway Books, 1996.

Mathews, James K. "The Spirit and the Church." In *What the Spirit is Saying to the Churches,* edited by Theodore Runyan, 125–37. New York: Hawthorn Books, 1975.

McClung, Floyd, Jr. *The Father Heart of God.* Eugene, OR: Harvest House, 1985.

——. *Holiness and the Spirit of the Age.* Eugene, OR: Harvest House, 1991.

McGrath, Alister E. *Christian Theology: An Introduction.* 5th ed. Chichester, UK: Wiley-Blackwell, 2011.

Merton, Thomas. *Disputed Questions.* New York: Farrar, Straus & Giroux, 1960.

Meyer, Joyce. *The Secret to True Happiness: Enjoy Today, Embrace Tomorrow.* New York: Faith Words, 2008.

Miller, Stephen. *The Peculiar Life of Sundays.* Cambridge, MA: Harvard University Press, 2008.

Moltmann, Jürgen. *The Crucified God: The Cross of Christ as the Foundation and Criticism of Christian Theology.* London: SCM, 1974.

——. *God in Creation: A New Theology of Creation and the Spirit of God.* Minneapolis: Fortress, 1993.

——. *History and the Triune God: Contributions to Trinitarian Theology.* New York: Crossroad, 1992.

Morinis, E. Alan. *Everyday Holiness: The Jewish Spiritual Path of Mussar.* Boston: Trumpeter, 2007.

Mosshammer, Alden A. *The Easter Computus and the Origins of the Christian Era.* New York: Oxford University Press, 2008.

Muller, Wayne. *Sabbath: Finding Rest, Renewal, and Delight in Our Busy Lives.* New York: Bantam Books, 1999.

Newhouse, Catherine. "Voice of the Hispanic Christian Vote." *Urban Faith,* October 21, 2011. No pages. Online: http://www.urbanfaith.com/2011/10/voice-of-the-hispanic-christian-vote.html/.

# Bibliography

Orsuto, Donna L. *Holiness*. New York: Continuum, 2006.

Oswalt, John N. *Called to Be Holy: A Biblical Perspective*. Nappanee, IN: Evangel, 1999.

Owen, John. *Triumph Over Temptation: Pursuing a Life of Purity*. Colorado Springs: Victor, 2005.

Padgett, Alan G. "Christianity and Postmodernity." *Christian Scholar's Review* 26, no. 2 (Winter 1996) no pages. Online: http://www.csreview.org/XXVI2/padgett/.

Paine, Thomas. *Common Sense*. January 10, 1776. The Thomas Paine Library. No pages. Online: http://libertyonline.hypermall.com/Paine/CS-Frame.html.

———. *The Thomas Paine Reader*. Edited by Michael Foot and Isaac Kramnick. Penguin, 1987.

Palmer, Michael. "Sabbath Living." Talk presented at Regent University faculty retreat, August 18, 2005. Online: http://www.regent.edu/acad/schdiv/assets/faculty/palmer /sabbath_living_2005-08-18.pdf.

Pascal, Blaise. *Pensées*. Translated by A. J. Krailsheimer. London: Penguin, 1993.

Pope Benedict XVI [Joseph A. Ratzinger]. "Paul's Conversion: We Are Christians Only If We Encounter Christ." Address during the general audience in Paul VI Hall, Vatican City, September 3, 2008. No pages. Online: http://www.vatican.va/holy_father /benedict_xvi/audiences/2008/documents/hf_ben-xvi_aud_20080903_en.html.

Powell, Samuel M., and Michael E. Lodahl, eds. *Embodied Holiness: Toward a Corporate Theology of Spiritual Growth*. Downers Grove: InterVarsity, 1999.

Religion Library. "Holiness and Pentecostal." *Patheos*. No pages. Online: http://www .patheos.com/Library/Pentecostal.html

Runyon, Theodore. "Holiness as the Renewal of the Image of God in the Individual & Society." In *Embodied Holiness: Toward a Corporate Theology of Spirit Growth*, edited by Samuel M. Powell and Michael E. Lodahl, 79–88. Downers Grove: Intervarsity Press, 1909.

———. *Sanctification and Liberation: Liberation Theologies in Light of the Wesleyan Tradition*. Nashville: Abingdon, 1981.

Rushdoony, Rousas John. *The Institutes of Biblical Law*. Nutley, NJ: Craig Press, 1973.

———. "Second American Revolution: Rousas John Rushdoony (1 of 9)." Youtube video posted by "jcr4runner," January 15, 2007, 2:15. Online: http://www.youtube.com/wa tch?v=jkQ6DlTQ114&feature=youtu.be.

Ryle, J. C. *Holiness: Its Nature, Hindrances, Difficulties, and Roots*. Moscow, ID: Charles Nolan, 2011.

Sanders, Cheryl J. *Saints in Exile: The Holiness-Pentecostal Experience in African American Religion and Culture*. New York: Oxford University Press, 1996.

Schor, Juliet. *The Overworked American: The Unexpected Decline of Leisure*. New York: Basic Books, 1992.

Searle, Alfred L. "Music in the Church." In *Friends' Intelligencer* 72. Philadelphia: Friends' Intelligencer Association, 1915.

Servant, David A. "Prayer for Holiness." *Shepherd Serve*, 2002. No pages. Online: http: //www.heavensfamily.org/ss/songs/prayer_for_holiness.

Seymour, William. "The Pentecostal Baptism Restored." *oChristian.com*. No pages. Online: http://articles.ochristian.com/article3481.shtml.

Spurgeon, Charles Haddon. "The Lord's Own View of His Church and People." Sermon delivered at the Metropolitan Tabernacle, Newington, London. Online: http://www .spurgeongems.org/vols31-33/chs1957.pdf.

Swanson, Dwight. "Holiness in the Psalms." *Re-Minting Holiness.* No pages. Online: http://holiness.nazarene.ac.uk/articles.php?n=11.

Synan, Vinson. *The Holiness-Pentecostal Tradition: Charismatic Movements in the Twentieth Century.* Grand Rapids: Eerdmans, 1997.

Tertullian. *On Baptism.* Translated by Sydney Thelwall. No pages. Online: http://www.earlychristianwritings.com/text/tertullian21.html.

———. "On Exhortation to Chastity." Translated by Sydney Thelwall. No pages. Online: http://www.tertullian.org/anf/anf04/anf04-15.htm.

Tesfamariam, Rahiel. "Is Gay Marriage a Crisis for the Black Church?" *Washington Post,* May 20, 2012. No pages. Online: http://www.washingtonpost.com/blogs/guest-voices/post/is-gay-marriage-a-crisis-for-the-black-church/2012/05/18/gIQAP3gHZU_blog.html?wprss=rss_guest-voices.

Tozer, A. W., *Born After Midnight.* Camp Hill, PA: Wing Spread, 1987.

Tramel, Terry. "The Beauty of the Balance: Toward an Evangelical-Pentecostal Theology." DMin diss., Assemblies of God Theological Seminary, Springfield, Missouri, February 2008. Online: http://search.proquest.com/docview/193491529.

Van Manen, Max. *The Tact of Teaching: The Meaning of Pedagogical Thoughtfulness.* Albany: State University of New York Press, 1991.

Wainwright, Geoffrey. *Worship with One Accord: Where Liturgy and Ecumenism Embrace.* Oxford: Oxford University Press, 1997.

Walker, Clarence Earl. *Breaking Strongholds in African American Family: Strategies for Spiritual Warfare.* Grand Rapids: Zondervan, 1996.

Wesley, John. "Circumcision of the Heart (1733)." In *John Wesley's Sermon: An Anthology,* 23–32. Edited by Albert C. Outler and Richard P. Heitzenrater. Nashville: Abingdon, 1991.

———. "Scriptural Way of Salvation (1765)." In *John Wesley's Sermon: An Anthology.* Edited by Albert C. Outler and Richard P. Heitzenrater. Nashville: Abingdon, 1991.

———. "Upon Our Lord's Sermon on the Mount: Discourse IV." In *John Wesley's Sermon: An Anthology.* Edited by Albert C. Outler and Richard P. Heitzenrater. Nashville: Abingdon, 1991.

———. *The Works of the Rev. John Wesley.* 10 vols. Edited by Joseph Benson. London: Conference-Office, Thomas Cordeux, 1811.

———. *The Works of the Reverend John Wesley.* Edited by John Emory. New York: J. Emory and B. Waugh, for the Methodist Episcopal Church, 1831.

Wethmar, Conrad. "Confessionality and Identity of the Church: A Reformed Perspective." In *Christian Identity,* edited by Eduardus van der Borght, 135–50. Boston: Brill, 2008.

White, John. *Flirting with the World: A Challenge to Loyalty.* Wheaton, IL: Harold Shaw, 1990.

Williams, Edward S. "Sexual Conduct of Christians." *Mountain Retreat.* No pages. Online: http://www.mountainretreatorg.net/apologetics/sexual_conduct_of_christians.shtml.

Willis, Timothy M. *Leviticus.* Abingdon Old Testament Commentaries. Nashville: Abington, 2009.

Wolfteich, Claire E. *Navigating New Terrain: Work and Women's Spiritual Lives.* New York: Paulist, 2002.

Wright, N. T. *After You Believe: Why Christian Character Matters.* New York: Harper Collins, 2010.

## Bibliography

Yoder, John Howard. *Body Politics: Five Practices of the Christian Community before the Watching World*. Scottdale, PA: Herald, 2001.

Yong, Amos. *Hospitality and the Other: Pentecost, Christian Practices, and the Neighbor*. Maryknoll, NY: Orbis, 2008.

———. *Spirit of Love: A Trinitarian Theology of Grace*. Waco, TX: Baylor University Press, 2012.

———. *Theology and Down Syndrome: Reimagining Disability in Late Modernity*. Waco, TX: Baylor University Press, 2007.

Xunzi. *Basic Writings*. Translated by Burton Watson. New York: Columbia University Press, 2003.

# Subject Index

## Subject Index

### M

Merton, Thomas, 103, 161
McGrath, Alister E., 63
Monastic, Monasticism, 7, 22, 23, 33, 37
Morinis, Alan, 49
Miller, Stephen, 24
Micah, ix, xiv, xv, 127
Muller, Wayne, 46, 47
Mussar, 49, 50,
Meyer, Joyce, 99

### O

Oppression, 29, 53, 66, 110, 122
Orsuto, Donna, 73, 74, 157
Owen, John, 162, 163

### P

Padgett, Alan, 12
Paine, Thomas, 137
Palmer, Michael, ix, 47
Paschal, Blaise, 36
Paul, 56, 57–58, 65, 68, 69, 70, 73, 74, 75,
    76, 79, 85, 86, 97, 101, 102, 103,
    105, 113, 118, 119, 120, 142, 143,
    151, 160, 162, 163
Pearson, A. T., 131
Peculiar, Peculiarity, xvii, 4, 6, 9, 10, 16,
    20, 22, 24, 25, 35, 36, 37, 38, 52,
    74, 139, 143, 152, 154–155
Pentecost, Pentecostal, ix, xiv, xv, 3, 5, 7,
    8, 15, 16, 18, 19, 28, 42, 47, 56,
    57, 59, 66, 78, 81, 85, 91, 106,
    116, 120, 127, 129, 132, 132, 133,
    134, 134, 135, 142, 149, 150, 160
Peter, 10, 13, 14, 24, 35, 44, 56, 58–60,
    62, 67, 68, 121, 140, 143, 156
People of God, xvii, 10, 25–26, 43, 48,
    49, 50, 59, 70, 92, 149, 155
Piety, xi, xvi, 6, 9, 10, 14, 26, 33, 41, 57,
    79, 97, 99, 148, 149

Political or Politics, 10, 12, 20, 21, 66, 80,
    93, 132, 134, 135, 136, 137, 139,
    144, 145, 146, 147, 148, 155
Poverty, 23, 66
Practical Theology, xvii, 30, 165
Prayer, 6, 9, 17, 23, 26, 29, 37, 38, 42, 55,
    57, 60, 73, 74, 79, 87, 92–95, 99,
    105, 106, 108, 113, 115, 130, 134,
    135, 157, 158, 162, 164
Psalms, 52-55, 123, 157
Psalmist, 53, 54, 55, 64, 128

### R

Rosa, Adolpha, 129
Runyon, Theodore, 69, 80, 107

### S

Salvation, 4, 15, 16, 18, 27, 33, 41, 62–67,
    69, 73, 74, 86, 100, 115, 116
Soteria, Soterion, 66
Sabbath, (also Sabbath Day), 36, 45–48,
    94
    Sanctification, xv, 3, 4, 12, 15, 16, 18,
        19, 21, 23, 24, 44, 62–67, 69–74,
        79, 80, 86, 129, 147, 160
Sanctify, Sanctifying, 3, 44, 56, 57, 69, 74,
    80, 86, 91, 113, 119, 120, 129, 145
Sanctified Church(es), xi, xiv, xv, 3, 4, 5,
    6, 7, 9, 15, 17, 44
Sanders, Cheryl J., xiv, 9, 150
Seymour, William, xii, xvii, 15, 80, 91,
    129
Sexual, sexuality (also sexual purity,
    sexual immorality, and sexually
    immoral), xvi, 8, 58, 84, 117, 118,
    119, 120, 124, 125, 137, 152
Slave(s), 27–29, 46, 48, 71, 94, 105, 120,
    138, 142
    abolitionist, 110
    Christian(s), Slave Christianity 22,
        27, 28, 29, 30, 31–32, 37
    Society, 22, 24, 25, 26, 27, 29, 30, 31,
        33, 34, 35, 36, 37, 41, 42, 43, 59,